W9-CEL-625

Fashion in Costume
1200–1980

Evening dresses designed between 1908 and 1977. Inspired by classical or oriental styles and using the minimum number of seams, these designs are almost timeless.

Fortuny 'Delphos' in pleated silk. Cape in cream and grey printed silk gauze.

Fortuny evening bag.- printed silk velvet in grey and pink with matching cord and beads

Yuki evening cloak in white rayon jersey with pleated organdie frills.

Draped silk jersey dresses by Grès (Alix)

Fashion in Costume
1200–1980

Joan Nunn

NEW AMSTERDAM
Lanham • New York • Oxford

NEW AMSTERDAM BOOKS
4720 Boston Way
Lanham, MD 20706

First edition published in 1984 by
New Amsterdam Books
by arrangement with The Herbert Press Ltd, London

ISBN 0-941533-79-4

Printed in the United States of America.

♾™ The paper used in this publication meets the minimum requirements of American
National Standard for Information Sciences—Permanence of Paper for Printed Library
Materials, ANSI Z39.48–1984.

Contents

To my brother John
and to the memory of my parents
Charles and Lilian

Acknowledgements

I would like to thank the staff of the libraries at the University of Kent at Canterbury, the Canterbury College of Art, the Kent County Library, the Museum of London, the Victoria and Albert Museum, and the research department of the Museum of Costume, Bath, for their help. Thanks are also due to Mrs Sidney Jowers for her research on my behalf in the USA, Miss Enid Billings for typing the manuscript, Mr George Maynard for the calligraphy on the illustrations, and Mrs Brenda Herbert for her kindness, patience and understanding as editor.

Introduction

Man's inventiveness in manipulating a length of cloth into a three-dimensional shape to cover the human body has been demonstrated with astonishing variety over the past eight centuries. The continuous desire for change in dress cannot be dismissed as arbitrary. Fashion, whether in art, architecture, furniture or dress, must rather be seen as the expression of ideas shared by a number of people at any one time, often linked to fundamental changes in moral or social values, and thus reflecting the essential characteristics of a particular period; and dress as an art form, a skilful arrangement of materials through which ideas or messages, both personal and social, are communicated.

Articles of clothing were first used in this way as symbols of rank, authority or occupation, a function that still survives in, for example, a king's crown, a bishop's mitre and cope, special robes for judges or men of learning, and the whole range of uniforms for military or specialized services. From these specific symbols developed the use of clothes to convey less obvious or direct messages such as the superiority of one individual over another, particularly in terms of wealth (which frequently also meant power), indicated by jewels, rich fabrics and furs, or garments in which it would be difficult to undertake physical labour. Even today the desire to wear a mink coat, diamonds or ostentatious clothing as a sign of financial and social success is not uncommon.

The need to achieve status and win admiration is a fundamental human instinct, however subconscious, and is reflected in our choice of clothing. Few people are completely indifferent to the clothes they wear; even those who choose to dress 'out of fashion' in what they consider a more aesthetic manner or one that is negligent or even slovenly often achieve a sense of superiority in being unconventional. But there is also a strong urge to belong; man is a social animal and needs to feel at one with the community. Fashion, particularly in the highly personal area of dress, is therefore an expression of the communal ideas or beliefs of a social group – as, for example, in the revolutionary casting-off of formality in the late 18th and early 19th centuries, the restrictive, often hypocritical formality of much of the Victorian period, the greater emancipation of women during the mid 1920s, and the deification of youth and revolt against the establishment in the 1960s.

The desire to be admired for physical beauty also plays an important part in costume. In seeking to achieve the ideal fashionable image, dress has been used to accentuate good points and disguise shortcomings. Success in attracting the opposite sex has been consistently admired and envied, but physical ideals have varied widely, noticeably rather more so for women than men during the 19th and 20th centuries.

Why should men and women dress differently? The assumption since the mid 16th century that skirts are correct for women and not for men (except in certain specialized dress such as the Scottish kilt) was fairly obviously brought about by roles they were called upon to play in society, underlined by religious pressures. Feminists may claim that masculine desire for superiority or dominance caused women to be dressed in garments that hampered their movements; but it may be that such garments were originally an indication of a lady's privileged position. However, most upper and middle class women, forced until comparatively recently to accept marriage as the only respectable career, had for practical reasons to look for social advancement or financial stability in a husband if they had any choice at all, while men, who had greater freedom, might be attracted into marriage by beauty alone; and this may have encouraged what has been referred to as the erotic or seduction principle in women's dress, with a constant change of emphasis on different parts of the anatomy to stimulate interest and attention. With less religious pressure and greater equality between the sexes in the last few decades, men and women have often worn similar clothes, so whether differentiation of the sexes by clothing will continue in the future is open to conjecture. I personally think that women's dress, like men's since the 19th century, will tend to change less dramatically and remain fairly practical; but on suitable occasions lavishly trailing skirts or robes in rich fabrics may still have a place, and perhaps convention and custom will alter to allow men also to wear such garments once again.

The study of fashion and costume is fascinating not only for the artistry and skilled craftsmanship it reveals but also for the many queries posed by the messages contained in dress. It requires careful observation of the construction and manufacture of original period garments whenever possible, and also of contemporary portraits, sculpture, prints and photographs to note how garments were· worn. Also essential for an understanding of the exterior image is a knowledge of the corset or underwear worn beneath the outer garment; many theatrical 'period' costumes have proved unsatisfactory because this has been overlooked. I have therefore indicated, where space allows, how garments were made and how they were supported; and for the illustrations I have in every case worked from contemporary sources to endeavour to catch a little of the spirit of the age. From the 13th to the early 19th century there were often marked differences between the clothes worn in different countries but later, with the development of fashion reporting, wider trade and travel and mass production, fashion became almost international. The illustrations therefore show the country of origin until c.1900; there is still a subtle variation in the way people of different nationalities look, but this is more to do with how the garments are assembled or, perhaps, with physical characteristics or grooming, than with the clothes themselves which are often internationally marketed. Some of the costumes drawn from American magazines of the late 19th century may have originated in France, but I have taken the risk on occasions of labelling them American. It should be noted, too, that examples taken from fashion magazines often represent very advanced styles; but they are not wholly misleading, since they represent an ideal to which the fashion-conscious may aspire.

The more one studies costume the more there seems to be to discover. A detailed study of the costume of the common or working-class people, which I have only touched on here, or of specialized costume for certain occupations or protective clothing from armour to the astronaut's suit, would, for example, extend the story of western costume still further.

1200–1450: Gothic

Few garments survive from earlier than the 16th century: our knowledge of the costume of the medieval period comes from contemporary memorial brasses, sculpture, paintings, frescoes and manuscripts. The Luttrell Psalter (completed 1340, now in the British Museum) and the Romance of Alexander (1338–44, Bodleian Library, Oxford) contain detailed illustrations not only of costume but of agricultural, sporting and manorial life. William Langland's *Piers Ploughman*, Chaucer's *Canterbury Tales*, and *Sir Gawain and the Green Knight*, all written in the 14th century, give us vivid verbal pictures of the costume and manners of the day.

The popular image of the later middle ages is one of magnificent cathedrals and romantic castles, religious fervour, crusades, chivalry, courtly love and people dressed in rich trailing garments whose slenderness and verticality echo the architectural style of the 12th to 15th centuries known as gothic. This somewhat romanticized image tends to obscure the manoeuvring for power among feudal lords, the hierarchy of the church, the rising bourgeoisie, the increasingly mercenary attitude of the crusading knights and their followers, and the discomforts of life in cold castles and houses with centrally-placed fires belching smoke, lit by flaring torches and tallow candles. The life of the peasants and serfs was hard, and the plague threatened all levels of society.

Nevertheless, this period saw a resurgence of art and architecture, religious aspiration, the invention of printing in *c*.1455, a greater intermingling of the peoples of Europe, wider and more intense trade, and the establishment of the Craft Guilds.

The attitudes and changing social patterns of the day were reflected, as in all periods, in its costume. It is difficult today to comprehend the extent of religious dominance during the 13th, 14th and early 15th centuries and its influence on thought and behaviour. The great Franciscan and Dominican orders established in 1214, which spread throughout Europe, were centres of learning at a time when schools scarcely existed and when the skills of reading and writing were as incomprehensible to the ordinary citizen as the computer still is to many people today. Art as well as learning was centred on the church; the monastic communities produced sculptures and frescoes to adorn their cathedrals and churches as well as exquisite manuscripts. Mosaics in coloured glass and precious metals inlaid with enamel vied with the richly woven and embroidered garments worn by the wealthy in the congregation.

Women's costume was strongly influenced by church doctrine, which held that sin entered the world through Eve and that women were the eternal cause of sinful lust and thus the source of all wickedness. Women were therefore urged to conceal their physical charms, occasionally without success. With the exception of very young girls and brides, the hair had to be covered and as little as possible of the anatomy revealed. It is interesting to note that even the Virgin Mary was invariably portrayed with her hair covered, and that many nuns' headdresses today are similar to those worn by most women in the early 13th century. Both men and women were attacked by the religious moralists of the day for their rich and extravagant dress.

The Crusades, in addition to bringing about a more cosmopolitan attitude and

9

English, first half of 13C. King wearing green cloak lined with vair (fur). Robe with bejewelled horizontal decoration. Richly decorated buckled belt with long tongue. Shoes of diapered material.

English musicians, 1340. Tunic with buttoned front and tippet sleeves. Chaperon with liripipe and turned-back front.

Amiens Cathedral, 1220

Shield saltire

Shield quarterly quartered

English, first half 13 C
Knight wears mail hauberk with mittens, coif and braies; lower hose covered with metal bosses, laced down back of leg. Surcote, fastened to hauberk under arm, to match standard and ailettes on shoulders.

Selby Abbey, east window, 1325.

French, after 1230 Fluted cap and barbette. Cape with roll collar. Robe fastened with jewelled brooch, jewelled belt.

French, 13C knight. Long surcote over chain mail hauberk with coif and mittens; low-slung belt supports sword with decorated hilt.

13C. Barbette worn with cap and veil

Pattern from 13C brocade

German, 1210-35. Foliated crown over flowing hair, mantle held by jewelled clasp

French, 13 C. Womens heads wrapped in linen strips

English, 13C. Young girls wearing sideless surcotes, one tucked up into side openings with underdress pinned up for ease of movement. Both have loose, flowing hair, one with a coif (left) and one a circlet.

Brooch and small purse hung from belt, c. 1230

French, 13 C. Men wearing coifs, one with a straw hat, Chemise split at front and tucked up into belt. Braies rolled around waist cord to which the legs are hitched up.

French 12-13 C.
Shepherds, both in single chemise, one with long, loose hose, the other with bare legs and boots. Chaperon stiffened at back.

French, 13 C. Women with hair in kerchief or strips of linen, one wearing sleeveless surcoat and striped hose.

English, mid 13 C. Chaperon stiffened at front. Hose without feet. (left.) Braies without hose, shoes drawn up at front to fastening.

breaking up to some extent Europe's provincialism, also introduced to the West the arts and crafts of the East – particularly, in dress, the beautiful richly woven fabrics. They also gave rise to the increased use of emblems: the armorial bearing or blazoning on a knight's shield and garments proclaimed his title or origin so that he was instantly recognizable to friends and followers. The popularity of the tournament extended their use, even to women's dress. Spectators at a tournament would have had a keen knowledge of blazoning. Emblems also formed part of the livery worn by the many escorts of a great lord when he and his household travelled from one of his houses or castles to another (a not uncommon event), thus advertising his importance.

The privilege and power of the aristocracy and feudal lords was to be challenged by the bourgeoisie or merchant class to whom increased trade meant increased wealth, and by the Latin-speaking scholars who travelled between the growing universities of Paris, England and Italy. Sumptuary laws multiplied during the 14th and 15th centuries as rulers tried to control the manner of living of the steadily rising lower classes. But whereas in the 12th century a bourgeois woman could be fined for dressing like a noblewoman, by the 14th century her clothes might even surpass the noble-woman's in richness and magnificence. Great fortunes were made from the import of woven textiles from the East, Spain and Italy, and from the export of raw wool, both important with regard to dress. Saracen weavers produced brocades in Granada from early times, and the Norman lords of Sicily brought Greek weavers to Lucca in the 13th century, from where they spread to Florence, Genoa, Venice (famous by the end of the 14th century for magnificent brocades of silk, velvet and metal thread), Bologna and Milan. These richly patterned fabrics were a revelation to Italy's northern neighbours. The strongest influence of these Italian city states came later, during the Renaissance, and later still the emigration of many weavers to France and Flanders made Paris, Rouen and Lyons the great silk weaving centres of the 17th and 18th centuries. Philippa of Hainault, wife of Edward III of England, established a woollen mill at Norwich in 1331 with Flemish weavers, but the raw wool which was England's largest export was woven almost entirely in Flanders. The protection of this vital trade was one of the causes of the Hundred Years War.

During the 250 years covered by this chapter, although variations existed in the style of clothing worn by different nationalities in Europe, it is possible to give a general description, commenting on any particular divergence from the overall pattern. Clothes changed from the loose flowing garments, very long for women and never above knee-length for men, of the 13th century to a closer fit, obtained by greater skill and knowledge of 'cut' and the use of buttons, during the 14th. (Buttons found in use among the Turks and Mongols by the crusaders were copied, and replaced the earlier buckle fastenings.) In the late 14th and early 15th centuries came a more rigid, stiffened appearance and more exaggerated styles, originating at the Burgundian Court, with elaborate headdresses for women, very short tunics for men, trailing sleeves, and shoes with long pointed toes. In contrast, the peasants' simple style of dress scarcely changed from the 13th to the 16th century. Of necessity the peasants were self-sufficient, spinning and weaving their own wool and linen and using skins from wild or domestic animals for warmth. Men would bandage twisted straw around their legs or use leather thongs, cross-gartered over their long hose to protect their legs. As materials manufactured in the towns became easier to obtain, untreated hides tended to disappear; but apart from admiring the rich and mighty as they passed by, or during an occasional visit to the town, country people were unaffected by fashion.

MEN

Undergarments consisted of a straight, loose garment with sleeves, usually made of linen, called a chemise and subsequently a shirt, about knee-length and often slit up from the hem at the centre back and front; and loose baggy shorts called under-hose or braies. The chemise can occasionally be seen showing at the neck and wrist in prints or drawings, and peasants appear to have worn chemise and braies, either alone or together, as their only garments. The under-hose worn by gentlemen were probably shorter and closer fitting, even before shorter tunics made this necessary.

Over the chemise was worn a cote (cotte or coat), a calf- or ankle-length garment, moderately full, belted fairly low and often decorated with bands round the lowish neck and the hem. The sleeves, cut in one with the body, wide at the top and tapering to the wrist (a shape known today as dolman or magyar) were at first wrapped over and fastened and later buttoned. The cote could be worn alone, but was frequently worn with a surcote (sur-coat) – originally a simple covering for armour (such as the vest-like hauberk of chain mail) – a rectangle of cloth with a hole in the middle for the head to go through. Known also as a tabard, it became part of ordinary dress, evolving into a sleeveless tunic reaching the knees or ankles, with armholes wide enough to give room for the cote sleeves, and might be slit up at the front or back and worn belted or unbelted. Later it appears to have had sleeves attached and looks like a robe. The habit of wearing one or two garments over another and of having detachable sleeves can make it difficult to distinguish one garment from another. Also, the same garment may be given different names, and this can be confusing.

Also adapted from military usage was the gibon (1290–1400) worn next to the shirt, taken from the gambeson, a thick padded or quilted garment worn under armour to prevent chafing. The civilian garment was also quilted or fur-lined, with or without sleeves, shortened from knee to waist-length by the second half of the 14th century; and by the end of that century it was called the doublet, a name originating in France.

In the mid 14th century there was a noticeable change in men's wear with the introduction of the cote-hardie (cote-hardy), a close-fitting knee-length over-garment buttoned down the front, with a low neck and elbow-length, set-in sleeves with a tongue-shaped extension behind. After about 1350 the cote-hardie became tighter (probably cut on the bias) and the elbow flaps grew into long hanging bands known in England as tippets and in France as *coudières*. These long streamers reaching almost to the ground often appear to hang from a detachable cuff around the upper arm, and are dagged (scalloped) at the edges. The cote-hardie was often particoloured, i.e. halved or quartered in different colours or in plain and striped fabrics. A belt supporting a pouch or purse was worn low on the hips. These garments obviously required considerable skill in making, and indicate the rapidly growing trade in tailoring, now an exclusively male profession; until the middle of the 12th century clothes had been made by women in their own homes. The first charter was granted to the merchant tailors of Hamburg in 1152, but by the beginning of the 13th century the guild was split up and a distinction drawn between one section of the craft and another: in France the Paris Tailors' Guild split into pourpointiers, who made common articles of apparel, and doubletiers who made the doublets worn with armour. Men also made women's clothes; in France in about 1300 the Queen and her ladies are known to have employed only men tailors.

In the late 14th and early 15th century the cote-hardie lost favour with the young and fashionable who adopted the houppelande, a garment opening down the front and

German, 1249-50. Coif over long hair. Centre-front clasp on cote, fringed fastening on mantle, studded belt; gloves hang from sword handle

English, 1245. Robe or cote striped horizontally. Foliated coronet over veil.

German, 1249-50 Coronet over stiffened cap. Mantle with French-style collar fastened with jewelled clasps.

German, 1230-40. Red cape, blue cote heavily studded with jewels.

English, 1245. Small cowl. Gown has front button fastening and sleeves slit at front.

German, 13 C. (left) Mantle fastened by clasps, small coronet over veil and wimple or barbette. (right) Sideless surcote over heavily decorated undercote or robe.

English, 1376. Sleeves on under-tunic extend over hands, and are richly embroidered. Fur lined cloak fastened on shoulder.

English, 1340. Peasants wearing hats over chaperons, one with short liripipe. Both wear working gloves; legs protected by bindings.

English, 1364. Chaperon, sleeves, hem and slit at front all edged with identical embroidery.

English, 1364. Cote-hardie buttoned at front and on sleeves; tippets hang from upper arm; fitchets on front of skirt. Lopped braids under fillet and veil.

English, 1338-44. Girls at play in sideless surcotes and cote-hardies, hair plaited over ears under chaperons or fillets and veils, skirts pinned up in various ways. One wears tippets.

After 1360. Cote-hardies belted low, one particoloured.
Chaperon worn under hat. Particoloured hose.

English, 1349. A rich
bourgeoise. Hair braided
over the ears, covered by
wimple and veil. Mantle
and surcote edged with
embroidery and lined
with fur or contrasting
material. Cote, richly
embroidered, has
tightly buttoned sleeves.

English, 1338-44. Jesters in loose tunics, one particoloured.
Exaggerated liripipes on chaperons.

French, 1390. French-style sideless surcote, fur
plastron at front with elaborate buttons; jewelled
belt on cote.

falling in voluminous folds from the fitted shoulders, varying in length from thigh level to trailing on the ground. Early versions were worn hanging loose, but by the mid 15th century the fullness was laid in formalized, often padded, pleats from shoulder or breast to hem, kept in place by a belt or secured from the inside by tapes or stitching. The stiffened collar, very high at the back, was either buttoned close under the chin or cut away to reveal the neck or undergarment at the front. As the period advanced, variations in the collar occurred. Several types of sleeve were attached to the houppelande – either very wide, expanding from a normal armhole to a funnel shape reaching almost to the ground, often dagged at the edge; or the bagpipe sleeve, also very wide, deeply pendent from a closed wrist to form a huge hanging pouch which might be used as a pocket: or a long, full sleeve gathered into a cuff and worn rucked up at the lower arm, but with a vertical slit richly ornamented or revealing a fur lining on its outer edge or slightly to the front, through which the arm might be thrust, allowing the sleeve to hang loose – sometimes referred to as bellows sleeves. The houppelande was always worn over the doublet (which by the mid 15th century might also be worn as an outer garment) and, being lined often with fur, could be used as an overcoat is today. Conversely, circular cloaks or mantles and short capes were also worn indoors for extra warmth. After 1450 the long houppelande was more generally called a gown, becoming a symbol of dignity worn by men of learning and officials right into the 16th century; the short version is then often referred to as a tunic.

In the 13th and 14th centuries, hose or stockings were made of wool, usually with feet but sometimes strapped under the foot, and cut high enough at the sides to be attached to a belt with metal-tipped ties called points. With the advent of the very short doublet in the first decade of the 15th century, the hose were joined at the crotch, with a wedge-shaped section at the front called a cod-piece attached at the fork and tied up with cords. According to C. W. and P. Cunnington the name derives from 'cod', the old name for a bag. These joined hose were kept up by the same method as the separate hose, although the points might now be attached to an under-doublet. Hose were often particoloured and although generally shaped from cloth and fitted to the leg with well-placed seams, it is believed that even at this early date some may have been knitted. Shoes, cut high and close fitting, following the natural contours of the foot, were often highly decorated with embroidery and jewels. By 1250 pointed toes had become fairly exaggerated and between 1300 and 1350 they went to greater extremes. The shoes of Burgundian dandies might have stiffened and padded points three times the length of the shoe, sometimes reaching such proportions that they had to be supported by a light chain attached to a band at the knee – though this was an extreme fashion and rarely seen. By the mid 15th century shoes began again to take a more natural shape.

Soft calf-length boots were worn out-of-doors, and for riding might be longer and pulled up above the knee. They were made of pliable leather and outlined the foot and leg like hose, often laced up on the inside or outside of the leg. Peasants or country folk would have boots roughly fashioned from cowhide. Pattens – overshoes consisting of wooden soles secured by leather straps – were worn with shoes or boots in the 15th century to keep them above the dirt.

In the 13th century men's hair was cut to about the jaw line or a little longer, with either a centre parting or a fringe, curled, waved and even dyed. Most men were clean shaven, and although towards the end of the century small beards were seen, neatly trimmed to a point or forked, accompanied by small turned down moustaches, they do

English, 1400. Houpplande with bagpipe sleeves falling back to reveal sleeves of under-robe

English, 1338-44. Gentlemen and musicians wearing 'rayed' cote-hardies with tippet sleeves chaperons, monogrammed pouches and embroidered shoes; gloves tucked through belt.

English, 1400. Houppelande belted at the normal waist and open at neck revealing the doublet. Bagpipe sleeves buttoned at wrist. Forked beard

English, 1404. Reticulated headdresses with veils English, 1413.

Italian, 1345. Short houppelande with bagpipe sleeves.

Flemish, 15C. Sleeves on man's houppelande have dagged edges; the woman's are open at the front. Man's chaperone draped up on to the head. Woman's turban style headdress is typical of 1410

English, 1410-1420 Houppelande with funnel-type sleeves. Striped hose

Florentine, first half of 15C. Garment similar to surcote called a 'guibberello'.

English, 1420. The beginning of the Horned headdress.

English, 1423. Wide templers and veil

Roundlet with drape over shoulder

Pattens or clogs - wooden sole strapped over the shoe to protect it.

Long points on shoes popular in Burgundy

Flemish, 15 C. Bellows sleeves; doublet sleeve can be seen under gown.

Dagging on sleeves.

French, 1409-16.
Blue houppelande blazoned with gold crowns, worn with red chaperon. Gown in light and dark blue brocade with plain border worn with feathered hat. Fringing on sleeves (new in 15 C.)

Bag hat

English, 1430. Horned headdress and veil with scalloped edge.

English, 1441 Horned Headdress

Franco-Flemish, 1438-40. Heart-shaped headdress with padded roll. High waisted gown with broad belt; contrasting fabric on cuffs, collar and edge of skirt.

Franco-Flemish, 1438-40. Pleats fixed in place without aid of belt. Roundlet. Bellows sleeves.

English, 1450. Heart shaped headdress

Burgundian court dress, first half of 15C.
Dagging on sleeves cut into leaf shapes

Flemish circa 1450
Small hennin with dark veil

English, 1446. Heart-shaped
headdress; armorial
bearings on mantle

Burgundian fashion with high steeple
hennins, 1389

not appear to have been generally popular. At the end of the 14th century and in the 15th, the lower part of the head was shaved to above the ears and the hair brushed from a centre point on the crown into a rounded bowl-like shape (as in the portrait of Henry V of England in the National Portrait Gallery, London).

Two head coverings, a close-fitting coif and a hood with cape attached, were worn throughout the period and continued with variations into the 16th century. The coif, a plain white linen cap rather like a baby's bonnet, which covered the ears and tied under the chin, was worn by all levels of society, the most costly being of very fine transparent linen. The hood, at first similar to a monk's cowl with a cape, evolved during the 14th century into a style called a chaperon, which was fairly close-fitting and had the point at the back extended into a long 'tail' known as a liripipe (confusingly this is sometimes referred to as a tippet, a name also used for the pendent streamers on sleeves, mentioned earlier). During the late 14th and 15th century, the chaperon was worn with the face opening placed over the head and the rest arranged as a kind of turban, held in place by twisting the liripipe around it and allowing the ends to fall on to the shoulder. (In World War II soldiers sometimes wore their balaclavas in a similar manner.) For convenience the draped-up chaperon began to be stitched into place, and this evolved naturally into the 15th-century padded roll, later called a roundlet, mounted on a cap and trimmed to resemble the original draped fashion. This type of hat is also illustrated hung over one shoulder and held in place by the streamers (liripipe); a relic of this fashion may be seen today on the shoulder of the English Garter robes.

There were many styles of felt hat, usually black until 1300 when they were dyed different colours, with a round shallow crown and a brim varying in width, sometimes turned up to form a long point at the front. Hats of similar shape were made from plaited straw, at first only worn in the country but later for formal wear. The huge hat shown in Van Eyck's portrait of Arnolfini (1434, National Gallery, London) is made from black plaited straw. Peasants also plaited rushes to make hats. Brimmed hats were often worn over a coif or hood.

Smaller hats included one with a rolled and padded or fur trim and a soft floppy crown of cloth or velvet, often referred to as a bag hat; another type, worn more in Italy than elsewhere, was brimless, rather like a fez, and its increasing height suggests that it must have been stiffened. Although the chaperon was also worn in Italy, it seems rarely to have had a liripipe. Wreaths and chaplets of flowers were worn by men as well as women on occasions, especially for weddings. Circlets of gold set with jewels were worn by the nobility, and jewelled brooches were used to decorate hats.

WOMEN

Women's costume at first followed similar lines to that of men. The chemise, like a man's but reaching to the ground, was later called a smock. Over the chemise, a cote, less wide at the armhole than the man's, with a fairly low neckline slit at the centre front, clung slightly over the breast, then hung full and loose to the ground or was belted with a long tongued girdle. This garment is occasionally referred to as a kirtle. By the 1360s a more closely fitted gown had evolved, with sleeves like those on the man's cote-hardie, including the tippets; it was often buttoned down the front, with a boat-shaped neckline and very wide skirts which suggest that gores were added at the side seams: this gown is referred to both as a surcoat and a cote-hardie. At the front were two decorated slits (fitchets) rather like pockets through which a purse hanging from a girdle on the cote underneath might be reached. Illustrations of this period seem also to indicate that some women adopted a bodice cut on the same lines as the male cote-hardie, attached at the hips to a pleated or circular skirt, the join covered with a decorated belt. A garment such as this can often be seen under a formal sideless surcote which was different from anything worn by men, low-necked and widely cut away at the sides from shoulder to hip to reveal the garment beneath. The wealthy edged the openings with fur, and had a front panel or plastron also of fur cut in a deep curve, variously decorated, which was known as a plackard or placcard. Some sideless surcotes hung loose, some were close-fitting, but the grand ones were extremely long, front and back, and had to be held up by the wearer when walking, thus revealing the lining of a contrasting rich fabric or fur. They were worn between 1360 and 1500 and as state apparel as late as 1525.

The houppelande was worn by women at the end of the 14th century, long and loose, high-collared and with sleeves like the men's (though not the bellows sleeve). The pleated houppelande was also worn, but the pleating started high under the breasts with a belt to emphasize the high-waisted effect. The high collar gave way to a V-shape, cut to breast level and outlined with a fur or a flattish collar, showing the undergarment at centre front. A similar neckline and collar featured on gowns worn in Burgundy in the late 14th century and becoming popular elsewhere in the 15th, which had high-waisted, closely-fitted bodices with long tight sleeves cut to cover the hands to the knuckles, broad belts and extremely long full skirts, semi-circular or pleated to the bodice, with a wide band of contrasting fabric or fur around the hem to match the collar.

For extra protection out-of-doors, cloaks or mantles were worn, hanging from the shoulders and caught across above the breasts by decorative cords. Indoors the mantle was worn on state occasions.

Women's hose were in fact stockings, held up with garters. They would rarely have been seen, except perhaps when riding. Shoes followed the same lines as the men's but without the exaggerated toes.

Women's headdresses, from modest beginnings in the 13th century, had by the 15th reached a rare level of fantasy and absurdity, increasing considerably the apparent head-size and height of the wearer. Italian women seem to have succumbed to these follies less whole-heartedly, although their headdresses were elaborate enough; in particular, draped turbans and complicated arrangements of jewels, hair and fabric were popular, and the hair was less completely covered. Elsewhere, uncovered hair was rare, being considered respectable only for very young girls, brides or a queen at her coronation, who might wear it loose and flowing under a small circlet of gold and precious stones or simply of flowers. A coif was worn by young girls over loose flowing hair, but less often under a cap by women until the 16th century though it may have been worn informally at home or as a base on which to mount other headdresses.

In the early 13th century the hair was taken into a small knot or bun in the nape of the neck and covered by a wimple, a piece of fine white linen draped over the front of the neck and swathed round the chin with the ends fixed to the hair at the crown, or to a band or fillet around the head. The French called the wimple a barbette but also used this name for a narrow band of linen worn in the same manner as the wimple. Over the wimple it was usual to place a veil, light or dark in colour, which hung down at the back and sides of the head. By the middle of the century a small round flat-topped cap was worn over the wimple or barbette; sometimes it was hollow-crowned and the neck

Figure from 15 C. tapestry. Blue gown lined with beige coloured fur; bandolier in red and green.

14 C. rings Opal & pearls

14 C brooches pearls and precious stones

Burgundian, mid 15 C Heart-shaped headdress with padded roll.

15 C Flemish, 15 C Butterfly headdress.

pearls and precious stones on gold

Flemish, 1460. Tunics with fixed pleats.

Flemish, late 15 C. Blue tunic, pinkish-red hat and hose.

drapery was pulled through and draped over the top. It is probable that this small cap evolved into the larger, turban-like style (as worn by the Countess of Holland in the 15th-century *Figures from a chimney piece* in the Amsterdam Museum).

By the 14th century the hair was braided over the ears, with the wimple taken up over it and held by a fillet or circlet shaped to fit the widened hairstyle, leaving the braided hair visible at the front. Hair braided in this way was later enclosed in decorative cauls of bejewelled gold network joined by a fillet or circlet, over which a veil might be worn. These reticulated cases, often referred to as bosses or templers, might be lined with silk, and since the nape of the neck and the upper forehead were shaved, no hair was visible: even the eyebrows were plucked to a fine line or shaved completely. By 1410 this type of headdress had evolved into the horned headdress with the widened templers further extended by wires from which a veil fell over the back of the head. This in turn changed to the templers being extended upwards above the head, forming a V-shaped dip over the forehead, secured by a decorative circlet and with a veil at the back, fashionable between 1420 and 1450 and later known as the heart-shaped headdress. This shape was also embellished by a padded roll attached around the inner side of the templers, dominating the headdress, worn with or without a veil. The hennin, generally thought of as typical of the gothic period, in fact only came into fashion in the mid 15th century; often worn with a large veil supported by a wire frame, it became known later as a butterfly headdress. The towering steeple shape, popular in Burgundy, was rare in England and Italy.

The chaperon and wide straw and felt hats were worn by women as well as men.

CHILDREN
Infants were swaddled in bands of cloth, often richly embroidered. Older children were dressed in replicas of adult garments but with less exaggeration in the length of skirt and sleeve. On formal or state occasions children of noble and wealthy families were dressed as richly as their parents. Both boys and girls wore the coif, the girls' hair flowing out from beneath it.

ACCESSORIES AND JEWELRY
Men and women, rich and poor, carried a purse at their belt, and might hang articles such as a sheath knife or keys from it also. A baldric or bandolier worn diagonally across the body, originally used to suspend either a script or sword but worn in the late 14th and the 15th century as an ornament by men and women, was often ornate, jewelled or even hung with bells. Gloves of kid, chamois or fabric, soft and wide at the wrist or with gauntlets, were often tucked through the belt if not worn. Working gloves would be made of hide.

An increasing demand for jewelry in Europe during the middle ages allowed jewellers gradually to liberate themselves from church patronage and form guilds, laying down rules of apprenticeship and setting high standards of workmanship. Jewelled belts, brooches (round, star-shaped or pentagonal), rings, and chains with jewelled pendants were worn by men and women. Lady Fee, in *Piers Ploughman*, is described as follows:

... Handsomely her fingers were fretted with gold wire,
And thereon red rubies, as red as any hot coal,
And diamonds of dearest price, and double manner of sapphires,
Orientals and green beryls [emeralds] ...

Hat worn over coif

Chaperone or hood with liripipe

Roundel with top drape, over Chaperon

Loose hose

Overskirt turned up and fixed at back

Small cap or hat

Short doublet to which hose could be attached

Short cape with hood

Pouch attached to belt

Knee length hose with bare legs and feet

Semi-fitted surcote with deep armholes

Cape with hood

French, 15 C. Peasants or country folk

Precious stones were thought to be antidotes to poison and a remedy for disease. Sword and dagger hilts represented fine examples of the goldsmith's art. With the lower necklines in the 15th century, women wore heavy, collar-like necklaces; and the 'collar' or necklace of an Order was worn by men who had the right to do so.

FABRICS AND COLOUR

The 13th and 14th centuries saw the introduction into western Europe of a great variety of fabrics, which became more widely available as European textile workers grew increasingly skilful during the 15th century. Linen weaves included sheer lawn and baptiste for veils and canvas for hard-wearing garments. Cotton, originally imported from Egypt via the ports of Asia Minor but from the 12th century grown and spun in Italy, was available in various weights, colours and patterns. Germany produced hand-printed fabrics from the 12th to the 14th centuries when monasteries developed mass-production methods for cutting blocks to print capital letters on manuscripts.

Wool was the staple material for men's and women's garments, in a great variety of weights and colours including serge, flannel, cameline (thought to be a textile made of camelhair, probably imported from Cyprus and Syria, first mentioned in 1284), and, in the 15th century, camlet, a kind of mohair. Langland's Lady Fee wears a robe 'full rich, of red scarlet dyed/With bands of red gold and of rich stones'. Scarlet was not a colour but a fabric of soft, fine wool dyed in the yarn with cochineal; after weaving it might be left red, or top-dyed black or any dark colour, hence references to 'black-scarlet'.

Among the silks were damasks, brocades, cendal – a coarser version of sarcenet which was a thin, soft silk of taffeta weave with a sheen variously coloured, often shot – and samite, a very expensive silk, often interwoven with gold and silver threads, which were also used to make gold or silver fabrics. A fine silk tissue was used for veils.

Velvet, known in Europe from about 1298, was figured, cut and brocaded. Wool velvet was manufactured in Venice, cotton velvet in Lucca. Fur was used extensively, sable, squirrel and ermine for the rich, rabbit, wolf or sheepskin for the poorer communities. Garments likely to receive hard wear were often made of leather.

Time has mellowed the colours in paintings and frescoes, but it is fairly certain that the original clothing had a gem-like brilliance since we read of 'vermilion samite embroidered with gold flowers', 'cloth of gold, red tinselled with gold and trimmed ermine', 'brown samite with little drops of gold'. All dyes were of vegetable origin. Heraldic devices were embroidered in gold across the front of a surcote, and a particoloured robe might be plain on one side and gaily embroidered with heraldic birds or fish on the other; or a garment might be 'rayed', i.e. striped horizontally or diagonally in different colours. In contrast were the sober homespun colours, often faded and stained, worn by the peasants and poorer citizens. Chaucer's Knight in the Prologue to *The Canterbury Tales* wears a tunic of fustian (similar to canvas) '... stained dark/With smudges where his armour had left mark'.

1450–1600: Renaissance

The intense preoccupation with attaining heaven which dominated people's outlook in the middle ages gradually gave way during the Renaissance period to a broader, more questioning awareness of the world. The Renaissance developed first in Italy where, in the mid-15th century, a rediscovery of the classical past and the spread of learning led to new ideas about the nature of the world and the importance of the individual; and it was there, under the patronage of rich merchant princes ruling over independent and rival city states, that a great upsurge of activity in all the arts occurred, spreading across Europe and reaching its final flowering in England during the late 16th and early 17th centuries.

Dynastic union with the Netherlands, Austria and much of Italy, together with her conquests in the New World, made Spain a great power with considerable influence in Europe, especially as regards costume, in the 16th century, and notably in England, the country which was to challenge her power and her authority in the New World.

The widening of horizons brought by the discovery of the Americas and Indies, a broader intellectual outlook, and the new interest in classical styles are all reflected in the transition from a vertical to a horizontal emphasis in architecture, and important buildings were now secular, not ecclesiastical. Houses, although better lit with clearer window glass and whitewashed ceilings, were still sparsely furnished; private chambers were now usually tiled on the ground floor and boarded on the upper floors, but the great halls were still covered with rushes whose lower depths might harbour refuse and ordure. Nevertheless, even if living standards were primitive in comparison with today, this was the age of such painters as Botticelli, Leonardo da Vinci, Raphael, Michelangelo, Titian, Holbein, Brueghel, Dürer, Cranach, Moroni, Veronese and El Greco and of writers such as Cervantes, Bacon, Marlowe and, of course, Shakespeare.

The emphasis in dress also changed from height to width, and the last of the medieval or gothic style can be seen in the transitional period of the late 15th and early 16th centuries. Men's long pleated gowns and pointed shoes gave way to square shoulders, short gowns and square-toed shoes; women's hennins, high waists, V neck-lines and long trains were replaced by lower headdresses, longer bodices, square décolletage, and skirts just reaching the ground. The extreme width seen during the reigns of Henry VIII of England, François I of France and Charles V of Spain was in its turn superseded by a more slender appearance, still wide at shoulder and hip to set off the long bodices and narrow waists.

There is considerable national variation in dress at this time, although with increasing trade and travel the exchange of fashion ideas was growing. In general, Italian dress was soft, fluid and elegant, reflecting the idealization of the human form so important in Italian Renaissance art; Spanish similar but quickly becoming more rigid; German over-elaborate, slashed and puffed, with hats loaded with feathers; French, influenced by Italy until about 1510, then more Spanish; English, influenced first by Italy, then Germany, and finally very strongly by Spain.

Styles of this period can still be seen in use today; for instance, the Swiss Papal

Guards' uniform, attributed to Michelangelo; the Yeomen of the Guard at the Tower of London, dressed much as they were in Henry VIII's time; academic gowns at Oxford University, priests' birettas, and many traditional peasant costumes. The court cards in a traditional pack of playing cards are a stylized version of mid-Renaissance fashion.

MEN

The shirt, worn next to the skin but seen through slashings and openings of the upper garment, was cut full and gathered at first to a low neckline and later into a band with a small collar or frill, from which the ruff (page 49) developed. The front, neckband and edges of the long full sleeves, also gathered into a band during the mid-16th century, were embroidered in black, red, blue or gold. The rich fabrics of the outer garments could not be washed, but the shirt, usually of linen, could; in addition to being decorative its purpose was probably more to protect those expensive fabrics from becoming soiled than for reasons of hygiene.

Body garments worn over the shirt were the doublet, jerkin and gown. As the doublet and jerkin are often similar in line it is necessary to define as clearly as possible the characteristics of each. Until about the early 16th century the doublet was an undergarment rather like a modern waistcoat, close-fitting to the waist, cut low and wide at the front to reveal the shirt and sometimes a stomacher or 'fill-in'; its sleeves, slim and to the wrist, were either sewn or tied by points into the scye (armhole). All that can be seen in portraits, etc. are the lower sleeves and the fronts. From the mid 16th century, however, the doublet was definitely an outer garment (comparable to today's jacket), tight-fitting to a very narrow waist, buttoned down the front from a high collar and developing skirts which varied from very short to hip-length; the sleeves were fuller at the head, their attachment being hidden by stiffened bands, often crescent-shaped, projecting over the shoulder and known as wings, or by a padded roll. Between 1570 and 1600 the somewhat absurd and ugly peascod-bellied doublet became fashionable (though not in Italy). The tight narrow waistline ran from normal level at the side to a low point at the front, stiffened and padded between the lining and outer fabric with buckram and bombast (a mixture of horse-hair, flock, wool rags, etc.) to form a bulge overhanging the girdle. Some sleeves were also bombasted in a leg-of-mutton shape.

The original doublet continued as an undergarment, called by mid-century a waistcoat or petticoat, i.e. a short coat, sleeved, often padded and worn for warmth but rarely visible except in informal half-dress. The Earl of Essex is said to have been executed in a scarlet waistcoat.

The early jerkin was fitted to the waist, its pleated skirts reaching to just above the knee; it might be high- or low-necked, but was always open at the front to reveal the doublet, shirt and cod-piece. It usually had sleeves, probably detachable. By the mid 16th century the jerkin was high-necked with a standing collar; worn either buttoned closely from neck to waist or falling open from a closed neckline, it was usually sleeveless, with wings or padded rolls at the shoulder, the skirts no longer pleated but flared and of varying lengths. A narrow scalloped or tabbed edging below the waist or around the armhole was referred to as pickadils. Jerkins of leather known as buff-jerkins were adopted by civilians from the military for informal wear.

The long gown was considered fashionable until about 1490–95, after which a shorter version appeared, and by 1540 its direct descendant was fashionably worn

Richly dressed dwarf:
pale blue brocade doublet,
buff-coloured hat,
belt, tabard or cape,
and hat grey under-
brim on hat.

Italian, early-mid 15C.

Queen. Hair drawn back
into a small hennin,
with short veil over
forehead and neck, worn
with a light coronet.

Workman. Dark,
close fitting tunic
with gathered
upper sleeve.
White cap, shirt
and braies. Hose rolled
down below knee with
points hanging loose.
Short boots laced in
front.

Man with short curled hair
and flat black cap with
decoration in turned — up brim

Back view of fighting
man, showing hose (one leg
green, the other red) attached by
points, revealing shirt and braies
at centre back. Ties at shoulders
for attaching extra sleeves.

Queen's attendant. Hair drawn back and wrapped in a roll around
the head. Soft pink robe with hanging sleeves and embroidered
belt over blue-green and gold brocade under-robe. Chemise shows
at neckline.

English, 1482. Hennin with butterfly veil. Fur collar and cuffs. Long pendent tab on girdle.

English, 1473. Butterfly veil, hair shaved back from forehead, fold of veil over front. Elaborate necklace.

English, 1484. Small hennin with butterfly veil. Bold elaborate fabric design for gown.

Italian, 15C. Dyed hair combed high and held in place by jewel. Sleeves embroidered with large flower motifs.

Italian, (Umbrian), 1465-6. Black gown with gold brocade sleeves, hair dressed with white and gold braid and jewels.

English, 1488. Cream hood embroidered in light brown and veiled in black, over white cap. Black wimple edged with white.

Italian, 1490-95. Short gown with wide sleeves and collar. Pleats on shirt held by braid. Particoloured hose. Gloves with cuffs weighted by jewel.

Italian, 1486-90. Tabard-like garment with low V neckline over short-waisted, full skirted gown, visible at sides. Shift puffs out through sleeve at shoulder and elbow fastening and at slashing on upper arm. Small jewelled pendant.

German, 1523-4 Scholar's cap and two gowns, the under one fur-lined, the outer one with deep collar and cuffs of contrasting material.

Italian, 1514. The Casa di Rafaello Rome, – later demolished

Flemish, 1490. Black velvet hood with brown crown, pinned with a brooch. Brown gown pinned up at back shows black kirtle; sleeve open on back seam to reveal puffs of shift.

Flemish, 1490 Large white beaver hat with high feather trim, held on by a lavender-coloured scarf, over a green cap and long hair. Red and green robe over black doublet, grey hose

English, late 16C. Hair brushed back and puffed out (possibly padded), uncovered except for jewel. Lace-trimmed ruff-like collar over supportasse.

Flemish, 1568. Peasants dancing

Wide black shoes, tasselled pouch on belt

Flemish, 1490. Gold turban, pink gown with grey-blue under-sleeves, green plastron or stomacher laced across with red cords, gold girdle with pommander.

Black beaver hat worn slung over shoulder, small red cap over long hair. Brown doublet. Upper part of hose striped white, pink and grey, lower part black, embroidered in gold. Black shoes. Decorative belt and pouch with tassels.

English 1560. Stone staircase at Burghley House Northamptonshire. Man in doublet and trunk hose.

short to above the knee, very full, pleated at the back from a yoke, open at the front and thrown back to reveal a rich lining, often of fur (snow-leopard or spotted lynx were popular). The lining also covered the widening collar spread over the shoulders to a squared-off shape at the back. The bulky square silhouette was emphasized by enormously puffed short sleeves reaching the mid-arm and disclosing the sleeves of doublet or jerkin from elbow to wrist. These gowns sometimes also retained the bellows sleeve hanging behind the puffed sleeve, presumably simply for decoration. Long gowns, plainer but of fine material and richly lined, again often with fur, were still worn by older men, but by 1600 were retained only by scholars and ecclesiastics, or as night or house robes.

The short gown remained fashionable for gallants until about 1570 when it was replaced by the cloak which became general wear, with great variety in cut and length. Some cloaks reached just below the waist, others almost to the feet; some were collarless, others had standing or falling collars, some even had sleeves inserted though apparently never used. The 'Spanish' cloak was short and hooded; the Reiter or 'French' cloak, long and circular or semi-circular, generally had a square flat collar or shoulder cape. Cloaks were worn in various ways – over both shoulders, slung from one only, or diagonally across the back. A counterpart of the sleeved cloak was the mandilion, fashionable around 1577 – a loose, smock-like jerkin with open side seams and sham sleeves, worn either as a cloak with the sleeves hanging over the arms or sideways with the sleeves hanging at the back and front. It subsequently became a livery garment.

In the late 15th and early 16th centuries, if the sleeves and a section showing at the front of a garment are of different fabric to that of the rest, this does not necessarily postulate the existence of a complete undergarment. Sleeves were detachable, and small pieces of material called stomachers, often heavily ornamented, were used to fill the V- or U-shaped gap at the front of the doublet. There is also evidence of garments having two pairs of sleeves set to the same armhole, the uppermost hanging loose and being uniform with the body garment and those covering the arm of a different material, pattern or colour – an agreeable and economical way of varying the appearance of garments, not infrequently used in later periods.

Hose continued to be worn, often visible to the waistline or partially covered by the jerkin. They might be striped, variegated, particoloured or embroidered; or with the upper portion differentiated from the lower to suggest short trunks. Hose were still attached by points to the under-doublet and contemporary illustrations show working men who have discarded their jerkins and untied the points joining hose to doublet at the back to give greater ease of movement – a practical solution, but probably not considered appropriate for a gentleman, except in unusual circumstances.

After 1540–50 hose became separated into upper and nether stocks. The upper stocks were in effect breeches, the nether, stockings. In Germany upper stocks reached the knee and were elaborately slashed, but in England, where they were to become known as trunk-hose, trunk-breeches or round-hose, they were fuller and at first only just visible under the skirt of the jerkin. A conspicuous feature of both styles was the protruding cod-piece, padded and often elaborately decorated. With the shortening of doublet and jerkin, the trunk-hose were fully revealed and between 1550 and 1600 took on a variety of shapes – very short, barely to the crotch; longish to the lower thigh; stiffened, padded or falling softly. They were constructed in three layers: a fitted base, over which any padding was arranged, an inner lining cut full, and an outer section, less full but slashed into long strips called panes, braided on the edge, between which the inner lining would show. Ribbon-like lengths of material might be used in a similar manner. About 1570, canions came into fashion; for these the inner or base section was extended to the knee or just below, and the section revealed below the short trunk-hose could be of rich material often of a contrasting type and colour. The stockings were worn drawn up over them, and during the second half of the 16th century a fashion for wearing a sash garter placed below the knee in front, the ends crossed behind the knee and brought forward to tie in a bow above it centrally or to the outer side, was referred to as cross-gartering.

Venetians – pear-shaped breeches, wide (often bombasted) around the hips, then narrowing to the knee – were very fashionable by 1580. They continued to be worn until the end of the century. Venetian-slops or great slops were voluminous throughout and were probably named after slop-hose, the loose wide-kneed breeches worn by seamen. Small slops, worn from about 1585 until the early 17th century, were similar to Venetians but with the legs only slightly narrowed and finishing loose above the knee.

Between 1490 and 1540 width was also emphasized in shoes. Firmly established by 1500 was a heelless shoe cut very low at the front, often only just covering the toes, and up to $6\frac{1}{2}$ inches wide, held by a strap across the ankle or instep. Made of leather, velvet or heavy silk, these shoes were slashed to show silken puffs, embroidered, bejewelled or with jewelled buckles. (This extreme fashion for width never found favour in Italy.) By 1540 a rounder toe and higher cut appeared, and also a wedge-shaped sole raising the back of the foot. The round-toed shoes were apparently pulled on like slippers; but later the side latchets were extended and tied at the front with a bow, elaborated in the late 16th and early 17th centuries to form a large rosette. Heels were introduced around 1600, low and often painted red (a fashion that was to become universal in the 17th and 18th centuries). Boots were worn for travelling, riding or hunting, hugging the calf and splaying out or split at the back behind the knee and turned over for ease of movement. If not turned over they might be attached to a belt, in the manner of early hose. From the late 15th to the mid 17th century, overshoes shaped like mules, called pantofles (pantables or pantacles), were worn to protect the front of the shoes.

In the late 15th and early 16th centuries men's hair varied considerably in length. Italian and Flemish dandies wore their hair falling to the shoulders, but in general it reached about chin length and, by 1550 or so, was cropped quite short, only to lengthen again slightly with soft curls around 1580. Shaven faces were fashionable at first but the fashion for beards increased; Henry VIII and François I, with their rather square short beards and small moustaches, had their followers, and during the reign of Elizabeth I the small neat beard, rounded in about 1560 and pointed around 1570, with a small moustache, seems to have been general, though forked, square and spade-shaped beards were also seen – but rarely a clean-shaven face.

The small round cap-like hat with or without a turn-up, worn by Italians in the 15th century, appears to have been the forerunner of that worn by Henry VII in the portrait bust by Pietro Torrigiano (1500), with the crown pinched into four lobes and the side flaps or half brim standing out slightly. In its turn, this cap was the ancestor of the scholar's cap worn late into the 16th century, and the priest's biretta. In contrast to this simple cap are the wide-brimmed hats of the Flemish dandies portrayed in the illuminated manuscript *Roman de la Rose* (1490, British Museum) with the brim turned up off the face and a huge feather shooting up from the crown. Apparently worn over a

German-Swiss, 16C.
Gauze drawn over an
embroidered cap. High collar
edged with ruching;
skirt caught up in front
reveals striped underskirt
or kirtle; Long girdle
with massive pendant
at back.

German, 1498. Italian-inspired costume: long hair; gold
grey and black embroidery on shirt; velvet bands on doublet.

German, early-mid-16C. Short gown with wide collar
and hanging sleeves,
banded with velvet.
Pleating at neck of shirt.
Slashed undersleeves.
Thigh-length doublet or
tunic, pleated and
trimmed with bands
of velvet.

German, 1514. Swiss and
German mercenary soldiers
adopted and influenced the
spread of slashed styles,
of which this is an early
example.

Venetian, 1495. High waist, low neckline; puffings on
sleeves; rich brocade kirtle.

French, early 16C. — Townswomen, one wearing early version of
French hood, the other a linen veil. Skirt hitched up over girdle (left).

Flemish, early 16 C. Robe in deep blue with cream decoration and lining, soft pink kirtle, embroidered chemise. Heavy gold and jewelled chain round neck and girdle. French hood decorated with gold.

Deep blue robe trimmed with gold, collar and sleeve lining deep pink, gold embroidered shirt. Cream hose, shoes and belt.

Heavy gold chain round neck.

Franco-Flemish straw.

late 15 C. early 16 C. hats (The man's worn over a hood), pouches. Tucked-up gown, common in peasant' costume with laced bodice.

German, 1525-30 Gown of velvet and brocade with laced bodice revealing chemise. Large plumed hat worn over a caul decorated with pearls.

Heavy necklace and gold chains.

German, c. 1525. Elaborate slashing favoured by mercenary soldiers.

small cap, these hats are held in place by a long scarf, and are also shown hanging from the shoulder, the scarf falling across the neck.

Throughout the 16th century there are many variations of a flat cap with a beret-shaped crown and a narrow brim, either straight or turned up, which was cut into sections, fastened up or allowed to droop, or sometimes widened and stiffened. This type of flat cap is shown in portraits of Henry VIII and Edward VI of England and François I of France, worn a little on one side, trimmed with jewels and feathers laid along the brim or a feather at the side – all emphasizing the width. But by 1570 it was no longer court fashion; known as the city flat cap, it was worn only by citizens, tradesmen and apprentices, who continued to wear it well into the 17th century.

By the late 16th century, when fashion decreed a longer, slimmer look, the cap grew in height and was worn slightly to one side; the crown was pleated and stiffened, with a band of metallic braid or twisted braid and ribbon round the base, the brim narrow and rigid (the French favoured a rolled brim). Trimmed with rosettes of gold and jewels and tall ostrich tips or osprey plumes, this hat supplanted the Tudor cap. By the 1670s hats of stiff felt or leather with fairly high crowns and increasingly wide brims foreshadow those of the 17th century.

Hats generally were worn indoors as well as out, and were rarely doffed except in the presence of royalty. A skull cap with a small upturned and decorated brim was worn informally indoors in the 16th century; and in bed, in the second half of the century, a plain washable nightcap called a biggin was worn with a nightshirt.

WOMEN

The smock or undershift, worn next to the skin, could be seen at the neckline, wrist or elbow or all three, and puffing out through the slashed sleeves.

With outer garments in the late 15th century, there is a marked difference between the Italian style and that of the more northern countries. The waistline of Italian gowns varied from high to normal, the neckline was low and rounded and some bodices laced across the front over an undergown or kirtle or a stomacher. Sleeves, slim and close-fitting or slightly fuller and wider at the head, were frequently tied into the arm scye and slashed between the upper and lower sections at the elbow to allow the smock to puff out. This sleeve was seen in other countries but not in England. A type of surcote, hanging loose from just below the bust and shoulder blades and open at the sides to show the gown, was retained by the Italians. Italy at this time was a group of city states each with its own individual fashions, such as the Venetian courtesan's gown of 1500–10, often very high-waisted, with a round, low neckline exposing most if not all of the breasts, tight sleeves slashed to reveal many puffs of the smock, and long trailing skirts over high pattens or chopines. These women, heavily rouged and powdered, their hair bleached and/or dyed in streaks, are vividly portrayed in Carpaccio's painting *Two Venetian Courtesans* in the Museo Civico, Venice. Later in the 16th century Italian women's dress came more into line with that of other countries, although neither the style fashionable in early Tudor England nor the extreme stiffness popular during Elizabeth I's reign was ever adopted in Italy by men or women.

The north European countries may be viewed as a group, although there were national variations. English and Flemish women kept the high-waisted wide V neckline, tight sleeves and long trailing skirts until the late 15th century, but by about 1500–10 the waistline dropped to its natural position, the neckline was squared, sleeves belled out from the elbow tapering to a narrow wrist, or were long and wide like the earlier houppelande sleeves. This transitional style evolved into that of Henry VIII's reign – a long stiffened bodice with a low, wide, square decolletage, the skirt spread wide over stiffened petticoats, sometimes open at the front to reveal the kirtle (now the name for an underskirt or petticoat). English gowns were trained at this time, Dutch and Flemish rarely. The sleeves further emphasized the appearance of width. The undersleeve, cut in two pieces usually in the same material as the kirtle, was flat and wide below the elbow with the back seam, curving into the wrist, left open and tied with points between which the smock sleeves puffed out. (Some costume historians think these undersleeves may have been part of the undergown, but as with men's clothes it is difficult to be certain about extra sleeves, stomachers, etc.) The oversleeves had a fitted sleeve head and upper arm, then spread out and turned back into enormous cuffs lined with fur or rich fabric. Henry VIII's daughters are both portrayed wearing this type of gown – Elizabeth, aged about twelve or thirteen, by an unknown artist, wears red and gold trimmed with gold and pearls, and Mary, by Hans Eworth in 1554, wears russet brocade and dark brown fur in the later style enclosing the low decolletage with a yoke and high upstanding collar. The drawings and paintings of Holbein, court painter to Henry VIII, are also an excellent source of information on both men's and women's costume of this period.

From the 1550s, while Italian, Protestant German and Swiss fashion preserved some national character, England and France adopted details of dress from a diversity of sources. The dominant characteristics of fashion throughout the West were Spanish, and in dress as in etiquette the Spanish style was in the grand manner. The long wasp waist, high collars, padded hips and general rigidity usually referred to as Elizabethan might more correctly be termed Spanish, as, indeed, it is by German historians.

The bodice and skirt became separate garments in the 16th century and it is easier to deal with them separately after 1550. The bodice, tight and flat across the chest, lengthened to a deep point at the front, reaching well over the stomach by the 1590s. To achieve this, an undergarment known first as a 'body' or 'pair of bodys' and by the 17th century as stays, was made of two layers of linen often stiffened with paste, stitched together and shaped to the waist at the sides. Later, whalebones were added at the sides and back; to keep the front rigid a busk (busc) – a flat length of wood, horn, whalebone or metal tapering to a point – was inserted between the layers of linen on the forepart and held by a lace. These stays were fastened at the back or front and covered by a stomacher when gowns open at the front became fashionable. The low, arched decolletage held its own for a while but was frequently filled in by a contrasting partlet covering the body from breast to neck and often matched to detachable sleeves, and increasingly the bodice itself was high-necked. Baring the bosom was popular again in the late 1570s; in England it was considered a sign of maidenhood and was much affected by Elizabeth I in her later years. The small waist and long point of the bodice was accentuated in the 1590s by the stomacher or plastron, an ornate V-shaped panel, often matching the kirtle, from the low decolletage to the point at the waist.

Sleeves varied; the bell sleeve with turned-back cuff and wide undersleeve was rare after 1560, being replaced by a slim-fitting sleeve closed at the wrist, the upper arm covered by a puffed section, often paned like men's trunk-hose, or by wings. By the last quarter of the 16th century full sleeves, bombasted like the men's, were affected by ladies of high fashion. Both types of sleeve frequently had oversleeves of various shapes, hanging to waist level or to the ground, partially covering or hanging well at the back of the upper arm or caught by brooches across the forearm.

English, 1537. Red Velvet gown lined with sable, embroidered in gold braid; huge puffed sleeves with unused hanging sleeves attached at back.

Black hat with white plume, underside trimmed with gold tags.

English, 1536. English hood, with one side of veil and both lappets pinned up.

English, 1540. French hood; white cap with frills of gold tissue and crescent band, narrow black velvet veil.

Satin gown with velvet yoke; slashed sleeves reveal gold-embroidered puffs and are caught with aiglets (tags of precious metal) Black embroidery on wrist ruffles.

English, 1527 A lettice cap

Jerkin with pleated skirt, trimmed with silver braid and cut low at front to show a high-collared doublet slashed on front and sleeves. Elaborate codpiece mounted on upper stocks — white lower stocks or hose. Shoes cut high over instep.

Russet velvet gown, the neckline edged with pearls and rubies; turned-back cuffs, front edge and hem embroidered with fine braid. Sleeves and kirtle of silver brocade, ruby clasps on sleeves between puffs of chemise.

Flemish, 1539. Over a tiny pearl-edged cap an oblong of lawn, then a larger cap embroidered with gold and pearls. Jewelled pendant pinned on left side.

Flemish, 1530. A bongrace headdress.

Cut-away front of bodice over a partlet reflects male jerkin fashion. High waistline and lack of train typically Flemish.

English, 1543. Gable hood, with lappets turned up, veil hanging at back. Fur-lined sleeves. Chemise revealed at neck and back seam of sleeves.

Italian, 1553-4 White satin gown embroidered with black galloon braid. Sleeves, with puffed tops, caught with cords and jewels; yoke a network of fine gold cord decorated with pearls. A similar net covers the hair.

English 1548. Red velvet gown, ermine-lined, trimmed gold braid; short sleeves, with loose hanging sleeves at back. Doublet of silver brocade has flared skirts to thigh level; horizontal cords, crossing the bands of decoration, button at front. Trunk hose, with codpiece, slashed to match doublet sleeves. Black dagger-sheath with large tassel.

Black hat with turned-down brim, white feather.

English version of French hood. High decorated neckband with ruff.

Tassel of girdle made of tiny pearls

'Pickadils' on collar, sleeves and skirt of jerkin, bound in gold.

White hose shoes still slashed and fairly wide

Italian, 1540. Hair uncovered, wrapped closely round head with a small jewelled band.

Paned trunk hose padded low.

Spanish 1551 jerkin shoulder double skirt; panes over slashed which are

Leather with short sleeve and slashed into doublet, the sleeves of caught by braid.

English, 1545. Gown with velvet yoke and lining to oversleeves. Red satin underskirt and sleeves, the latter with embroidered bands and aiglets. A book hangs from girdle.

Pinkish-red gown with huge puffed and ruched sleeves; lower sleeves, possibly of an undergown are Burgundy colour, slashed to show yet another sleeve, black with gold braid. Crimped yoke, fine gauze with gold trim.

English, mid 16C. Doublet of
orange-red silk trimmed gold
braid and pearl buttons,
slashed on sleeves and chest
to reveal shirt. Very high collar
with ruff; collar-wings and
short skirts edged with pickadils.
Black hat with higher crown,
jewelled band and coloured
feather to match doublet.
Belt has attachment
for sword and dagger.

Necklace of
white and black
pearls with
medallion.

English or French, 1560. Hair
parted in centre and arched
over temples, caught into
small cap or caul of same
material as yoke and lower
sleeves of gown. Unusual upper
sleeves - short to elbow, large
puffs above. Kirtle of brocade
or damask
over Spanish
farthingale.

Pearl
necklace
knotted at
front.

Spanish, 1560. Cap decorated
with pearls. Cape of rich brocade
edged and banded with braided
decoration has hanging
sleeves and is lined with
ermine. Standing
collar cut with a
'step'- an early
form of lapel.

French, 1569.
Black velvet
cape and jerkin
with long skirts,
decorated with gold
embroidery. White doublet,
sleeves with pinked
decoration.
Padded

trunk
hose, paned
and pinked.

Spanish, 1567. Jerkin
with peascod belly, wings,
collar and skirt trimmed braid,
sleeves slashed and pinked. Well-
padded trunk hose, paned and
with codpiece. Lace-edged
ruffles and wrist ruffles.

Shoes fairly natural shape
and slashed.

During the second half of the 15th century, in Spain, a structure known as a farthingale was devised for holding out the skirt. Hoops of rushes, wood, wire or whalebone, graduating in size from hip to hem, were stitched into a petticoat which was gored so that it sloped stiffly and smoothly from waist to ground in a dome or bell shape. It was adopted in England in the early 16th century and referred to as the Spanish farthingale, and was worn in England and France until the middle of the century; but from contemporary portraits it appears that in those countries extra padding was added to give a more rounded appearance to the hips. This evolved into a large padded roll called a bum roll or barrel, tied round the waist to distend the skirt at the hips, which replaced the Spanish farthingale (although it was retained in Spain well into the 17th century). By 1580 the large roll had become cumbersome, and cane or whalebone encased in a petticoat returned, but now in a wheel-shaped structure placed high on a level with the waistline to hold the skirt out horizontally and then allow it to fall vertically to the ground. The long busk point of the bodice rested on the front, causing the structure to tilt up slightly behind. This wheel or Catherine farthingale, and another similar in construction but wider at the sides and flattened at the front which was known as the French farthingale, remained in fashion until about 1620.

These huge skirts might be of the same material all round, or open at the front to display the kirtle or a forepart or decorative panel mounted on a coarse underskirt. The effect of the wheel and French farthingales was further emphasized in the 1590s by a projecting flounce of material matching the skirt, set in radiating pleats from the waist and resting on the extended hip or the rim of the wheel. Most skirts were ground length, and trained for ceremonial wear; later, around 1610, ankle-length skirts were seen, but they died out in the next decade.

Headdresses, like garments, varied in style between countries. The Italians seem never to have adopted the enveloping headdresses popular in northern countries, and during the 15th and 16th centuries usually displayed their hair, often arranged in elaborate coils and braids decorated, rather than covered by, silken caps and cauls or ribbons and jewels. Particularly characteristic of Italian fashion, however, was a large round turban-like headdress, ruffled, netted and knotted, worn set back on the head to reveal the front hair parted in the centre.

The Germans draped up elaborate structures of stiff white linen and later wore large hats, festooned with many plumes in magenta, scarlet, orange, yellow, black and white, over jewelled cauls, as depicted in the paintings of Cranach.

The English favoured an architectural style covering the hair, although stress was laid on the flowing hair of maidens. Hennins continued until the late 15th century, steeple-shaped in France and small and fez-like in England, worn far back on the head, with a wire frame supporting a gauze veil – a continuation of the butterfly headdress. Folds of velvet or gauze placed over the front of the steeple or butterfly headdress foreshadowed the shape of the English hood, known also as the gable, pediment or kennel headdress (1500–43), wired to form a pointed arch above the forehead. The early form hung in folds to the shoulders; the front sections around the face, slit up from the bottom and longer than the back, were called lappets or chaffers. The hood was mounted on an undercap but the front hair was left exposed, smoothed down from a centre parting, until about 1525 when it was concealed by folds of silk, often striped, crossed over under the gable point. Also, at this time, the back drapery was replaced by two long pendent flaps, sometimes pinned up, and the front chaffers were shortened and also often turned up, and a frontal of gold and jewels outlined the gable shape. This type of headdress may be seen in the Holbein drawings at Windsor Castle and in his portrait of Jane Seymour in the Court Museum in Vienna or that of Lady Guildford (attributed to him) in the Metropolitan Museum, New York.

The French hood was to challenge and oust the English hood and remain in fashion from 1521 to 1590 – understandably, as it was considerably more becoming. It was a small bonnet made on a stiff frame, worn far back on the head, the sides curved forward to cover the ears; the inner edge usually had a ruched edging behind which was a decorative border of goldsmith's work called the nether billiment and, further back, arched over the crown, a second band of gold and jewels called the upper billiment. From this a veil of formal pleats or a stiffened flap fell over the back of the neck and could be turned up and worn flat over the crown, the straight edge projecting over the forehead, when it was known as a bongrace.

An English variant of the French hood was flattened across the head, projecting wide at the temples, then turned in to cover the ears, as seen in portraits of Mary Tudor. Later, in the 1580s, Mary Stuart, Queen of Scots, wore a similar style. (18th-century indoor caps following this line were called Mary or Marie Stuart caps.)

Informal coif-like caps can be seen in Holbein drawings dated about 1527, sometimes worn under a hat, but also made of fur and called lettice caps or bonnets or miniver caps (lettice was a fur resembling ermine).

From the 1560s, even in northern countries, there was a tendency to uncover the hair, even out of doors: the centre parting lost favour and the front hair was brushed straight back into an increasingly high coiffure with a small caul or cap confining the back hair. Padding and false hair were often used, and from the 1570s the hair was generously sprinkled with jewels and/or pearls. Coinciding with the fashion for uncovered hair (and to the horror of contemporary moralists), hats and caps in masculine styles were worn by women, particularly for hunting or travelling. Lower-middle, working-class or country women wore simple linen caps much as they had worn the coif – and continued to do so until the 19th century.

Women's shoes, often of rich brocade and jewelled, resembled men's. Pattens (over-shoes) with thick cork soles were in favour from about 1575 to 1600. Chopines, another type of overshoe with a pedestal-like sole, were fashionable in southern Europe, especially in Venice, though they must have been known in England since Shakespeare refers to them in *Hamlet*.

From the second half of the 16th century stockings (previously called nether stocks) might be knitted. Queen Elizabeth received in 1561 a gift of black knitted silk stockings which, it is said, 'tickled her taste so greatly that thereafter she wore no other kind'; silk for leg coverings, however, had apparently been used earlier (although probably woven rather than knitted), as 'one pair short hose of black silk and gold woven, one pair of purple silk and of gold etc.' appear in an inventory of Henry VIII's wardrobe taken after his death. Machine knitting on a stocking frame was invented in 1589.

For protection against the weather women used cloaks, usually hooded, during the whole of this period. The small stiffened shoulder capes favoured by the Flemish in the mid 16th century were probably worn as much indoors as out, as were the loose gowns or coat-dresses common in Germany, with puff sleeves and often lined with fur. Short loose jackets of similar cut to these loose gowns, trimmed with fur and bands of velvet, were a late-16th-century fashion worn for additional warmth.

English, 1577. Sleeveless leather jerkin and padded Venetian breeches, with pickadil finish at armhole, waist and knee. Jerkin fastened with points, left open below neck to reveal the almost skirtless doublet with a row of tiny buttons. Doublet sleeves padded and ruched up the lower arm.

Small ruff above high collar of jerkin.

Large gold jewel on ribbon is caught to one side; small chain and jewel worn under collar

Spanish, 1570. Hat trimmed with small pearls mounted in gold; plumes beige and red. Close-waisted gown in gold brocade with very short paned sleeves.

English, 1569. Hair caught in a caul under small black hat trimmed with groups of small pearls mounted in gold; cream and red feathers. Gown and sleeve portes red, trimmed with black, red and gold braid.

Spanish, 1585. Masculine style hat, high and not gathered, trimmed with pearls and a high plume. Hair dressed high and slightly puffed above the temples.

Light-coloured shoes cut high on instep.

English, 1585. Mandilion worn like a cape with sleeves hanging at back and front. Falling band, a fore-taste of 17C style.

Bell sleeves, split along inner seam, trail on the ground.

Gown fastened at front with ribbon loops and aiglets and worn over a Spanish farthingale.

CHILDREN

Babies continued to be swaddled and children were still dressed as replicas of adults, though the very young may have been allowed to play in their shifts in the seclusion of the nursery. Young boys and girls were dressed alike in long skirts and coif or bonnet. At the age of three or four, boys discarded both for more masculine styles; girls wore the bonnet until their ninth year.

ACCESSORIES AND JEWELRY

Civilian men usually carried a dagger and also, by the early 16th century, a sword, on a girdle or belt. The girdle was at first slung diagonally over the hips, supporting a pouch with a strap through which the dagger could be thrust, or the dagger might be attached direct to the belt or girdle. By 1510, with the introduction of the dress sword carried generally by upper-class civilians, the sword-belt was slung obliquely, often connected to a horizontal girdle, the dagger being worn as before or hung by a chain or tasselled cord. By the mid 16th century, the girdle followed the line of the waist on the doublet and must therefore have been cut on a curve; the sword was then carried by a side strap and hangers carefully arranged to hold it at the correct height and angle, and the dagger might be attached to the girdle at a slanting angle at the back.

A walking stick of polished wood or lightweight cane with a decorative knob was carried by men during the latter part of the 16th century, and was to become part of the fashionable man's attire until early in the 20th century. The watch, introduced in the 16th century, was a much-prized valuable: Charles V is said to have owned an earring containing a small chiming watch, and Henry VIII wore one on a gold chain around his neck. In England in Elizabeth's day it was considered the height of elegance to wear a watch.

Many accessories were common to both men and women. Gloves, either worn or tucked into belt or girdle, of leather (stag, kid, suede, doeskin), satin, velvet, knitted silk or worsted variously coloured, were scented and increasingly elaborately embroidered or decorated and fringed, some slashed to reveal a finger ring. Purses in the shape of small soft bags were often tucked through the girdle (clothes had no pockets). Handkerchiefs, carried from the 16th century, were costly articles of fine linen or silk, familiar to so few that Erasmus urged their use for hygienic reasons; certainly most were carried for display and might be embroidered or edged with fringe, or have tassels at the corners. They were often presented as gifts.

Masks were worn from about 1550. The vizard, covering the whole face to conceal the identity of the wearer or to protect the skin from the weather when riding, was more popular among women than men and in England and France than elsewhere. The half-mask covering the upper part of the face in the mid 16th century was called a loo-mask. The muffler or chin clout, mentioned by Shakespeare as part of Falstaff's disguise when impersonating the fat woman of Brentford, was a square of material folded diagonally and worn over the mouth and chin and sometimes the nose.

Fans and pomanders were carried by women, but by only extremely foppish men. Fans, in common use from the mid 16th century, were rigid, made of feathers, silk or straw fixed to a decorated handle. Queen Elizabeth's wardrobe list of 1600 contains 'Item: one fanne of white feathers, with a handle of golde, havinge two snakes wyndinge aboute it, garnished with a ball of diamonds in the ende, and a crown on each side with a pair of wings garnished with diamondes' and 'Item: one fanne of divers colours, the handle of golde with a bear and a ragged staffe on both sides and a lookinge glasse on throne side.'

English, 1575. Cloak with hanging sleeves, worn over shoulder. Slashed doublet

High-crowned and wide-brimmed hats, later to become associated with the Puritans in England.

Short paned trunk hose with 'tucked' canions tucked into cross-gartered stockings

High-crowned hat has jewelled band and plume

Black pantofles worn over shoes.

Folding fan hangs from girdle on knotted coral-coloured ribbon

French, 1581. Ladies wearing French farthingales, long pointed bodices with collar-shaped ruffs, large bolster-like sleeves. Men's peascod-bellied doublets and Venetians have narrow bands of vertical slashing.

Crown, necklace and pendant of coral, pearl and jet set in gold; long ropes of pearls. Wired veil of gold gauze edged with pearl-sewn lace; pink rose pinned to lace-edged white ruff.

Overskirt and backs of hanging sleeves in gold and cream brocade or cut velvet.

White satin shoes

Fans from portraits of Elizabeth I.

Gloves embroidered and fringed.

English, 1592. Low-cut, stiffened and pointed bodice, padded sleeves and kirtle in cream satin, with criss-cross decoration of rose-like puffs caught with studs of coral, pearl and jet set in gold, also on lining of hanging sleeves edged with pearls. Shorter skirt, also edged with pearls, is mounted on a wheel farthingale.

English, 1586. Hat with high crown trimmed with bands of crêpe-weave fabric called 'cypress', a jewel, osprey and ostrich tips. Hair longer and fuller. Cartwheel ruff.

English, 1596. Girl wears open ruff revealing the bosom. Decorated stomacher on long pointed bodice; double pleated frill over wheel farthingale; loose girdle around waist matches decoration down front of skirt, which is short to reveal a petticoat. Bombasted sleeves with turn-back lace cuffs.

Hair dressed high and puffed out, covered with only a jewel and ostrich tips.

French, 1570. High crowned hat, draped band and rosette with jewel at centre. Small ruff above high collar of doublet.

Type of beard called a 'pick-a-devant' or 'barula'

Boy, still in skirts, wears doublet with peascod belly, sword and sword belt, a sash and a lownecked lace collar (or unstiffened ruff).

Supportasse or under-propper to support huge ruffs worn in the second half of 16 C and early 17 C.

A whole mask, called a vizard

Soft crowned hat trimmed with jewelled band, brooch and ostrich tips.

English, 1582. Paned trunk hose over richly decorated canions, stockings drawn up over knees. Doublet with slightly peascod belly. Ruff split at front. Collarless cloak decorated with pattern similar to that on panes of trunk hose.

A bum-barrel or bum roll tied round the waist to extend the skirt at the hips.

Spanish Farthingale 1550 - 1620.

Pantofles over high-cut shoes

Pomanders, carried or hung from the girdle between 1500 and 1690, were small perforated receptacles of goldsmithing, either circular and flat or spherical, containing perfume or sweet herbs thought to protect against infection and helpful in warding off unpleasant smells. A sable or marten skin with head and claws mounted in gold and jewels, hung from the girdle or worn loosely around the neck, was thought to repel fleas. Small muffs appeared late in the 16th century.

The ruff, so characteristic a part of both male and female costume between 1560 and 1640, originated from the gathered frill above the neck-band of the shirt, but by 1570 it was a separate article. It consisted of a straight band of cambric or lawn pleated into regular tubular folds, starched and goffered, then gathered to the neck size and fixed to a band which could be slipped inside the collar of the doublet or bodice. The folds, known as sets and formed by means of setting sticks, might be held close like a honeycomb or in large open curves. It fastened with tasselled strings and was worn open or closed at the front. Ruffs reached huge proportions in the late 16th and early 17th centuries and had to be supported by a wire frame, generally whipped over with gold, silver or silk thread, fixed at the back of the neck, called a supportasse or under-propper. An alternative to the ruff, sometimes worn with it and eventually replacing it, was the falling band, a separate turn-down collar varying in size and shape and worn by men between 1540 and 1670 and only very occasionally by women before the 17th century.

The amount of jewelry worn by both sexes increased steadily throughout the period and included chains, earrings, brooches, aiglets (metal tags), Orders and finger rings. Jewels were worn in women's hair and decorated the edges of headdresses, hat bands, sword and dagger hilts, fan and mirror handles and girdles and buttons. Eventually whole garments were lavishly sprinkled with jewels; Elizabeth I's gowns for state or gala occasions, covered in embroidery and myriads of little jewels, have never been equalled in extravagance.

FABRICS AND COLOUR

All the materials available in the gothic period continued in use, but weaving skills increased. England, the leading producer of wool, had weaving centres in East Anglia, Yorkshire and the west, and English broadcloth and kerseys were exported throughout Europe. Patterned woollens and linens were also imported from the Netherlands. The majority of silk was still produced in Italy, including some plain stuffs and taffetas (travellers were advised to wear taffeta-lined doublets to discourage fleas). Sarcenet, satins and velvets were, like the woollens and linens, often enriched with embroidery, gold and silver braid and spangles, or might be slashed and pinked (a form of decoration consisting of small holes or short slits cut in the fabric or in the finished garment, arranged to form a pattern and revealing a different-coloured lining). Patterned silks included damask with designs in a single colour, brocades in one or two colours often embroidered with gold, and patterned velvets which, in the 15th and 16th centuries, achieved a technical perfection never surpassed; the pattern, often with a gold background, was in a sumptuous silk pile woven in two or three levels, with groups of gold loops to provide the final accent. These velvets were typical of Renaissance luxury and ostentation.

The English had been famous for embroidery since the 10th century, principally lavished on church furnishings and vestments until the Reformation, after which it was more often used for dress. The skill of Tudor embroiderers, heirs to a long and vigorous

49

tradition, can be seen in the precise detail of contemporary portraits and in the textiles that survive today.

Colours were strong, often dark, at the beginning of the period; red, deep blue, wine, gold brocade, and black continued to be fashionable throughout the period, but were joined after about 1550 by brighter colours such as scarlet, yellow, tawny orange, flame, parrot green and sky blue. Black with white, gold or red were admired combinations, and white with silver was much favoured by Queen Elizabeth in her later years for herself and her ladies.

The age and its people are brought vividly to life in contemporary paintings and literature and in records of pageantry and spectacle. Edward Hall records in *Chronicle* (1542) his eye-witness account of Henry VIII's meeting with Anne of Cleeves in 1540, describing Henry's dress in great detail, including 'a coat of purple velvet all over embroidered with flat gold of damask ...' and 'the sleeves and breast outlined with cloth of gold and tied together with great buttons of diamonds, rubies and orient pearls'. Philip Stubbs, an eloquent Puritan, lists the many excesses of fashion during the 16th century in his *Anatomy of Abuses* (1583).

The clothes of the peasants changed very slowly, but the paintings and drawings of Brueghel in the 1550s–60s show variations from the clothes illustrated by 15th-century artists; though Brueghel's peasants are Flemish, their dress may be accepted as fairly general, especially in the more northern countries. The men, in addition to hose with a cod-piece, wear slops or full breeches and jerkins with pleated skirts. Women's skirts are full and pleated to the waist, sometimes with aprons; bodices are often buttoned or laced over a shift or under gown; their heads are wrapped and they sometimes wear boots like the men. Hats with low or high crowns, wide or narrow brims, in straw or felt, are often worn over coifs; both men and women are hung about with a variety of pouches, bags, knives, bottles, or the tools of their trade. Brueghel gives us as much information about the dress of the common man of his day as Holbein does about that of the court of Henry VIII.

Peasant after 1564.
Skirted tunic, over full
shirt. Long boots.

After 1565. Large
hat and long
tunic. Belt
carries bag of
animal skin bottle,
spoon, knives etc.

Fairly loose hose
or breeches, worn with
boots.

c. 1559-63 Woman with hoe and basket
in long jerkin, patched apron.

1565 or later.
Small bodice
over loose gown or
shirt. Straw or
felt hat worn
over wimple.

c. 1565. Head wrapped in kerchiefs
under fur or sheepskin hat.
Short jacket over very full
skirt or gown.

Market woman,
c. 1558-9. Fur or sheepskin
hat over scarf wrapped head.

c. 1559 - 63.
Loose breeches, jacket
with ragged sleeve.

Netherlands, 16 C. peasant costume.

The seventeenth century

The seventeenth century was an age of experiment and scientific discovery, of increasing freedom of thought and speech, and of wider communication through advances in printing and literacy. As foreign trade and colonization spread, the known world continued to widen; trading links with Russia, India and China, as well as contacts with Africa and the Americas, brought great wealth to England and Holland and great power to the noblemen appointed to administer the new territories. Of the spoils acquired by European conquests around the world – silks, spices, precious metals, jewels, tropical timber, tobacco, sugar and industrial raw materials – it was the English merchants and slave traders who took the largest share.

It was also a time of constitutional, religious and political ferment throughout Europe. Although England was comparatively withdrawn from the disruption of the Thirty Years War (1618–48) and her aesthetic life changed little during the first forty years of the new century, two influences of fundamental importance were growing, one religious, the other constitutional. Puritanism was becoming hostile to the Anglican church established under Henry VIII and threatened the whole political fabric, leading to Civil War and the execution of the King in 1649. But in 1660 the monarchy was restored, and by 1688 a parliamentary monarchy – something quite new – was established.

France became a great power under the absolute monarchy of Louis XIV (1643–1715), and the brilliance and extravagance of his court at Versailles had enormous influence. From the 1660s the French style dominated manners, dress, furniture and decoration, as well as literary and artistic taste, through most of Europe (though not in Holland). To promote French fashion, Paris sent dolls dressed in the latest designs to London and later to other European capitals. Charles II of England, whose mother was French and who had spent his years of exile in France, naturally favoured the French style, and the gaiety and wit of his court gave a lead to the English nobility and followers of fashion. At the same time, a certain amount of religious tolerance allowed the Puritans, although driven from political power, to flourish in trade and colonial enterprise.

The Dutch, freed from Spain's dominance, became immensely wealthy through trade and colonial expansion. Reacting against the rigidity, pomp and formality of their former rulers, their preference for more comfort and freedom of movement had considerable influence on 17th-century style. Details of their domestic interiors and dress are recorded in delightful detail by painters such as Jan Steen (1626–79), Pieter de Hooch (1630–77) and Vermeer (1632–75). Under William of Orange (1689–1702) the Dutch influence was also strong in England.

Spain retained a more formal and severe style than the rest of Europe and her influence on European costume weakened during this period although it was still felt in Italy where the importance and power of city states such as Venice declined with the discovery of new trade routes by sea.

Throughout the century, the New World offered both opportunity and refuge for the religious dissenter. America at this time was a mixture of different nationalities, each bringing with them their own styles and fashions. Much importance was given to dress as a status symbol, though fashions changed more slowly than in Europe. The poorer settlers would weave their own cloth and make their own clothes; the rich ordered garments from England or France.

In Europe, wealth was no longer the prerogative of the landed aristocracy, and as the upper classes expanded there were considerable changes in the way people lived. Large families, often including uncles, aunts and cousins, lived together, with a great many servants who now had their own quarters. As privacy became more important the planning of great houses included more rooms. Furniture became more plentiful and finely crafted; wall panelling replaced hangings, and carpets covered the floors. A new appreciation of craftsmanship, comfort and elegance ousted to some extent the rigid ostentation of 16th-century dress. The introduction of the levée, which took place in the ante-room or dressing-room of a nobleman's or lady's bedchamber, often while the elaborate ritual of the *toilette* was being completed, made a dressing gown or wrap more essential.

The gradual swing away from stiffness and elaboration in dress began during the first decade of the century. First to go were bombasting and the farthingale (except in Spain). Starched ruffs continued well into the 1630s for conservative men and women, and American colonial governors wore them with the long gowns associated with men of learning during the 16th century. As rigidity was relaxed, excessive ornamentation went out of fashion; small slashes replaced the long vertical slashes of garments. Rich plain or textured fabric, notably velvet and satin, in natural folds and soft deep hues or light clear tints, wide lace, narrow braid and rows of small buttons were the outstanding features of dress between 1630 and 1650.

In England, under the Commonwealth, Puritan beliefs produced a severity in dress in contrast to the Cavalier style of Charles I's reign, with subdued colours and plain white collars; and this severity also distinguished sober religionists in France, Holland, Germany and, notably, in the Massachusetts Bay Colony in America. The same influence may have led to the use of woollen cloth for fashionable men's day wear as, perhaps, did the gradual infiltration into the upper ranks of society of the minor gentry and merchant class. Tailors were quick to appreciate the value of a cloth with such good manipulative qualities, and the status of woollen cloth rose steadily until it eventually became, for many years, the only fabric used for men's outer garments.

From 1660 to 1680 the courts of France and England presented a dazzling exuberance of dress, with a flourish of ribbons, curls, flounces and feathers and a general loosening of garments and studied negligence reflecting a change in social attitudes. The pendulum was to swing back, however, and by the late 1680s stiffness and formality returned with the sober rectitude of the court of William of Orange and the almost pietistic atmosphere surrounding the later years of Louis XIV.

MEN

Throughout the period men wore linen drawers under their breeches, and shirts, full in the body and sleeves and slit at the side seam, which were at first still only visible puffing between the slashes of the doublet but by mid century were exposed at the lower arm, the waist and the centre front under a much reduced doublet. The sleeves were gathered into a band at the wrist and cuffs, often lace-trimmed, turned back over the sleeve of the doublet. Later, if not finished with a plain buttoned wrist-band, the sleeve had a lace or lace-trimmed ruffle falling over the hand. By about 1615 the large stiffened ruff was in decline, often replaced by an unstarched softly falling ruff; but by 1640 both had been ousted for fashionable wear by the falling band. This was really a collar, which gradually widened to fall over the shoulders by 1630–40; made of plain linen or, for the wealthy or more pretentious, lace-edged, it was tied with fine cords at the front and was worn outside armour, cloaks and gowns. With the fashion for longer hair in the 1650s–60s the collar narrowed at the shoulders, where it would have been hidden by the hair, and lengthened into long tabs at the front (worn in shorter form by ministers of religion until the end of the 19th century and by the legal profession in France and England until today).

By 1670 the collar or falling band had given way to the cravat, a long strip of linen or lace or a combination of both wrapped round the neck with the ends folded one over the other at the front; alternatively, the strip could be attached to a plain linen neckband with the two ends left hanging at the front and folded in like manner. In the 1690s two variants of the cravat appeared. The first was the Steinkirk, a long cravat generally edged with lace, loosely knotted under the chin with the ends either threaded through a buttonhole of the coat or pinned to one side. The second was a large stiff ribbon bow, light or dark in colour, tied under or behind the cravat ends.

During the 17th century men's clothes gradually evolved into what we now call a suit. To give as clear an impression as possible of the general look, the doublet (jacket) and breeches are therefore described together. The stiff, exaggerated style of the previous period continued until the second decade of the century. By the 1620s the peascod belly and trunk-hose had been discarded by fashionable men, but the doublet was still stiffened with buckram and closely buttoned down the front and retained the wings or crescents at the shoulders over fairly narrow sleeves, and the deeply pointed waistline. The skirt of the doublet, formed by a series of overlapping tabs (usually eight), flared out over large or medium-full breeches gathered in just above the knee (sometimes referred to as cloak-bag breeches) and still attached to the doublet by points passing through visible eyelet holes in the tabs at the waist, or concealed under the skirt. The points, tipped with aiglets, were very decorative and might also be used as decoration at the lower edge of the breeches.

By 1630 the style was easier and unstiffened. The waistline, high at the side and back, still retained a modest point at the centre front and wings on the shoulders. The sleeves were full above the elbow and slashed vertically two or three times at the front, once or twice at the back, to reveal the shirt, which might also show through long vertical slashes on the body of the doublet at breast level. Skirt tabs were longer and reduced to six or four in number. Breeches were high-waisted, longer and slimmer, attached by hooks and eyes to the doublet, but points still appeared around the waistline as decoration.

The late 1630s' doublet, cut without a waist seam, looked more like a jacket, having a high undefined waist, a slightly flared skirt slit at the side and back, and still often slashed at the breast. The sleeves were now usually open along front and back seams from armhole to wrist, revealing more of the shirt; buttons and buttonholes often edged these openings but seem rarely to have been fastened. More of the shirt was also revealed by leaving the doublet unbuttoned below breast level. Some sleeves, cut extra long, were left unbuttoned for approximately 5 inches and turned back to show a contrasting lining or facing – an interesting precursor of the coat cuff that became so important during the late 17th and 18th centuries. Breeches known as Spanish hose,

English, 1605. Tall-crowned hat, jewelled band.

Small slops trimmed with braid and ribbon loops.

English, 1615. Hair swept back and puffed out a sides, with a light coronet and a jewel on the forehead. Bodice and skirt of cream satin embroidered with red, green, deep blue silk and gold thread; very low neckline edged with lace.

Small wired whisk and matching cuffs of fine lace.

English, 1613. Hair fluffed out, small beard and moustache. Tasselled earring of black jet. Large stiffened collar or whisk and matching cuffs, lace trimmed.

Diagonal cloak, red lined with blue.

English, 1627. Small ruff. Doublet with pointed waistline, deep shoulder wings and skirt of overlapping tabs. Sleeves paned above elbow.

Cream satin shoes with gold rosettes.

Cloak embroidered in gold, coral and grey-blue on black; red-brown lining also embroidered.

Great slops embroidered in in same colours as cloak. Doublet in gold material with a high sheen, embroidered pale blue with touches of coral, is worn unbuttoned and has a slit through which a baldric-like band is slotted. Pale gold hose, brocade shoes with large, gold rosettes.

Points at waist and at lower edges of cloak-bag breeches

Boots folded down under knee to form a cuff.

Dutch, 1600-25. Broad-brimmed hat trimmed with ostrich feathers. Small lace-edged falling band, plain linen cuffs. Paned wings on doublet, sleeves open at upper arm and wrist with buttons and buttonholes. Undecorated cloak-bag breeches; garters with longish ties; long ties on square-toed shoes.

Large spur leathers

English, 1634. Broad lace-edged falling band over a military gorget. Leather jerkin with fabric sleeves attached under wings and open on forearm with buttons and buttonholes to show shirt.

Sword carried on decorated baldric.

Pale-coloured hat with braid and feather trim.

English, 1628. Hair drawn back, leaving small curled fringe, curls over ears. Drop pearl earrings; single strand of pearls with drop pearl high on neck, another on shoulders finishing with a brooch between the breasts. High-waisted bodice with bow at centre front, matching those on virago sleeves. Long stomacher extends over underskirt, the gown opening to reveal both. Sparkling braid trimming on sleeves and underskirt is used diagonally on edge of gown.

Wide lace-trimmed collar wired up at back, triple lace ruffles above wrist.

English 1639. (left) Highwaisted doublet partly unbuttoned and slashed on chest and sleeves to expose shirt. Slashes, hem and front edged with braid. (right) Lace-trimmed velvet cloak lined with silk.

Long hair worn with fringe.

English, 1633. High-waisted bodice with tabbed basque; full gathered sleeves finishing just below elbow, neckline edged with lace-trimmed collar. Bodice and skirt in pale blue satin, sash and rosette coral colour. Pearls earrings, necklace and bracelets.

Wispy fringe, curls over ears, small pearl-edged comb.

Both men have lace-trimmed falling bands, Spanish hose fringed with ribbon loops, boots with bucket tops, lace boot-hose tops and butterfly spur leathers.

English, 1643. Broad-brimmed hat, shoulder-length hair. Broad linen collar over gorget.

Buff jerkin with wings and wide-tabbed basque. Cloth sleeves (perhaps of an under-doublet, or attached under wings) buttoned at wrist, plain linen cuffs.

Full breeches, narrowing at knee, and gathered into a band. Plain linen boot-hose tops over cuffs of boots.

Butterfly spur leathers

English, 1640. A lady at her toilette. Heavily draped table carries a dressing-box with mirror lid.

English, 1643. London merchants' wives. Wide-brimmed, high-crowned hats over caps. Deep kerchief collars.

Fairly full sleeves with lace-trimmed cuffs finish just above wrist.

Dutch, 1645. Merchant class. Man wears tall narrow-brimmed hat trimmed with cord, over fairly short hair. Lace-trimmed falling band and cuffs. Long, easy-fitting velvet doublet, slim breeches finishing below the knee with ribbon bows at sides.

Overskirts held bunched up to reveal embroidered underskirts.

Woman wears small cap over severely drawn-back hair; deep double kerchief collar; long pointed bodice, full, long sleeves and open skirt of heavy silk or taffeta; underskirt trimmed with braid.

Bucket boots and lace-trimmed boot-hose tops

English, 1650-1700. Jackboots in stiff black leather with bucket tops.

were fairly full at the waist, narrowing to below the knee, and decorated at the lower edge with ribbon bows, loops or pleated lace frills.

The many wars in England and Europe during the late 1640s and early 1650s had an influence on men's dress. The buff-jerkin, adapted from a military garment in the 16th century, was now cut like a fashionable doublet and often worn over it, still made of leather and sleeveless; or, with sleeves of contrasting material, it might take the place of the doublet. Boots and military-style sashes worn diagonally across the chest were also popular.

In its final phase in the 1650s and 1660s the doublet was reduced to a short-sleeved, bolero-like jacket, unbuttoned and reaching to just above the waist, with voluminous folds of fine cambric shirt flowing out negligently at the lower arm and the waist. It was worn with petticoat breeches (also called Rhinegraves or pantaloons), very wide in the leg, pleated or gathered into the waistband, and falling like a divided skirt to the knees or just above. They appear to have had a lining forming baggy underbreeches gathered into a band above the knee. The lavish use of ribbon loops on the shoulder and sleeves of the doublet and round the waist and down the sides of the breeches contributed to a total image which may seem effeminate to modern eyes; but contemporary writing confirms that these gentlemen were not lacking in heterosexual inclination.

Alongside the short doublet and petticoat breeches there developed a style which was to be the forerunner of the 18th-century coat – a collarless doublet, more like a coat, with easy-fitting body and knee-length, slightly flared skirt cut in one and closely buttoned down the front, and fairly wide sleeves turned back to form cuffs. It appears to have been based on a military garment, and Fairholt (*Costume in England*, Vol. 1, Glossary) calls it a cassock (a name also used for an overcoat worn by men and women at the end of the century). It was worn, with full breeches gathered to the knee, but very little of them could be seen.

Towards 1670 coats and vests became fashionable – and from them evolved the coat and waistcoat worn with modifications until the present day (in America a waiscoat is still called a vest). The first coats were very like the cassocks, collarless and reaching mid thigh but slightly more flared in the skirt. Their successors were longer, the hemline just above the knee where it was to remain until the early 18th century. From the first these coats had close-set buttons and buttonholes from neck to hem, increasingly left partly undone. During the next decade the body of the coat was cut closer, the skirt more flared, and slits with buttons and buttonholes appeared at the back and sides around 1680 for convenience when riding. By 1690 the coat was full-skirted with two groups of fan-shaped pleats gathered under a button at the back, and a stiffened interlining. The buttons were to remain on men's coats long after they were of any practical use, and still survive on the back of tail coats and morning coats today. The sleeved vest followed the cut of the coat but was less full in the skirt, and the back (not seen) was often made of inferior fabric. It reached to just below the waist at first, then gradually lengthened until, by the 1680s, it was as long as the coat. It was closely buttoned until the 1690s but by 1695 the fashion was to wear it buttoned only at the waist, exposing the shirt. Both vests and coats had slit pockets, occasionally with a vertical opening but generally horizontal and placed low with flaps, increasing in width throughout the period, which could be buttoned down on to the garment.

Coat sleeves were fitted smoothly to the arm scye and widened at the bottom to turn back (like those of the cassock), forming a split cuff above or below the elbow,

English, 1645. Sugarloaf or copotain hat over long hair. Loose short doublet in gold and black brocade trimmed black braid, shirt revealed at slit forearm and front opening. Black breeches trimmed with black and gold gauze ribbons and black (jet?) beads.

Pale beige gloves with soft gauntlets.

Child's frock in tawny taffeta, high-waisted with points, braid trim down front; paned sleeves. White coif embroidered in gold

White, lace-trimmed lawn or linen falling band and cuffs

Pale blue hose; black shoes tied with black and gold ribbon.

Spanish, 1659. Very wide farthingale, flattened at back and front, ('garde-infante').
Bodice with long basque and paned sleeves matches skirt of deep blue velvet trimmed silver braid. Deep collar and wrist ruffles in sheer white fabric.

Blue ribbon rosette behind large brooch at centre of bodice, blue ribbons in hair and as trimming on beige gloves

Large fur muff.

English, 1639-40 Street costume: mask, hood, cassock with deep capes, and muff. Long-handled fan of feathers may have had a central mirror.

Low neck outlined with deep lace-edged collar.

Dutch, 1654. Peasants' costume hardly changed from the previous century: flat caps, long hose, long tunic or short jerkin; short hair

French, 1645. Hair drawn back into small knot, curls hanging over the ears to shoulder level. Long pointed bodice laced at front, short sleeves above puffed shift sleeves with lace-trimmed cuffs. Skirt open to reveal patterned underskirt. Small box and mirror hang from waist.

English military dress c. 1640
Generals in Cromwell's
army

Lace-edged
cap under
large wide-
brimmed hat.

English or colonial America,
mid 17th century. Man
and woman in 'Quaker'
costume.

Linen falling band,
jerkin over doublet,
mailed gauntlet glove

Lace-trimmed
falling band, jerkin
over doublet with slashed
sleeves.

Colonial America, 1650-60.
Golden brown satin striped
over-dress and brocade
under-petticoat, flame-
coloured turn-back on
sleeves; narrow
stomacher of beaded
galloon with
spangles and
bugle beads.
lace at
neck and
for under sleeves

Colonial America
1674. Woman's dress of
greenish-yellow with black and red ribbon loops on sleeves;
vermilion red under-petticoat or skirt decorated with silver
and yellow embroidery; elaborate lace edging to collar.
Jet bracelet, amber necklace. Baby's dress in pale yellow
with leading strings and white lace undersleeves; lawn apron.

Colonial America,
mid 17th century.
Tobacco planter in
simple cloak, doublet,
short breeches and
tall-crowned, wide-
brimmed hat.

sometimes caught back with buttons which were retained later as decoration. Sleeves increased in length throughout the period and after 1680 the cuff became very bulky. Vests had similar sleeves and appear to have been turned back over the coat cuff, but these additional cuffs might have been simulated and do not necessarily imply the presence of a vest sleeve. In the 1690s the vest occasionally had a close-fitting sleeve reaching the wrist.

Full breeches were inconvenient with the long coats and gradually fell out of favour completely by about 1680. Breeches of moderate width gathered at the knee around 1670 gradually evolved into the plain close-fitting breeches of the 1690s, cut fairly full over the seat, gathered to a waistband and fastened at the front, with no other form of support, the legs fastened above or below the knee with a buckle or a row of buttons. They were plain and undecorated, in the same material as the coat or in black velvet.

Over the lower part of the leg, stockings of silk, linen or wool, of a lighter tone than the breeches, were gartered at the knee or above and appear somewhat wrinkled. The rich and fashionable wore silk only, sometimes several pairs at once for warmth. Boot-hose of stout linen thread were worn between stockings and boots to protect the former, and often had a wide decorative border of thread, gold or silver lace or ruffled linen falling over the top of the boot just below the knee. During the 1660s–70s, with petticoat breeches or breeches not confined at the knee, cannons or port cannons were worn without boots; these were stockings similar to boot hose with wide decorative frills turned down over the garters in a broad flounce below the knee. Between 1665 and 1680 garters below the knee had bunches of ribbon or a gathered flounce of lace at the side; by the 1680s these went out of fashion and for the next two decades stockings were drawn up over the knee and held by simple buckled bands, usually hidden in the rolled top of the stockings.

From 1620 to 1655 boots were almost universally worn, not only for riding or out-of-doors but even on fairly formal occasions indoors, complete with spurs – another military influence. At first they were long and close-fitting but with a wider top turned down or folded below the knee in a broad 'cup'. About 1625 a shorter boot with a bucket top was introduced. Spur leathers assumed a quatre-foil shape in the 1630s and grew to huge dimensions. By the 1660s fashionable men generally wore boots only for riding. The prevalent style was the rather cumbersome jack boot made of rigid leather hardened by boiling or applications of pitch paint; tubular in shape, it had an expanding bucket top above the knee, a deep square heel and square toe. A lighter version in softer leather, laced or buttoned at the side, came into fashion later. Also laced, buttoned or buckled were spatterdashes, in use from the 1670s; they were made of leather, canvas, cloth or cotton and reached from the ankle to above the knee. Since the join with the shoe was covered by large spur leathers it is difficult to distinguish between boots and spatterdashes in contemporary illustrations.

Shoes had long vamps and round toes until 1645 when a tapered square toe was used for shoes and boots. The sides were fastened across the tongue (which grew in length and by about 1700 often turned over, being cut in a scallop shape with a red lining) and tied with latchets of leather or ribbon. Huge shoe roses were, at first, fastened over the top, but by mid century these were obsolete, replaced by lavish bows of ribbon, which a dandy in the 1680s might have wired out on each side of the foot. In the last decades of the century, buckles replaced bows, small at first, then growing larger and rectangular.

From the 1670s boots and shoes were almost invariably black with red heels, though brown leather was occasionally used for hunting when close-fitting calf-length boots called buskins might be worn. Red heels were retained for shoes (but not boots), with a red sole edge, into the 18th century.

During the 17th century, men wore their hair longer than at any other time in the history of western culture. In the first two decades a longish bob was fashionable, brushed straight back in the manner favoured by the Elizabethans, or with a centre or side parting and sometimes a fringe cut straight or in light ringlets. From 1630 dandies, including Charles I, wore their hair cut asymmetrically, one side to below ear level, the other with a long lock of hair falling forward on to the chest and tied with a ribbon, known as a love-lock. Between 1640 and 1660 long hair falling on to the shoulders was associated in England with the Royalist cause, and a short cut to just above the shoulder or shorter with the followers of Cromwell during the Civil War; however, the short cut reflected a sober, puritanical taste for austerity shown by people of similar religious beliefs, notably those in New England. By 1660, the habit of adding false hair when natural hair was deficient led to the introduction of the periwig, which became an essential part of a fashionable man's attire. At first hanging in curls from a centre parting, it grew more and more artificial; by the 1670s it had become a huge arrangement of corkscrew curls hanging over the neck, back and breast, and in the 1690s it rose above the head in two peaks, no longer only a camouflage for lack of hair but a fashionable necessity. For comfort and perhaps hygienic reasons men cut their own hair short or shaved their heads. The wide bow worn under the cravat caused the wig to be pushed back at the sides; and as early as 1678 it might be tied back for convenience by soldiers, or when hunting, a fashion which was to become universal in the 18th century.

Beards and moustaches gradually declined in favour; from 1625, small neat beards, and moustaches turned up at the ends, got progressively smaller, and by 1650 the beard was only a small tuft on the chin, disappearing completely by 1680. A thread-like moustache lasted a little longer, but by the final decade of the century this too had disappeared, and fashionable men entered the 18th century clean-shaven.

Stiff, steeple-crowned hats with medium or broad brims called a copotain or sugarloaf, fashionable in the early part of the century, were retained by conservative men, particularly Puritans, throughout the period. A similar style returned as high fashion around 1660 when sober-minded men such as priests and Quakers adopted also a softer-brimmed and lower-crowned hat often represented in portraits of William Penn, the founder of Pennsylvania. In court circles during the 1630s–40s fairly low-crowned, soft, broad-brimmed hats were worn, cocked up at the front, back or sides according to personal taste and trimmed with jewelled bands and long ostrich feathers curling around the crown and over the brim. The stiffer hats of the 1650s might be decorated with bunches of ribbon; but in keeping with the rest of their attire the Puritans avoided any show of extravagance and their hats had a simple band and buckle, as did those of the lower classes.

By the 1690s it became smart to turn up the hat brim at back and sides, a style which developed into the 18th-century tricorne; a fringe of feathers around the edge of the brim was later replaced by metallic lace or braid. Hats were made of felt or beaver and were usually black. During the fashion for huge wigs, they were frequently carried under the arm rather than worn.

Nightcaps, simple and washable, had been worn in bed from earliest times but now the name was also used for a skull cap with a close turned-up brim, often made of embroidered fabric, which was worn informally indoors to replace the wig, as was the montero, a round cap with fur-lined peak and earflaps turned up or let down and fastened under the chin. Unlike the nightcap, this was occasionally worn out-of-doors when travelling or hunting.

Semi-circular cloaks continued to be worn indoors and out. They were longer and softer than in the 16th century, draped in a variety of ways, often over one shoulder, and fastened by cords under the arm. Some apparently still had fake sleeves, but the collars were unstiffened and fell softly on to the shoulders. The advent of the coat and vest put an end to the cloak as a fashionable indoor garment, but it was retained for travelling in bad weather into the 18th and 19th centuries. From about 1676 top coats or greatcoats began to be worn: the Brandenburg, calf-length, loose-fitting with frog fastenings (cord loops and braided buttons), or the very long, loose cassock (not to be confused with the coat of military origin, page 58), which buttoned down the front and might have cape collars.

WOMEN

Women continued to wear a chemise next to the skin, and the more prosperous would now also have a night-chemise to wear in bed. (Until the mid 16th century, they had slept naked or in the day chemise.) A night-coif, often embroidered, might also be worn during the day as negligée, as was the night-rail or rayle, a short cape to waist or hips made of lawn, holland, silk or satin. Some confusion may be caused by the use of the term 'nightgown' (and 'morning gown') for a loose, unboned comfortable dress worn at all times of the day, indoors and out, and even on formal occasions.

Outer garments changed from the rigidity and over-elaboration of the later 16th century (retained in Spain until well into the 17th) to a soft simplicity, especially in England, until the 1670s when a certain rigidity returned with the long, narrow line that clearly reflected both the architecture and furniture of the time.

Essential to the shaping of the bodice was the corset (stays) or a boned lining. Norah Waugh in *Corsets and Crinolines* tells us that the term 'corset' was only rarely used in the 17th century, not coming into general use until the end of the 18th century, and her book is splendidly instructive as to their construction. At first the corsets were similar to those of the previous century; in the 1620s a higher waistline became fashionable and they were shortened, but the long stomacher was retained, showing through the gown opening with a narrow sash often passing across it with a bow or rosette slightly to one side. (Fashionable Dutch women continued to wear very long stomachers until the late 1660s.) A short bodice with tabs like those on the man's doublet, worn roughly between 1630 and 1640 (longer by the bourgeoisie and lower classes), might be mounted on a stiffened and boned lining in place of a separate corset, and this practice of incorporating the corset into the gown was used as the bodice lengthened again during the 1640s–50s, almost causing the corset to be dispensed with as a separate garment. The foundation was made of layers of linen or canvas reinforced with whalebone, then the fabric of the gown was stretched over it, seamed where necessary, and the sleeves were inserted into the combined foundation and bodice. Bodices in the 1650s–60s often had a deep point at the centre front tapering back to waist level just in front of the underarm, the sides and back being cut to hip level and then slit to form tabs spreading over the hips. The stiff pointed front was worn over the skirt and the tabbed sections under it, hooks on the skirt being slipped on to loops on the tabs. In the 1670s, when the over-gown or mantua found favour, the boned bodice worn under it again became the stays and was an essential part of a lady's toilette for many years.

63

Dutch, 1641. Hair drawn back under small cap, fluffed out at sides. Black velvet gown, full sleeves open at forearm, laced over corset and underskirt of cream and gold brocade, low neck filled in with lawn and lace tucker or chemise.

Gold drop earrings, pearl necklace, and bracelets, jet brooch and buttons. Kerchief collar worn over a flat collar, both lace-trimmed as are the cuffs.

Gold lace folding fan

English 1650-60 Bodice in pale blue moiré silk with seaming which does not match that of the lining

Boned bodice lining laced at centre front.

Sleeves set low at shoulder reach below the elbow.

Basque made of small sections joined together.

Long curled hair, small beards and moustaches. Plain linen falling bands

Sword carried on baldrick.

Dutch, 1641. Lawn and lace kerchief collar (over flat collar) and cuffs. High-waisted bodice with deep basque and full sleeves with turn-back cuffs in pale figured silk trimmed with gold braid; matching skirt

Pearls at neck and wrist

White feather fan

French, 1633 High-waisted doublets unbuttoned to reveal shirt, seen also at sleeve openings. Long slim breeches, one pair finished with sash garters

Plain boot-hose tops

Butterfly spur leathers.

Large shoe rosettes.

Hair decorated with ribbon loops.

English, 1645. Long pointed bodice with tabbed basque and full short sleeves, skirt gathered mainly at the back. Lightweight satin with a high sheen, very simple, no decoration except for lace on collar and sleeve flounces.

Short-waisted interlining made from two layers of stiffened linen with whalebone inserted between them.

English, 1630 Bodice in white satin, basque with gussets; full sleeves gathered to armhole, very deep at back. Position of interlining is indicated by dotted lines

German, 1660. Stiff wide-brimmed, tall crowned hat over long hair or wig. Falling band drawn into pleat at front (forerunner of the cravat). Short doublet revealing very full shirt at waist, forearm and wrist. Looped ribbons on sleeves and at waist and sides of petticoat breeches.

Cannons

shoes tied with broad ribbons.

Long hair, falling band.

Dutch, 1663. Woman (left) close-fitting cap or coif and fur-trimmed, full sleeved jacket.

Woman (centre), low necked bodice with draped collar, small hood, paned sleeves and long sash.

Large high-crowned hat

Man: short doublet with tabbed basque. Petticoat breeches trimmed with ribbons show full under-breeches gathered to knee.

Dutch, 1650-60. Hair twisted into coil caught with ribbon bands, curls over ears.

English, 1660. Hair dressed with full curls over the ears, possibly wired to increase width.

Pearls for hair ornament, drop earrings, necklace, brooch and bracelets.

French, 1665. Similar to German costume above but with cravat ribbons on shoulder and baldric on shoulder belt to carry sword.

Soft-brimmed hat profusely trimmed with ostrich feathers.

Rigid long pointed bodice with low circular décolletage and sleeve set in well below the shoulder, is fastened with jewelled clasps.

Deep velvet collar on bodice laced at centre back, its seams outlined with velvet. Very full sleeves set in deep at back with cartridge pleats.

English, 1660-80. Man's mules, red satin embroidered with rose and thistle pattern in coiled gold and silver thread.

Stays did considerable harm to the health not only of women but even small girls; when John Evelyn's two-year-old daughter died in 1665, the surgeon who examined her body found the breast bone pressed very deeply inward and two ribs broken.

Sleeves in the late 1620s were often double-puffed and slashed or paned (virago sleeves), caught between the puffs with a bow or rosette to match a sash. They were inserted into the bodice low at the shoulder (wings having by now been discarded), and this continued until the 1650s–60s when the single puff sleeve of moderate dimensions, often open at the front seam to reveal the shift and caught with clasps, was inserted well below the shoulder and the armhole scye taken right into the back so that the bodice, at shoulder-blade level, became very narrow. Sleeves and skirts were often gathered into cartridge pleats, made by one or two lines of regularly spaced gathering threads pulled up to give a group of rounded or ridged pleats, which enabled a considerable width of cloth to be drawn into a small space. In the late 1670s sleeves began to lose their fullness, and by 1690 they were fairly narrow and straight, often terminating in a cuff, and set higher on the shoulder as the neckline changed from a low circle to a square.

The shortening of sleeves during the 17th century was a radical change; never, since the early Christian period, had western women revealed their arms. Sleeves began to shrink back from the wrist in the early 1620s, and from 1650 they reached only just below the elbow.

Ruffs and wired fan collars remained in favour until the early 1630s, and older women and the bourgeoisie still wore the great ruffs; but by 1635 the broad falling collar, either high-necked or décolleté, was almost universal. A great variety of collars existed; often two were worn together, of fine lawn and lace, falling to the shoulder and emphasizing the sloping line from neck to shoulder. A kerchief of fine linen and/or lace folded diagonally to form an independent collar was much favoured in the 1640s by the middle class and Puritans, and by English colonists in America during the mid 17th century. In the 1660s, collars on high-necked dresses were somewhat wider over the shoulders and formed a straight line across the chest, characteristic of Dutch costume in paintings of this period. Modest women might tuck a folded kerchief into a low neckline, but the fashionable ladies portrayed by Lely reveal neck, shoulders and much of their breasts above their low circular décolletage, lightly masked by the frill or lace at the top of the shift or by a light gauze scarf. Ruffs at the wrist gave way to turned-back funnel-shaped cuffs of linen or lawn and lace, and some really short sleeves in the 1670s revealed a ruffled chemise sleeve reaching just below the elbow.

The farthingale continued until about 1620, although some portraits suggest that in England it was discarded earlier in spite of the actual style of dress remaining unchanged. The padded roll did not completely disappear until the 18th century; small versions were in use around 1640, when the slim line then coming into fashion suggests it was dispensed with, but if so it was for a brief period, as some form of padded roll or hip pad was needed from mid-century to give skirts the shape and 'hang' seen in contemporary paintings. Spain retained the cone-shaped Spanish farthingale until well into the 17th century, when it developed into the wide flat shape magnificently represented in the court paintings of Velasquez, particularly those of the young Infanta in a huge farthingale known as a *garde-infante*.

The open-fronted skirt exposing a decorative underskirt (the term kirtle was dropped by mid century) was replaced by a closed style in the 1630s–40s, but was to return later. These closed skirts worn by court ladies and the wealthy bourgeoisie became

English, 1640.
Country woman.
Small cap with
embroidered edge,
large kerchief
collar. Bodice with
basque and full
sleeve to wrist
Skirt embroidered
around hem.

Flat cap or tall cone-shaped hat.

Dutch, 1654-70.
Peasants. Women wear caps,
short bodices laced at
front, full skirts and
aprons; men wear
old-fashioned long
hose or breeches.

Fishwife
in flat cap
almost like
a beret.

Pattens worn
over shoes.

French, 1650-1700. Peasants or country
folk from near Paris
in their best clothes,
the woman's showing
what we now call
'folk costume'.

Lace cap or hood
under one of plain
linen: lace collar,
heavily embroid-
ered bodice, short
sleeves revealing
chemise sleeves
with lace ruffles;
apron; skirt
tucked up to show
underskirt
with deep band
of embroidery.
(A woman of
this class
would be
skilled in emb-
roidery and lace-
making, so her
dress would
feature her
own work.

English, 1686. Servant.
Close-fitting cap, black bodice, large
kerchief, sleeves pushed up to reveal
chemise sleeves. Large apron over full
plain skirt.

The man wears his own hair long;
ribbon loops tie his cravat and
decorate his petticoat breeches and
broad brimmed hat.

Dutch, 1667-9. Woman's hair dressed wide and trimmed with ribbon. Satin gown with long pointed bodice, wide low décolletage; graduated bows down front forecast 18 C. fashion. Skirt gathered with cartridge pleats. Pearls at neck and wrists.
Man's doublet in its final form, buttoned at front; collar gathered into pleats at front; petticoat breeches.

Dutch, 1650. Serving maid, basqued bodice with sleeves set in with cartridge pleats. Small cap, large apron, mules with shaped heels.

Sash garters with looped ribbons.

Dutch, 1670. Man in full periwig and cravat.

Woman; hair dressed in the 'taure' style with comb in back coil, has low circular décolletage, long pointed stomacher, gown looped up over underskirt

Tasselled handkerchief hangs from low pocket.
Shoes with high tongues and broad bows

Early type of coat and vest, loose sash. Petticoat breeches trimmed with lace.

Dutch, 1660. Woman in black jacket edged with white fur, tied with pale blue bow; red skirt trimmed gold, large white apron, white shoes.

Child in white gold-embroidered cap, grey gown with blue bows at elbow and skirt tucked up over bright yellow underskirt trimmed black braid.

extremely long and had to be held up or looped over one arm when walking, revealing richly decorated petticoats. Poorer or more active women, whose skirts might only reach the ground, tucked them up into a belt or pinned them up at the back. The habit of looping up the skirt became formalized in the elaborate drapery on gowns of the 1680–90s with their bustle effect and long trains. The mantua (manteau or manton), a development of the night or morning gown, had an unboned bodice joined to an overskirt draped back in this way to show the lining and form a long train, and was open at the front to expose the petticoat. It was worn, with variations, from the mid 17th century until the mid 18th century on all social and formal occasions.

A fairly easy-fitting jacket reaching to just below the hips, usually of velvet edged with fur, was often worn in the Low Countries betwen 1650 and 1670, as seen in many Dutch paintings of the period; it appears to have been less popular in England and France.

Fashionable women wore their hair uncovered throughout most of the century, indoors and out, though out-of-doors they might cover it with a headrail (a large form of kerchief or veil) or a primitive form of bonnet or hood consisting of a strip of cloth gathered at the back edge to fit the head, the front tapered to strings tying under the chin. Less fashionable widows and elderly ladies covered their hair with linen or lawn caps, as did Dutch burgher's wives, peasants, Puritans and colonists in New Amsterdam, New England and Virginia.

Hair was at first brushed back over a roll or pad and coiled into a flat bun on the back of the head. By the 1620s the padding had gone and the hair was drawn back tightly above the forehead but with a fringe running into bunched side curls. In the 1630s these were worn longer and the fringe was separated into single curls. After 1645 hair was still brushed back but with two side partings and no fringe, with curls still low over the ears, the back coil decorated with ribbons or pearls or covered by a small close-fitting embroidered caul. During the 1660s the side curls might be wired to stand out from the head, then hang to the shoulders. In the bull head or bull tour (from the French *taure*), a hairstyle of the 1670s, the front hair was cut and worn in short curls, the rest coiled at the back as before though possibly a little lower. During the 1680s the cap again became high fashion, covering the hair except for curls bunched high over the forehead or worn in two peaks. Called a fontange, a commode or a tower, this type of cap had a small round crown in front of which frills of lace or linen and lace on a wire frame rose in several tiers, projecting obliquely forward; two long streamers (lappets) of matching material hung down at the back or might be pinned up to the crown. This style of headdress was to remain in fashion until the end of the century; the kerchief and hood were adapted in size to cover it when out-of-doors.

Hats, if worn at all, were masculine in style, at first 'cavalier' hats with or without feathers, for riding or travelling. By the end of the century women adopted not only the three-cornered hat for riding but also men's coats, vests and cravats, including the Steinkirk, so that for the first time a special style of dress was worn for a particular activity. Merchants' wives and Puritan women wore broad-brimmed, high-crowned, sugarloaf hats like the men's over their caps (still seen in Welsh national costume).

During most of the century, women's feet were rarely visible under their very long skirts, but their shoes followed the masculine style, with a moderate heel, perhaps a little narrower and lighter than the men's, large shoe roses, ribbon latchets and high tongues. From 1660 very high heels of the shape now called Louis came into fashion, combined with toes tapering to a narrow squared-off point and fastened with ribbons

French, 1670's
Full-bottomed wig with corkscrew curls under wide-brimmed hat trimmed with ribbons. Coat has buttons down entire front but is fastened only to waist; skirt slightly flared with slits at the sides emphasised with braid matching the front decoration; larger cuffs, horizontal pockets set low. Loose shirt and petticoat breeches (no vest visible). Garters with ribbon ties. Fur edged gauntlet gloves.

French, 1680s. Woman shopping.
Long shawl worn over cap, leaving the frontage jutting out at the front. Gown folded back over underskirt.

French, 1680s - 90s.
Mantua gown of variegated stripes with wide neckline dipping at the front; short sleeves reveal ruffled lace sleeves of chemise. Narrow sash, under which the stomacher of the corset can be seen at the front. Skirt looped up to reveal matching underskirt. Long close-fitting gloves, mask hanging from waist. parasol.

French, 1680.
Royal page. Costume similar to that above, but hat brim turns up and is trimmed with feathers. Lace ruffles appear through the opening of the coat above which a sash is worn. Breeches gathered in just above the knee, trimmed with ribbon bows.

Long walk-ing cane attached to wrist with ribbon loop.

English or French, 1690s.
Fontange with Lappets

Shoes have a more delicate heel and a glove-like fitting.

French, 1680. Woman's shoe in light tan leather; dark olive satin and yellow straw appliqué simulating gold.

French, late 17 C. Woman's shoe in white kid with silk embroidery.

Periwig

Fontange with lappets tied with a bow under the chin.

French, 1690s.

Long full coat with wide buttoned cuffs.

Lace cravat worn over wide bow.

Flapped pockets.

Long full-skirted coat and vest over close-fitting breeches.

Shoes fastened with large buckles

Mules

French, 1690s. Long periwig; early form of tricorne edged with feathers. Plain cravat. Large muff. Sword with sash at hilt is slotted through slits in coat.

French, 1690s.
Hair dressed very high above forehead under fontange. Satin mantua gown with straight wide sleeves finished with cuffs above elbow and lace ruffles. Open front reveals decorated stomacher of corset extending over embroidered and fringed underskirt. Long close-fitting gloves small muff.
Huge periwig, long full coat buttoned only at the waist. Steinkirk cravat, buttoned vest. Large hat trimmed with braid and feathers. Large muff on belt.

Both man and woman wear face patches.

or buckles. They were made in various weights of leather or, for grand occasions, of satin, brocade or embroidered fabric. There is evidence that women wore buskins for travelling, made of velvet, satin or Spanish leather. High-heeled mules or slippers covering only the front of the foot were mainly for indoors.

Outer wraps were usually large circular or semi-circular cloaks, often with a hood, or huge shawls; but a long loose cassock overcoat like the men's was worn around 1640.

CHILDREN

Children continued to be dressed in replicas of adult garments, and the fashionable long hanging oversleeves served as leading strings to control a child's efforts in walking; these eventually evolved into long strips of material and continued in use during the 18th century. Boys still wore skirts until at least four years of age but did not suffer the discomfort of stays as their sisters did.

ACCESSORIES AND JEWELRY

Make-up, already in use in the 16th century, became increasingly popular among women of the wealthy and leisured classes, as from the 1640s did patches, small spots of black velvet or silk in a variety of shapes applied to the face with mastic. Both were also adopted by dandified men towards the end of the century. Cork balls or 'plumpers' were worn in the cheeks to produce roundness, lead combs were used for darkening eyebrows. Masks were worn out-of-doors to protect the skin, and night masks were coated inside with ointment to smooth the skin and prevent wrinkles. Restricted to the wealthy and frivolous, these practices were the constant target of puritanical denunciation. The lower classes and country folk had neither the money nor the time for such self-indulgence.

Certain accessories were common to both men and women. Gloves, stiffly gauntleted, embroidered and fringed, became progressively softer and lost the stiff gauntlet; women's gloves, made of pale glacé kid or silk and, right at the end of the century, of lace, were long, to meet the elbow-length sleeves, and were worn both out-of-doors and on formal occasions indoors. Muffs of silk, cloth or fur were used throughout the century, by men more frequently after 1650. Women's muffs were often of moderate size (snuftkins or snoskyns) and often worn pushed up on one arm, but some, like the men's were large; men hung them from a narrow belt or a sash to leave the hands free.

The sash was associated more with men than women, although a small narrow type was worn by women in the 1620s–30s as previously mentioned. The man's broad sash, tied in a great bow at the back early in the century, was a military style rarely worn by civilians; but by the 1660s–70s it had become general wear, tied loosely at hip level over the coat and gradually becoming more formal with short tied ends hanging level and worn over either vest or coat.

Canes, plain and a convenient walking length for men, longer for women, had bunches of ribbon or tasselled cords added in later decades.

For men, the shoulder belt or baldric, which took the place of the sword belt and hanger around 1625, was richly decorated and grew in width, length and splendour until its demise about 1695, when a small sword (similar to a court sword today) was hung from a sling beneath the vest with the hilt and sheath peeping out from the vest or coat skirts. Extravagant ribbon bunches worn between 1660 and 1680 diminished into a single shoulder knot, sometimes of cord, worn on the right shoulder. By mid century snuff boxes of various sizes and designs were used by fops or beaux, as were elegant

English, 1616. Young boy. Wired collar and cuffs, lace-trimmed. Doublet has long hanging sleeves (or leading strings) over slashed sleeves, and tabbed basque skirt is looped over a circular farthingale.

High-crowned, wide-brimmed hat trimmed with feathers.

English, 1611. Girl's bodice has wings over close-fitting sleeves and leading strings. Flounced skirt over farthingale is open at front to show underskirt. Apron with bib, cuffs, ruff and coif are lace-edged.

Ostrich tips trim coif.

Dutch, 1652. Boy, perhaps an apprentice, whose clothes look too big, and probably originally belonged to someone else.

Lace trimmed falling ruff and cuffs.

English, 1635. High-waisted doublet with sleeves open at forearm to reveal shirt; decorative points at waist. Falling band and cuffs trimmed with lace.

Spanish hose, slash garters tied with rosettes.

Large shoe roses.

Dutch, 1655-6 Large hat in two different fabrics trimmed with feathers, own hair worn long

Short sleeves revealing large puffed shirt sleeves.

Shaped belt has rosette at centre front.

English, 1627. Boy's high-waisted doublet with wings, hanging oversleeves and tabbed basque, and full long skirt, both fastening at centre front. are of pale blue and gold brocade trimmed with braid. Undersleeves of plain gold satin slashed to reveal pale blue satin lining.

Small boy wears plain falling band on gown trimmed with braid, fastened down centre front; leading strings from shoulders.

combs with which they ostentatiously fussed with their coiffures. Lace and tasselled handkerchiefs hung from their coat pockets.

For women, the folding fan came into use in the late 16th century and both it and the earlier rigid type were popular until the 18th century when the folding type became *de rigueur*. Aprons of fine lawn and lace were occasionally worn by the wealthy bourgeoisie (for servants and peasants they were of linen or coarse material) until 1690 when short aprons of lace, rich fabric, or embroidered and edged with gold lace became high fashion even on formal occasions. Long, broad scarves were worn round the shoulders, and parasols of Chinese pattern were carried towards the end of the century.

In contrast to the 16th century, jewelry was sparingly used, although men's hatbands, brooches, buttons, studs, rings and sword hilts were decorated with jewels. Men entitled to do so wore bejewelled Orders such as the Garter of England or the Fleece of the Low Countries hung on a broad ribbon around the neck. Earrings were still worn by some men of fashion, but increasingly long hair styles and wigs discouraged their use.

Pearls were the most popular jewel for women — pear-shaped drop earrings, barely visible under their side curls, single strand chokers and, until the 1660s, long chains of pearls worn around the shoulders and caught up at the centre front with a brooch, with loops of the pearls hanging below. With shorter sleeves came bracelets; pearls were twined around the wrist, and were also interwoven in the hair and used to edge decorative combs. Brooches of all kinds were worn by all classes except the very poor as clasps to fasten collars.

FABRICS AND COLOURS

Between 1630 and 1680 plain fabrics were used more than patterned, although some brocades can be seen in Van Dyke portraits. The fashionable delighted in rustling silks and satins and in the effect of the light breaking across these shining fabrics; but matt surfaces and monochrome sobriety were also appreciated. Velvet and satin were great favourites — velvet in burgundy, sapphire blue, crimson, purple, brown and black; satin and brocaded satin in white, cream, sky blue, almond green, tan, rose and grey — all trimmed lavishly with white or cream lace.

Woollen, cotton and linen fabrics were usually plain; scarlet-dyed woollen occurs constantly in hoods, cloaks and petticoats among the middle class and the strict religious groups whose choice was otherwise for fairly sober colours including rust red, brown, light and dark grey, leather-colour or buff, wine, dark green and black.

The revocation of the Edict of Nantes in 1685 caused the emigration of large numbers of Huguenots from France and these industrious and skilled craftsmen greatly benefited textile manufacture in Holland. After 1690 there was a revival of patterned fabrics in rather bright colours and of gold and silver brocade, and a tendency to use several colours in one outfit. Painted and dyed Indian cottons, finely textured and brilliantly coloured, were exported to England and the colonies by the East India Company; they were used at first for hangings, but as smaller floral patterns were introduced they became increasingly used for dress, initially by the lower classes and later, in 1680, by the fashionable upper class — thus reversing the usual rule that fashion descends through the strata of society.

Costume in the 17th century is particularly interesting as an example of how fashion will frequently swing from over-elaboration to comparative simplicity and back again, and also of how styles which are basically the same may be varied in colour and decoration to express religious or political beliefs.

The eighteenth century

The Age of Enlightenment, a name often given to the 18th century, cannot be strictly limited to the years 1700–1800. The rationalism of writers like Voltaire and Johnson may already be detected in the Dutch Republic of Spinoza's time or in the England of Pepys and the Royal Society. Nor was the intellectual development associated with it synchronous throughout Europe. But although its germination was restricted to certain western countries, the seeds of rationalist thought spread widely during this century, possibly striking the deepest roots in the English colonies across the Atlantic. Wars, plagues, torture, poverty and drunkenness were still rife, the slave trade prospered, and life for many was still brutish and short. Nevertheless, a spirit of humanitarian reform continued to spread. American colonists cast off the English yoke in 1776 and established their own government; and the French Revolution, starting in 1789, deposed king and aristocracy in the name of Liberty, Equality and Fraternity. The widening belief that liberty and happiness were man's natural right, embodied in Jefferson's Declaration of Independence, would eventually allow an increasing number to enjoy the pleasures and ease formerly confined to a limited elite.

The rococo style in art and architecture which flourished c.1730–80 particularly in France under Louis XV, was characterized by delicate curvilinear ornament and elegant artifice; and a corresponding change of style is evident in the dress of the period. Among painters, Boucher, Watteau and Gainsborough portrayed the charm, frivolity and often pastoral quality of upper-class life, Chardin middle-class domestic detail, and Hogarth and Rowlandson the coarser aspects of life among the less cultured or fortunate. Society was becoming more cosmopolitan, and in pursuit of cultural refinement and pleasure the gentry adorned their houses with elegant furniture and porcelain and passed their time in a round of concerts, assemblies, visits to spas or the seaside, travel and sport. A more gracious life-style was also apparent in many of the established and prosperous American colonies; hundreds of ships crossed the Atlantic each year carrying furniture, books, clothes, fabrics and all the things needed to make life agreeable in the seaboard communities of the New World.

Fashion was avidly followed by all but the poor; those living away from capital cities such as London and Paris, or in America, were eager for knowledge of the prevailing style popular with the beau monde, and to meet this demand magazines and fashion moppets or dolls were circulated, more easily as transport improved but still slowly enough to cause some delay in the arrival of the latest trends in more distant areas. New influences were also at work. Popular actors and actresses influenced fashion. In France, Marie Antoinette's dressmaker, Madame Bertin, may be classified as the first couturier: although only a woman of the people, her word on fashion was law. In England, Beau Nash, a man of birth but no fortune who lived by gambling, became Master of Ceremonies at the Assembly Rooms in Bath in 1705 and established rules of behaviour and dress; by the 1730s Bath was the most fashionable city in England, a meeting place for artists, writers, actors and the nobility.

European fashion was still dominated by the French. During the first years of the century no particular changes occurred, but the transition to rococo elegance and delicacy began with the accession of Louis XV in 1720. Even the Spanish succumbed to its charms. The English, although conforming in general, showed a preference for a simpler or more 'rustic' style, particularly apparent in men's clothes. Americans seem to have shown a similar preference although looking rather more keenly to France for women's fashion. By 1770, England's lead in masculine fashion was established, and it continued until the mid 20th century.

While men's clothes became progressively simpler and slimmer throughout the period, women's, until the 1780s, became more exaggerated, with enormous hooped petticoats, elaborate decoration and towering powdered wigs. Then came a radical change to simplicity: simple sashed dresses in muslin and calico, soft fichus and unpowdered hair. This change may be traced to various factors: Marie Antoinette's pastime of playing at milkmaids in her rustic village at Versailles, the English love of country life, the revival of interest in classical form engendered by the excavations at Pompeii in 1755, the romantic movement fostered by Rousseau and the Gothic revival associated with it, or the sexual permissiveness which ran, according to Professor Lawrence Stone in *The Family, Sex and Marriage in England 1500–1800*, from about 1670 to 1810 and may have encouraged the fashion around 1800 for thin, loose dresses revealing much of the body. All these influences combined with the general feeling for egalitarian reform and against any form of suppression to bring about the swing away from formality and elaboration.

MEN

Drawers, fairly full and short or to the knee, were usually made of linen but by the very end of the 18th century they might be of cotton flannel or woollen stockinette. Shirts of cambric or muslin, cut full with wide sleeves, were gathered into a band at the neck (over which a neckcloth or stock was worn) and into bands fastened with buttons at the wrist to which ruffles of cambric and/or lace would be attached; double ruffles might also be attached down the front of the shirt concealing a buttoned opening. Wrist ruffles were smaller in the second half of the century and after 1790 virtually disappeared apart from very formal wear.

Fashionable men discarded the long neckcloth or Steinkirk cravat around 1730 (although the former was worn unfashionably until about 1765) in favour of the stock, a high made-up neckcloth of stiffened linen or cambric tied or buckled at the back; the buckles, although rarely seen, were often ornamental. A black ribbon called a solitaire was worn over the stock; it might be broad, draped around the neck and tied in a bow under the chin, or tucked into the shirt front, or pinned in place, or loosely knotted; or narrow, tied close with a stiff bow in front. It was almost invariably worn with the bag wig, continuing in fashion until the 1770s when a new form of cravat was introduced, a square or kerchief of lawn or muslin folded into a triangle and then into a band and tied round the neck with a bow at the front. It continued well into the 19th century and was usually made by the ladies of the household. This type of cravat was highly favoured by the Macaronis, members of the Macaroni Club founded in 1764 by much-travelled wealthy young Englishmen back from Italy, who affected a fastidious and exaggerated style of dress: their short skimpy coats with flat collars, short waistcoats, a profusion of braiding, large ruffles, spy glasses, tiny tricorne hats and large nosegays of flowers pinned to the left shoulder were the subject of frequent caricature during the 1770s.

French, 1724. Stiffened coat with deep open cuff buttoned to sleeve. Long waistcoat. Dress sword. Bag wig tied with bow. Solitaire worn over stock.

English, 1732. Girl, simple country style. Straw hat over cap; closed robe with laced front, short robings, apron and mittens. Woman wears hooded mantlet over a cap; face patches.

French, 1724. Pinner cap. Sack of wide striped brocade; beribboned corset. Black ribbon bracelet with medallion. Mules.

Pearls in hair and above neck ruffle.

French, mid-18C. Open robe in champagne-coloured taffeta with matching flowered petticoat, ribbons and trimming. Echelles on stomacher. Elbow-length sleeves finish with self-ruffles over three layers of lace ruffles.

French, 1758. Lightly powdered hair drawn back with two curls falling on to shoulder.

Scottish, 1755. French style: unpowdered hair decorated with blue ribbon and tassels, blue neck ruffles; white lace cape over deep pink sack.

The coat style established in the late 17th century became more pronounced, cut without a waist seam, fairly close-fitting with flared skirts, pleated side vents and a centre back vent between deep inverted pleats; it reached just below the knee, although the ultra-fashionable might vary the length and opt for a tighter fit. Between 1720 and 1750 the skirts might be stiffened with buckram or similar material, the widened effect complementing the hooped skirts of the women. The coat was still cut high to the neck, collarless and with vertical fronts until 1740 when they curved away somewhat below the waist. Although rarely buttoned except at the waist, buttons and buttonholes ran from neck to hem until they were omitted below waist level around 1745. Horizontal pockets with shaped flaps moved up almost to waist level and then slightly down again. Sleeves, cut in two pieces, were fairly neat-fitting and short, gradually growing longer; large wide cuffs held their own until the 1750s. Buttons, down the front, on pockets and cuffs, and at the top of the pleats, might be gold or silver or covered with the coat fabric or with the braid or embroidery used for decoration.

The waistcoat followed the lines of the coat but without pleats or hip buttons, and a few inches shorter; the front skirts might also be stiffened. Often the waistcoat fabric matched the coat, but it might also be patterned or of a lighter colour, or embroidered. The sleeves and back, rarely seen, might be of a cheaper material.

Breeches were cut as in the late 17th century, full over the seat and gathered into a band, the fitting adjusted by a buckle at the back; the front fastened either with buttons down the front, without a fly, or with small or whole falls (a buttoned flap) which became general after 1750. The legs, fairly close-fitting over the lower thigh, reached to just below the knee, fastening at the outer edge with buttons and perhaps a band and buckle. If stockings were drawn up over the knees, the knee fastening might be eliminated for a neater fit; garters to hold up the stockings were hidden under their rolled tops. With the earlier long coats and waistcoats very little of the breeches could be seen.

Around 1730 the frock became increasingly popular. In previous centuries this name was used for a loose, sleeved outer garment of coarse material worn by farm workers, etc., later known as a slop-frock (and in the 19th century as a smock-frock); but during the 18th century a frock was an undress coat, easier in fit and shorter than the coat and distinguished by a small, flat, turn-down collar (called until the end of the century a cape), often of different material from the rest of the garment. At first only worn in the country or for riding, the frock was gradually used more frequently for town wear. It was usually of plain cloth, fustian, plush or serge, with metal buttons, whereas the formal full dress coat was made of brocade, flowered velvet, embroidered or gold and silver materials.

During the 1740s–50s, coat and waistcoat became shorter and tighter fitting. The coat was cut away at the front, the side seams curved backwards, and the buttons heading the side vents moved to the back; the waistcoat only reached mid-thigh and in most cases lost its sleeves. More of the breeches could now be seen and they also were tighter-fitting. By the late 1750s only the elderly or old-fashioned wore long full-skirted coats and waistcoats.

In the 1760s–70s the coat, worn for full dress only, was unwaisted and had no flare in the skirt; pockets, placed just below the waist, had small flaps, and the close-fitting sleeves finished at the wrist with narrow closed cuffs. Around 1765 both coat and waistcoat had small standing collars which increased in height during the next decade. The 1770s saw the front of the coat curved back even further, the buttons and buttonholes becoming merely decorative with possibly those at breast level remaining functional; this exposed the lower half of the waistcoat, its foreparts now cut back at an angle. The waistcoat, still growing shorter throughout the 1780s, reached waist level and was square-cut during the 1790s. It was always single-breasted until 1730, but a double-breasted style became common in the 1780s and usual during the 1790s; rectangular pockets without flaps were retained.

The frock also followed the more fitted style but kept its distinctive turned-down collar. From 1770 it might be worn on all occasions save at court, when a decorated version called a French frock was acceptable. The English frock was decorated only with braid and buttons (usually larger than those on a coat). Its skirts, shortened for riding, were at first buttoned or caught back and later cut away in a curve to become a tail coat by 1790. The fronts might occasionally be cut across horizontally but this is more typical of the 19th century. The sleeves lost their cuffs and were buttoned perpendicularly, though sometimes left unbuttoned. By 1780 the collar gained more 'stand and fall' and revers appeared, increasing in width and curving back from a double-breasted fastening. In effect, frock and day coat had merged, becoming an early form of frock-coat.

Fashion now decreed that breeches should be as tight as possible; doeskin riding breeches during the 1770s were said to have fitted 'with never a wrinkle'. The introduction of braces (suspenders) to support breeches in the 1790s led to a change in cut to a tighter fit with no need for an adjustable waistband.

A wig (periwig or peruke) was worn almost universally by men of all classes throughout the 18th century until about 1790. They were usually made of hair, human or animal; but there are references to wigs made of feathers, and metal wigs were invented around 1750 – but these were rare and their use short-lived. Styles varied considerably. Full-bottomed wigs, the fullness curving back somewhat, continued to be worn fashionably until 1730 and later by elderly men. The Duvillier (falbala or furbelow) was very long and high ('Huge falbala periwigs' are mentioned in *The Tatler*, 1709). The Adonis was a long bushy white wig 'like the twigs of a gooseberry bush in deep snow' (*The London Magazine*, 1734). Related to or directly descended from the large wigs were the campaigne (1695–1750), a bushy wig framing the face, with a centre parting, its short side ends sometimes tied back, worn for travelling and popular with the elderly; and the physical (from 1750), a larger version of the long bob, often worn by the learned professions. Bob wigs were bushy, informal or undress wigs, just covering the neck (long bob) or above the neck (short bob). The scratch bob or cut wig (*c*.1740 until the end of the century) was like the bob but covered only the back part of the head, the natural front hair being brushed over it. The cauliflower, like the bob but closely curled, was commonly worn by coachmen.

Wigs tied back in a queue, a tail of hair at the back of the neck, were in fashion from about 1725 until the end of the century; the front hair was at first parted in the centre, then, during the 1730s, brushed back from the temples and forehead into a roll called a toupee. Until 1740 it was not infrequently accompanied by 'pigeon's wings', bunches of hair brushed out or irregularly curled over each ear; during the 1750s–60s these became one or two stiff horizontal rolls, and the whole would be referred to as a pigeon-winged toupee. The toupee grew steadily higher from the 1770s and during that decade was carried to excess by the Macaronis.

A great variety of other wigs included the bag-wig (from 1725) worn for dress or undress occasions, its queue enclosed in a square silk bag drawn into the nape of the

English, c.1750. Men's coats with large cuffs, inverted pleats at back and flapped pockets, braid trimming. Bag wigs and tricornes.

English, 1742. Coat with round cuffs. Embroidered waistcoat. Late version of full bottomed wig.

Shirt ruffles show at front and wrists.

Dutch, 1742. Red velvet coat lined pale blue. Waistcoat of gold satin embroidered in silver and dark grey, matches cuffs. Dark orange breeches. Solitaire at neck. Long queue

English, first half 18c. Hat of black cloth with a deep nap; brim-edged metal braid and feathers

English, 1725-50. Man's green silk slippers, embroidered silver thread, with red leather heels.

Pale blue stockings, black shoes.

English, 1718-22. Sleeved waistcoat in gold and silver fabric with a little red, blue and green silk woven with a pattern of formalised foliage; the back to waist level and the upper sleeves of cheaper yellow silk. Green silk lining.

English 1720-40. Man's shoes in heavy black leather.

English 1745. The contrast between aristocratic youth and wealthy upper-middle-class citizen:
Young man in blue coat with pink and gold brocade waistcoat and cuffs. Bag wig and solitaire. White stockings; shoes with high red heels.
Elderly man in red coat, plain grey waistcoat and breeches, ribbed wool stockings, old-fashioned full-bottomed wig and Steinkirk. Both wigs are powdered.

French, 1770. Brigadier wig, the queue tied with a large bow. Coat has seo-trimmed toggle fastening

French, 1746. Open robes and capes. The lady's robe is mid-blue, her negligée light grey. The modiste's gown is striped mid-and light green, her black-hooded cape is lace trimmed; she also wears a pinner and apron.

English, 1754. Turban-like velvet 'night-cap'

English, mid-18C. century. Long bob wig

neck with a running string, concealed by a stiff black bow; the major (1750s) – called a brigadier in France – adopted by civilians from the military, which had two corkscrew curls tied together to form a double queue; the catogan or club (1760s–70s), with a broad flat queue turned up on itself and tied around the middle with a black ribbon; and the caxon, worn informally, with curls drawn back and bunched together to form a queue, occasionally also worn by women. Also informal but rather smarter was the pigtail (1760s–70s), with a long queue spirally bound or interwoven with black ribbon and tied above and below with black ribbon bows. Rather smaller was the ramillies, with a long queue of plaited hair diminishing in size, also tied with black ribbon bows either above and below or sometimes only below; from 1780 the plait might be turned up and bound by a ribbon at the nape of the neck or looped up high and secured by a comb to the back of the head.

Wigs were made in various colours – blonde, brown, auburn, black and white – and were frequently powdered. Hair powder made of starch was white for formal wear, but other colours such as blue might be used. After 1760 powdering lost popularity and by 1790 was rarely seen except on older or very conservative men. The head was shaved or close-cropped, with possibly a fringe of hair left at the nape or at the front. The former would be caught into the queue, and the latter pomaded and dressed into the toupee.

A few men such as members of the non-conformist religious groups did not wear wigs; others who wore their own hair had it pomaded and dressed to resemble a fashionable peruke. By the end of the century natural hair had become fashionable and in the 19th wigs were a thing of the past.

Western Europeans and colonial men, apart from the odd eccentric, countryman or peasant, were clean-shaven. In Poland, Rumania and eastern Europe moustaches appear to have been worn.

The three-cornered cocked hat or tricorne (a 19th-century name) worn throughout the 18th century varied only in its proportions and the elevation of the corners. The Dettingen cock had its brim cocked equally at the front and back, the Kevenhüller (1760–70) had the front peak turned markedly upwards; the Fantail (1780s) had the back section turned up very flat to form an open fan shape across the back and was originally worn for riding, occasionally by women as well as men. Kevenhüller was probably an ancestor of the bicorne, a two-pointed hat turned up and flattened back and front (1770s and early 19th century). A hat with a round crown and flat brim, at first worn only in the country, gradually became tapered and higher with a flattened top and narrower brim, leading to the top hat of the 19th century. With wigs, the tricorne was frequently carried rather than worn; a flat version introduced towards the end of the century was called a chapeau-bras and was made to be carried under the arm when wearing court dress. (The name was also used for a crescent-shaped hat used in the same manner but occasionally worn during the next century.)

Beaver was used for the most expensive hats. Beau Nash had a great cream-coloured beaver hat, but most were either black or brown. Tricornes were often edged with gold or silver braid or with lace, and on formal occasions a decorative button and loop held the cocked brim.

Nightcaps were fuller than those of the 17th century, more like a turban, and were often of the same material (wool, damask, velvet, etc.) as the nightgown (i.e. dressing gown). They were the usual wear for indoor negligée.

Square-toed shoes were superseded by a more normal, rounded shape. The tongue became shorter and rounded at the corners, the buckle larger, reaching its greatest size

English, 1766. Coat with slight stand collar, coat and waistcoat trimmed braid. Untrimmed frock with velvet top collar.

English, 1765. Gown with sack back in a French fabric: blue and pink shot silk brocaded with floral sprays in green, white and pink over white serpentine background pattern.

English, 1745. Mob cap with Kissing strings, and early form of round-eared cap.

English, 1745. Mob cap with kissing strings. Cream satin peterlair and matching corset. Pale pinkish lavender petticoat. Brocade shoes.

Child in white hood-like cap over a frilled cap. Pale blue cape trimmed with darker shade of blue over soft pink closed robe.

French, 1741. Bourgeois costume. Black cape with hood, over cap; sack-back gown striped dark orange and white, the skirt tucked up and drawn through the pocket slits, worn over olive-coloured quilted petticoat.

in the 1770s. Buckles – oval, square or oblong – were interchangeable. The oblong Artois buckle, fashionable between 1775 and 1788 and often very decorative, was made of Sheffield plate, steel or pinchbeck (imitation gold, an alloy of copper and zinc or, preferably, silver). Heels were fashionably red until 1750 and grew lower, as did the cut of the shoe over the instep, so that the buckle moved nearer the toe. By the end of the century shoes had a slipper-like appearance; and real slippers – the mules introduced during the 17th century, without a heelpiece – continued to be worn indoors for negligée. Shoes were generally black, made almost exclusively of Spanish leather.

Jack boots, by 1725 worn only by postillions, coachmen, etc., were succeeded by a close-fitting boot shaped to the leg and cut away behind the knee, and by jockey tops or half jack boots which ended below the knee with a turn-down top of softer, lighter-coloured leather; after 1780 they were called top boots. Spatterdashes were still worn in the country, as were gaiters, introduced for the infantry around 1710–20 and worn by civilians during the 1770s but considered unfashionable after 1790. Hessians – short riding boots, calf-length behind and generally curving to a point in front below the kneecap and decorated with a tassel – appeared after 1790 but are more a feature of early 19th-century dress. Boots were not worn indoors by men of fashion during this century until after 1780 when they became suitable for all occasions.

After 1730, stockings worn during the day might be ribbed or checkered and varied in colour, knitted by hand or machine from worsted or thread (twisted flax). *Read's Weekly Journal* (1735) states that at a royal wedding 'all the gentlemen's stockings were white'. Boot-hose, now long white woollen stockings, were still occasionally worn. Silk stockings, often clocked in gold or silver, were worn for formal evening dress. A fashion for striped stockings during the 1780s–90s followed the trend for striped fabric for coats and breeches which emphasized the slimmer line.

Cloaks remained in fashion for outdoor wear and were not completely discarded until the 19th century, especially with evening dress. In addition to the earlier circular style gathered to the neck under a turn-down collar, there was the knee-length roquelaure (or roculo) cloak, shaped to the neck with a single or double cape collar and fastened down the front; it had a back vent for convenience when riding. The Brandenburg coat, without frog fastenings, became known by 1730 as a surtout or wrap-rascal; still long and loose, it had one or more spreading collars. The term overcoat was not used until the 19th century, but a greatcoat implied a garment of heavy cloth worn for travelling while a top coat was of lighter-weight material more suitable for walking.

WOMEN

Fundamental to the shape and fit of women's dress in the 18th century were stays (or whaleboned bodices) and hooped petticoats. Stays or corsets at this time reached a very high standard of craftsmanship: the whalebone was cut into strips, as many as forty or more of varying thickness and length according to their position, and held in place with backstitch worked by hand. They were laced either at the centre front or back; front lacing might form a feature of the design of the dress or gown, or be covered by a decorated stomacher. Stays were often covered with silk or brocade, or embroidered, and were made to be seen when worn under a loose robe. A busk was still used, often of wood carved with emblems, and might be pushed down a busk sheath stitched into the front of the bodice. English stays were rather more rigid than those

German, 1750-55. Decorated panier, showing rows of whalebone.

Stays late 1790s, probably French (worn in England into the next century).

French, 1776. Stays with extra busk and shaping bones across the front and the shoulder blades.

1748-50. Method of lifting paniers

German, 1775. Whaleboned stays, laced at front over chemise; separate side hoops (pocket hoops) as worn for 'undress' over under-petticoat

English, 1775-85. Pink satin shoes with floral pattern in green, yellow and terracotta

English, 1770-80. Crimson damask slipper trimmed ruched satin ribbon striped in green and cream

English, 1750. Blue satin shoes with detachable buckles

1755-60. Paniers constructed as a hinged metal frame to allow hoop to be lifted under the arms; tapes hold the metal at required angle.

worn in France, but the aim of both was to achieve a long slim line with a small waist and somewhat raised bust given roundness by bones placed laterally across the front. To flatten the back, straight bones were also placed across the shoulder blades until the 1780s–90s when, with the more negligée style and higher waistline, more lightly boned cotton stays were cut higher and narrower at the back. The front neckline then became lower and the waist tabs either began from a raised waistline or were dispensed with altogether, and by the end of the century boned stays had disappeared, only to return in a slightly different form with the 1820s corsets.

Hooped petticoats to replace hip pads or heavy, stiffened petticoats apparently started in England. They are first mentioned in English journals dated around 1709. The early dome-shaped form soon became flattened, reaching a fantastic width by the middle of the century in spite of male ridicule and opposition. Called in France *paniers* and sometimes in England improvers, these petticoats were made of rich material with three or four rows of whalebone inserted at intervals from the waist down; extra hoops laid on the sides, with tapes tied at intervals from front to back inside, kept the outline wider and flatter. French *paniers* were wider at the base; in England the hoops were of equal size below the widened hip level. The very wide hoops were worn for court dress in France until the Revolution, but, remarkably, remained obligatory for full court dress in England as late as 1820, looking somewhat ludicrous when combined with the currently fashionable high waistline.

Skirts and petticoats naturally followed the line of the hoops. As the skirt was usually full and pleated to the waist, the waist seam had, in effect, to be extended over the *panier* to obtain the extreme width at the sides, with the pleats or gathers taken into it as required. Openings in these seams between the actual waist and the *panier* 'hip' enabled the wearer to reach her 'pocket', a separate small flat bag, or pair of bags, hung from a tape around the waist next to the shift or under-petticoat. The length of skirts varied, generally reaching the ground and trained for formal wear, but occasionally shortened to instep or even ankle level. The petticoat, usually of a different colour and fabric to the gown, was often embroidered and, between 1730 and 1750, quilted. Between 1750 and 1780 petticoats were often profusely decorated with flounces, ribbon loops, tassels, flower festoons, etc., particularly in France; the English and Americans on the whole favoured a simpler style.

For undress occasions, from the late 1750s or early '60s until as late as 1775, cotton pocket-hoops replaced the large hoops; these were fairly small, separate side hoops, rather like rounded boxes, worn on each hip and reaching to just above the knee. As drapery on skirts moved to the back, pocket-hoops gave way to a large pad called a 'bum' or 'rump' often made of cork, which continued to be worn, decreasing in size, through the 1790s to prevent the skirt from falling into the small of the back below the raised waistline. Having dwindled to a small roll it was worn into the early 19th century when it became known as a bustle.

Between 1700 and 1770 the gown, formed of a bodice and skirt sewn together, might have the skirt left open at the front to reveal a petticoat (sometimes referred to as a 'coat' which can prove misleading); this can be called an open robe, although the name is really of 19th-century origin. A gown with a closed skirt was known as a round gown or closed robe. The boned bodice of the open robe had the neck and front opening edged with robings, a flat trimming similar to revers, sloping from the wide neckline to a point at the waist in a V shape. This opening revealed either a stiffened and decorated stomacher, pinned in place under the robings, a plain stomacher, over which the bodice was laced, or back-fastening stays (or corsets) with embroidered fronts. Echelles, a series of ribbon bows decreasing in size from décolletage to waist in a ladder-like formation down the centre of the stomacher, were first seen in the late 17th century and continued in popularity until nearly the end of the 18th. Occasionally, until about 1720, the open robe might have a rounded décolletage and be buttoned down the front to the waist. Throughout most of the century the décolletage on formal gowns was lightly edged with narrow lace or gauze, but bourgeois or provincial women frequently wore a kerchief (later called a fichu), a square or strip of linen folded round the neck. The buffon, a larger version of this in gauze or very fine linen swathed around the shoulders and puffed over the bosom, became high fashion in the 1780s. The Medici collar, occasionally seen in the 1770s–80s on formal gowns, was generally of lace or net, upstanding round the back of the neck and sloping down to nothing on the front of the bodice.

Variations of the open robe included the mantua, its bodice unlined as in the 17th century but with the skirt no longer draped up, made in the richest of materials and worn on all social occasions and at court until the 1820s; the nightgown, similar to the mantua but with the décolletage covered by some kind of drapery, worn informally; and the slammerkin or trollope, a loose, unbuttoned, informal morning gown with a train, worn over a short petticoat, often without hoops.

The bodice of the round gown or closed robe of 1730–40 had an edge-to-edge fastening at the centre front; the skirt was made with a short 'fall' (similar to the falls on men's breeches) pleated into a band tied with strings under the bodice. The wrapping gown (1735–50) had a bodice front cut in one with the skirt, wrapped across and caught with a brooch or clasp at the waist; its low rounded neckline was filled in with a frilled edging of lace, lawn or other soft material.

A distinctive gown, worn in England between 1720 and 1780, earlier in France where it originated, was the sack (sac or saque). It was closed until 1750, then open. Between 1720 and 1730 it hung in voluminous folds all round from neck to hem; unpressed pleats on the front shoulders were drawn down and caught together at a point at or a little above the waist, and back pleats, caught at the neck, spread out freely into the skirt. The full loose back characteristic of the sack was to become formalized into single, double or treble box pleats either side of the centre back, stitched down for a short distance from the neckline, then hanging loose from the shoulder blades to merge into the fullness of the skirt. After 1730 the bodice was shaped to the body, its lining laced under the back pleats. Both styles revealed a stomacher, and the petticoat or underskirt worn with the open style appears generally to have been of matching fabric. From 1770 two variations of the sack appeared: the *robe a l'anglaise*, in which the back pleats were sewn down to waist level, and the *robe a la piémontese* (Piedmont gown) in which the box pleats were detached from the back of the bodice, forming a kind of bridge between the shoulders and the waist where they merged into the skirt.

Sleeves on closed, open and sack gowns from 1700 to 1770 were more closely fitting than those of the 17th century and set well in at the back scye with a little gathering or easing; they finished just below the elbow and were edged with a small turned-back cuff, pleated across the front, until around 1740, when the cuff grew larger and was then replaced by one or two flounces of the gown fabric, longer at the back than the front, from under which flowed ruffles of lawn and lace, detachable for washing; there was no room under the tighter sleeves for a ruffled chemise sleeve. In the 1770s the

English, 1768-70. Open robe trimmed narrow pleating. Scalloped edge on sleeve flounces over triple lace flounces. Apron of sheer fabric. Kerchief over high-dressed hair

Major Wig; Coat with small cuffs; tighter fitting breeches.

Round-eared cap

English 1743-5. Open robe in satin with a high sheen, with a plain short robings and turn-back cuffs; quilted petticoat.

English, 1768. Dark blue coat and breeches, white ribbed stockings. Vermilion red waistcoat trimmed gold braid with early type of revers.

English, 1750-60. Leghorn straw bergère hat trimmed with cream ribbons, over gauze cap. Pearl choker. Lace-trimmed sheer neckerchief

English, 1750. Sack gown in floral patterned brocade. Bergère hat over cap. Elbow length gloves.

1764. Rose-pink open sack gown with matching underskirt; trimming of pleated self material. Lace-edged gauze ruffles at neck and sleeves. Mixed flower posy on bodice.

Small lace-edged cap; hair tied with dark green ribbon.

1767. Matching coat and waistcoat, plain linen at neck and wrists. Toupee wig.

1753. Child's dress with long bodice and short cuffed sleeves. Fine gauze sleeve ruffles and pleated neck trimming.

1761. Small round-eared gauze cap trimmed with ribbon. Pearl necklace tied with ribbons. Fine gauze and lace wrapped across bosom over closed satin gown.

Bag wig.

1748. Dark brown coat with white lining to match long waistcoat embroidered with gold coloured silk. Plain, fine linen shirt and cravat.

1766-7. Hair dressed higher and decorated with pearls. Pleated gauze decorates stomacher and sleeves.

Large shawl.

Colonial American dress of the wealthy classes 1748-70.

Austrian, 1776. Court dress:
Powdered hair
dressed high,
entwined with
pearls.

Neck frill
forms a
'Medici'
style
collar

French, 1776. Court dress:
huge hooped skirt,
elaborately dressed hair
decorated with plumes and gauze.

French, 1777.
Walking
dress: polonaise,
puffed band
finish on sleeves;
hat of gathered
silk trimmed silk
drapery and feathers.
long gloves.

French, 1777.
Full court dress: pale
blue gown embroidered
with silver.
Powdered hair
decorated with
white plumes, blue
ribbon pearls and
brilliants.

French, 1777. Informal dress: polonaise in striped
fabric caught up with cords; underskirt shirred
up in smaller sections with tassels between.
Different striped fabric for petticoat.

English country style, 1779. Straw hat trimmed white ruched silk and pink ribbons. Pale yellow open robe over soft pink petticoat; white kerchief, sleeve ruffles and apron.

Unpowdered hair

Unpowdered hair

English country style 1770s. Grey-brown frock, waistcoat and breeches; buckled straps support brown half jack boots.

Little girl all in white with red shoes

Boy in dark green suit, white ruffled collar on shirt, pale green stockings, black shoes.

English, 1775-7. Fanciful style favoured by the English aristocracy. Oyster-coloured satin looped up in polonaise style, matching hat. Gauze sleeves with satin ribbon trim. Pink ruched petticoat.

Lightly powdered hair

English, 1778-80. Calash of black glazed cotton lined pink glazed cotton.

French, c.1780. Hood of sheer fabric large enough to cover the huge wig or hairstyle.

Embroidered satin shoes

English, 1786. Frock with high stand-fall collar, sleeve opening buttoned perpendicularly, and skirts cut away at front.

French, 1788. Woman: White muslin with lace ruffles at neck; narrow blue ribbon on sleeve, wider for sash. Hair curly over crown, longer at back, fashionable for undress.

Man. Velvet coat, satin breeches and silk stockings, all black.

English, 1770. Dormeuse or dormouse cap.

English, 1775-80. Polonaise in Indian painted cotton, purple and red on white; blue silk collar with white muslin over. White muslin cap, sleeve-ruffles and apron.

French, 1780. Leghorn straw hat trimmed with ribbon.

Buffon and sash

Black velvet hat trimmed black feathers and ribbon.

Powdered hair.

English, 1785. Blue and white striped gown, blue buffon, sash and wrist trimming; gold-coloured shawl, light brown fur muff.

ruffles tended to become gathered together at the bottom to form puffed bands.

Between 1770 and 1785 the bunched-up overskirt returned, and the polonaise (or polonese) became high fashion, worn at first with hoops and then exaggerating the new bustle shape. The overskirt might simply be turned back and pinned behind, revealing the lining, or tucked under itself and drawn out through the pocket holes; but the typical polonaise had the the overskirt looped up at the sides and back so that it fell in festoons over the petticoat, held in place by invisible tapes or by vertical running strings, with bows of ribbon or tassels placed to suggest that they held the festoons in place.

The simplification of women's dress began in the late 1780s. The open robe became high-waisted with a sash, a buffon puffed out the bust, and the trained overskirt was no longer bunched up. The closed or round gown was also high-waisted and began to be known as a frock in the 1790s. The most stikingly simple was the chemise dress (gown or robe), which resembled the undergarment of that name, its low round neckline gathered in with a drawstring, the high waist defined by a gathering thread over which a sash was essential, and the skirt hanging in an increasingly straight line. These dresses usually had tight, wrist-length sleeves.

Throughout most of the 18th century a separate bodice or jacket and skirt were worn on informal occasions. A jacket bodice, known as a casaquin in France, was close-fitting to the waist with a round or square décolletage and flared out over the petticoat to just below hip level, fastened by lacing or concealed hooks and eyes at the front. A similar jacket was referred to as a caraco, but the caraco *à la polonaise*, fashionable in the late 1770s–80s, was pleated and flared at the back and cut away at the front. The petenlair (called by some authorities a caraco *à la française*), worn in France in the 1740s and in England between 1745 and the 1770s, was simply a sack shortened to thigh length. All these styles were worn with fairly simple petticoats or skirts.

The riding habit, first introduced in the 17th century, had a jacket similar in cut to a man's, even buttoning left over right. Without a collar until 1730, and then with one, it was worn with a long full petticoat and often a waistcoat. By mid-century fine woollen cloth began to replace grosgrain or other silk for this garment; it was worn not only for riding or hunting but as a morning costume, and was probably part of the wave of anglomania in France during the 1780s which introduced English-style riding coats with collars, lapels and capes and long, short or cut-away skirts.

Small shoulder capes of fine lace or silk worn by women during the early-mid 18th century, particularly for negligée, are called pallatines by some authorities, but this is really the name for a sable shoulder wrap in the 19th century. A similar name, palatine, was used for a wrap worn around the neck and reaching to below the waist.

High-dressed hair, with or without a fontange, remained in fashion for the first few years of the 18th century, as did masculine-style wigs, usually worn with a riding habit. Around 1715 a small natural-looking hair style became the vogue, and remained so with some variations until 1760; the hair was drawn back close to the head into a small bun at the back, from which a few long or short curls fell on to the neck or over the shoulder, particularly for court wear, to soften the nape. This style was worn by Madame de Pompadour. Hair was always powdered on full-dress occasions (when small bunches or wreaths of artificial flowers, perhaps combined with pearls, were often added) and quite frequently on less formal occasions. For riding the hair was drawn back into a queue.

During the 1760s hair began to be dressed higher again, in an 'egg' shape with formalized curls. In court circles and among the ultra-fashionable the size and height was to reach monstrous proportions during the late 1770s. Padded with cotton-wool or other material and false hair, plastered with pomade and then powdered, the whole edifice towered above the head; ribbons, flounces, bands, scarves and feathers were added and even, according to contemporary reports, models of ships, coaches or windmills! Since so much time and money was spent on its erection, the coiffure might remain untouched for several weeks. These extreme styles, worn by only a few, are associated more with France than England, and in particular with Marie Antoinette. Others wore their hair dressed high but fairly simply: in *School for Scandal*, Sir Peter Teazel remembers his wife 'when I first saw you, sitting at your Tambour, in a pretty figured gown, a bunch of keys at your side, your hair combed smooth over a roll.'

Around 1780, width rather than height was favoured, with the back hair hanging down in a large chignon or catogan or, for undress occasions, a full curly mop over the crown and very long hair hanging behind. Powder was less often used, and a natural look became fashionable. Further simplicity and reduction in size complemented the simple dresses of the 1790s – short hair, loosely curled and arranged in studied confusion, or long hair drawn back into an imitation of ancient Greek and Roman styles.

With the fontange outmoded, caps were no longer worn for state occasions except by widows or the elderly, but they remained popular even in court circles for undress wear and were habitually worn by the middle classes. Until 1730, caps were fairly inconspicuous; the pinner, circular and flat to the crown with a frilled edging, was then joined and replaced by the round-eared cap (1730–60), and the mob cap (1730 until well into the 19th century, and even later for servants and national costumes). The round-eared cap, similar in shape to a bonnet, curved round the face to ear level or just below, the front bordered with a single or double frill, the back drawn together by a running tape, exposing the hair; side lappets might be attached to the lower borders of the front frill. The mob cap had a puffed up crown worn high on the head, and a frilled border with, until 1750, side lappets hanging loose or tied under the chin, called kissing strings or bridles; later it was fitted loosely to the head and had a ribbon band. Its size increased to accommodate the hair styles of the '70s and '80s. During the 1750s, however, tiny butterfly or fly caps made of lace and lawn wired to the shape of a butterfly and perched on the forehead became popular.

The dormeuse or dormouse, an undress indoor cap characteristic of the 1770s, had a high puffed-up crown trimmed with ribbon, and deep falling flaps at each side trimmed with ruched lace, called wings or sometimes cheek wrappers, which curved back to reveal the forehead and front hair but framed the face; it was often tied under the chin. The turban, folded around the head in a similar manner to the eastern style, was worn for dress or undress from 1760 until the 19th century, when it became evening attire only.

Hats in a great variety of shapes and sizes were made from felt, silk or straw. The popularity of straw may reflect the appeal of the 'simple life', but the straw hats of the peasants were of plaited coarse straw or rushes, whereas those of the upper classes were made from a fine yellow straw manufactured in Leghorn. During the 1840s–50s charming shallow-crowned, medium-brimmed hats trimmed with ribbon were worn straight or slightly tilted to one side, or cocked in a variety of ways, often over a cap. The slouch hat also had a shallow crown but the brim was floppy (the name continued in use during the 19th century for any hat with an uncocked and drooping brim). The

1777. Pale blue bodice, yellow skirt; cream pelisse with fur edging. Apron in sheer white material, cream drapery at neck.

Red drapery on head

1779. Red coat lined pale blue. Powdered hair or wig with long queue.

Snood-like headdress.

1786. Short coat with wide revers faced with white

Yellow coat and breeches.

1786. Pale grey gauze over satin, caught up with white ribbons and bunches of pink roses, which also appear under neck frill; pink ribbon sash. Powdered hair dressed very wide; cream straw hat with white ribbons. Low cut shoes with low heels. Typically Spanish.

1797-9. Hair natural colour with dark blue-green ribbon. Cream buffon held with pink rose and pale blue ribbon. Dark blue and green striped gown embroidered at wrists.

1792. Frock with high collar and wide floppy revers in narrow striped silk; breeches have buttoned side pockets.

1795. Pale creamy-grey silk coat with typical wide Spanish revers; blue and silver brocade sash.

Spanish Costume, last quarter of 18C.

American, 1788-90.
Elaborate cap of pleated
gauze and looped
ribbon. Hair falling
in tendrils on to
shoulders. Watered
silk open gown
with matching
underskirt, trimmed
with pleating.
Separate black
lace and gauze
shawl worn under
white buffon.

English, 1780-90. Pink silk gown
figured in red spots; collar has
bound Vandyked edging. Muslin
kerchief fills the open neckline.
Hair dressed
high and
rather
loose.

Cream hat
trimmed
deep pink
feathers.

American, 1792.
Light brown/dark
green shot silk
gown with pink
sash, cream gauze
pleating round
neck.

High-crowned hat
trimmed with
feathers and
large tassels.

American, 1790. Pale pink gown
with narrow three-quarter sleeves,
beige belt. White buffon edged with
small loops of fine black gauze.
Grey wig, trimmed with grey and
black feathers.

American, c. 1790.
Riding coat or redingote with pale buttons matching
edging on lapel and collar. Boy's skeleton suit.

American, 1792. Woman's pale grey satin open robe with long tight sleeves and matching underskirt. White muslin buffon and mob cap trimmed white ribbon.
Man's black frock with red facing to collar, large gilt buttons. Black breeches, white waistcoat and stockings.

English, 1785-90 Black kid slippers with pink kid heels.

American, 1793. White muslin buffon and mob cap trimmed satin ribbon.

English, 1775-90 Black and white satin shoes.

English, 1785-90. Black suede slippers bound and trimmed with green ribbon; green leather heels.

French, 1795. Woman's muslin gown shirred at waist and neck; neckerchief tucked into neck of bodice. Leghorn straw hat lined with lace valance. Man's, English styling: early form of cut-away tail coat with high turn-down collar and wide lapels; short double-breasted waistcoat.

Hat, forerunner of the 19C. top hat.

English, 1790. Rust-red redingote over pale cream gown. White stock, black hat trimmed rust and black ribbon.

Breeches fasten with small falls. Strings replace knee buckles. Top boots.

bergère or milkmaid hat, a big straw hat with a flexible or rigid flat brim and very shallow crown, tied on securely with ribbons, was worn from 1730 and by many women until 1800.

Fashionable hats during the 1770s were very small or very large, of straw, velvet or shirred silk, trimmed lavishly with plumes, feathers, ribbons and flowers, worn tilted and cocked at every imaginable angle on the high coiffures. With the wider hairstyles in the 1780s came wider brims and moderate crowns, familiar from Gainsborough portraits, and the *ballon* or Lunardi hat (named after the balloonist) with its large balloon crown and wide brim, made of gauze or similar material over a wire foundation.

For riding and hunting the masculine tricorne was often worn, and towards the end of the century a broad-brimmed, tall-crowned beaver or felt hat decorated with buckles or bows of ribbon also reflected masculine fashion.

The small hoods of the 17th century remained adequate with a little modification over the closely-dressed early coiffures; but of necessity, in the 1770s, hoods grew to enormous proportions. The calash (calèche) was a large folding hood built up on arches of whalebone or cane covered with silk; (its original name in France was a Thérèse, but this probably referred to a similar hood of gauze or very thin material).

Shoes, around 1730, had pointed toes, front fastenings with latchets and buckles over high tongues, and very waisted, rather solid heels of medium height. They became lower cut with tall, slender though still waisted heels which originated in France around 1745–50 and were known as French or Pompadour heels. From 1760 heels tended to be lower for undress, and high fronts and latchets gradually disappeared as ornate buckles were replaced by ribbon ties or rosettes and toes became less acutely pointed. Fashionable shoes were made of brocade, satin, or kid decorated with metallic braid; those worn by the lower classes were of sturdy leather. Mules continued to be worn indoors, and clogs or pattens – overshoes secured by leather straps raised on a metal ring – out-of-doors during muddy weather. Riding buskins were still worn, but boots very rarely. Stockings knitted from thread, worsted or silk were brightly coloured or white.

Outdoor garments were cloak-like wraps, capes and scarves, until the demise of the hoop allowed for masculine-style greatcoats buttoned down the front during the 1790s. The cardinal was a three-quarter-length hooded cloak, usually of scarlet cloth. The pelisse, also three-quarter-length, had a shoulder cape or hood and armhole slits; it was lined, and edged with ruchings of silk or satin or with fur. The mantlet or mantelet, worn from 1730 until the 19th century, was a scarf-like cape of taffeta or other silk, wide at the back and narrow at the front, crossed over the front waist and sometimes, if long enough, carried round to the back. The redingote, introduced during the 1790s, was a light-weight, full-length overcoat, often with capes, buttoned across the bosom; it continued in various forms throughout the next century.

CHILDREN

The attitude to raising and educating children changed considerably during the 18th century, but was not reflected in their clothing until the last two or three decades. At first, children seem to have worn replicas of adult garments at an even earlier age than in previous centuries. Boys were dressed like their fathers from the age of three, girls like their mothers from the age of two; the very young of both sexes were dressed alike in a boned bodice and (usually separate) long, full skirt, possibly shorter for boys. Both boys and girls wore stays stiffened with cane or, for poorer children, made of leather.

One of the first changes in children's clothing was the abandoning of swaddling. The Americans and the English were the first to relinquish this ancient practice around 1770–80; the rest of western Europe was a little slower to follow, but by the end of the century most babies were dressed in 'long gowns' a metre or more in length until about twelve months of age. Caps were worn day and night from birth, usually two, a close-fitting undercap and then a more decorative one.

By the 1760s, dress for girls began to differ increasingly from that of women, at first only for the very young; but by 1780 girls well into their teens were wearing low-necked, high-waisted, often short-sleeved muslin dresses, usually white with a coloured sash, the skirt hanging straight to ankle or instep. When this style became adult fashion from around 1785, a girl born in the 1780s might wear a similar type of dress from babyhood until her late twenties.

New in the 1780s were trousers, worn by boys after they had discarded the frock of babyhood and before adopting the coat and breeches of manhood at the age of ten years or so. Trousers were not a completely new garment: similar garments had been worn by sailors around 1760; however they did not become general fashion until adopted for small boys. At this time they either had a rather wide leg or were tight-fitting pantaloons; both types varied in length between calf and ankle but by the end of the century were always long to the ankle or just above, the slim style being slit up a little at the side. With them, boys wore a shirt with a frilled collar and a jacket without skirts or tails, sometimes accompanied by a broad sash but with no waistcoat. As women's and girls' waistlines rose, boys' jackets shortened, and by 1790 the trousers, now cut well above the waist, were buttoned over the jacket, a style known as a skeleton suit, fashionable for boys between three and seven years of age until around 1830.

Older boys, like men, wore wigs until about 1750–60 when a more natural look was introduced, and by the 1770s their hair was cut fairly short. Girls' hair, caps and hats followed adult styles. Shoes also followed adult styles but were always low-heeled; clogs or pattens were worn in the country.

ACCESSORIES AND JEWELRY

Accessories common to both sexes included knitted 'miser' or stocking purses; canes, of normal length for men throughout the period, taller for women after the 1770s, finished with a knob at the top and occasionally decorated with a tassel; muffs, usually large for men but rarely carried after 1760, small or large for women; handkerchiefs of delicate fabric trimmed with lace or embroidery; gloves, short and utilitarian for men, elbow-length for women, sometimes embroidered, and in white kid for evenings.

Women also wore mittens made of kid, cotton or silk, usually elbow-length, with a single opening for the fingers and a pointed flap covering the back of the hand which often had a decorative lining, visible when the flap was turned back; plainer, more work-a-day styles would be made from worsted wool.

Men wore dress swords with elaborate and beautiful hilts, often set with gems, until around 1770 when the fashion became less common. Throughout the century and into the next, men carried snuff boxes, often extremely beautiful, in various sizes and designs.

Folding fans were considered essential for fashionable women. Apart from its practical use at crowded assemblies, a fan was also used as a kind of sign language, as suggested by Soame Jenyns in *The Art of Dancing* (1730):

Its shake triumphant, its victorious clap,
Its angry flutter and its wanton tap.

A lady might carry a parasol, but it was more likely to have been held over her head by an attendant; and though she might don an expensive and decorative apron for house dress, aprons were more common among the lower classes; a large, enveloping apron with a bib was worn by servants.

Make-up continued to be fairly generously used by extremists of fashion, including the Macaronis. *The Connoisseur* commented in 1754, 'Our modern belles are obliged to retouch their cheeks every day, to keep them in repair ... our polite ladies have thought fit to dress their faces as well as their heads à la mode de Paris.'

The use of jewelry was fairly restrained, especially for men, and during the first half of the century for women also. Men wore rings and carried fairly heavy watches. Heavy seals of gold and semi-precious stones hanging from the fore-pocket of the breeches (the watch pocket) were a typical late 18th-century and early 19th-century fashion for men, copied by women.

Pearls were particularly favoured by women. Madame de Pompadour wore them entwined in her hair, twisted about her wrists and worn above a small lace or gauze ruff tied with ribbons. Brooches in the shape of a flower spray were an alternative to the popular flower posy (artificial or fresh) worn at the bosom, and in France and Germany brooches were skilfully designed to follow the shape of a stomacher and almost cover it. By mid century cameos were in fashion as brooches or as part of a rigid bracelet, a style that became popular during the 19th century. In the elaborate hair styles of the later 1770s, sparkling jewels were arranged in circles, looped in chains, or inserted at random. Americans wore strings of small gold beads, close to the throat. Increasingly popular was the chatelaine, an ornamental chain fastened to the belt or pocket, composed of elaborate linked and moulded elements in various shapes and sizes, from which chains hung from projecting points terminating in spring hooks to carry keys, a little prayer book, scissors, etc. This was worn as day jewelry only, and later became associated with housekeepers or housewives.

The manufacture of imitation gems became a huge industry in the 18th century, especially in France and England where remarkable results were achieved.

FABRICS AND COLOUR

Louis XIV did much to encourage the development of the silk trade, and by the late 17th century and during the 18th Lyons was producing silks, velvets and brocades of luxurious quality. Improvements in the English textile industry, particularly in dyeing and finishing, were helped by the invention of some important machines: James Hargreaves invented the spinning jenny in 1764; Richard Arkwright set up his spinning frame in 1769; Edmund Cartwright patented a power-loom in 1785; in America Eli Whitney devised the cotton gin in 1792, and in France Joseph-Marie Jacquard patented in 1801 the weaving loom that made possible the production of elaborately figured textiles at lower cost.

Men's undress coats were made from woollen cloth, plush (a long-napped velvet of cotton or wool), velvet, silk or satin; their frocks were of fustian, plush or serge. For full dress, gold and silver materials, brocade, velvet and embroidered fabrics were used, and even after 1780 when woollen broadcloth was generally replacing all other fabrics for undress coats and frocks, satin and particularly velvet was considered suitable for

Transitional style, late 18C. - early 19C.
(from Nicholas von Heideloff's
'Gallery of Fashion')

1799.
Formal open robe
in white muslin
embroidered in silver;
silver buttons hold
the gathered sleeves.
Petticoat of
embroidered muslin
with a Vandyke
(dentate) edge.

Riding costume, 1796,
following masculine
styles.

1799. Formal closed robe like a
tunic, in muslin with tinsel and
scarlet spots; gold buttons on
sleeves and front, high ruff,
red and
white striped
sash with
fringed ends

gathered ruffle
at neck

1799. Formal robe in black crape (a transparent
crimped silk gauze) with Vandyke
decoration on wrapped edge and sleeves.
Swansdown muff.

1797. Informal striped
over-robe with high sash
and ruffled cape.

court dress. Waistcoats for full dress were of heavily embroidered satin and velvet, those for undress of cloth, serge and calamanco (single worsted, glazed). Full-dress breeches were of silk, satin and velvet; for undress, cloth, plush and buckskin, the latter particularly for riding.

Fabrics used for women's gowns and petticoats included silks, satins, tabby (a course kind of thick taffeta, glossy and watered), brocade, damask, chintz and Indian cottons, with fine silk gauzes for scarves and trimmings. Between 1750 and 1780 there were also block-printed linens and cotton woven in checks and stripes. During the war between France and England which started in 1793, silk became extremely expensive, wool was needed for uniforms, but Indian cotton textiles were available and cheap – another reason why simple, white muslin, cambric and calico dresses became the mode, even in mid winter.

Colours, whether bright, dark or light, were never harsh: pale green, yellow, pink or blue, maize or lavender; or stronger shades, black backgrounds with flowers in crimson, gold or purple; or darker, such as snuff brown (a brownish-grey), puce (a purplish-brown), dark blue, dark green and burgundy. Woven and printed motifs were smaller than in the 17th century, usually floral, but ribbon motifs were popular, woven in loops and bows or in bands alternating with flower posies, foreshadowing the vogue for stripes for both men and women in the second half of the century. The classical revival produced patterns of small dots and circles derived from late Roman ornament. Applied pattern included embroidery, quilting, ruching, quilling (small round pleats of lace, ribbon or tulle ending in open flute-like folds), braiding, lace and ribbon bows.

It must be stressed that only the favoured few enjoyed the pleasures of elegant houses and gardens, music, literature and art, assemblies and sport, the benefit of travel and education, and the delights of fashion. Probably more than half the population of Europe still lived meanly, owning little, toiling hard, often hungry and usually wretchedly clothed.

German, 1780. Poor men
wearing old-fashioned
cast-off clothes.

French, 1740-44. Bourgeois style.
Hair almost completely covered by cap.
Linen neckerchief; dark grey apron
with bib; light brown casaquin over
dark grey petticoat.

Brown shoes

German beggar,
1772

Child: orange-brown cap with roll,
over white cap; cream robe
over light brown petticoat;
natural-coloured apron.
Light-brown shoes

French, 1742.
Woman trader
of the poorer
class. Cap,
neckerchief,
overskirt
pinned up.

Italian, 1750.
Workman in large black hat,
coat made up of patched
leather and blue cloth, tan
coloured breeches, drab oversocks.

1800–1850

The French Revolution was followed by twenty years of war involving the whole of Europe. Napoleon's 'continental system', which endeavoured to strangle British trade in Europe, and Britain's blockade against France, resulted in severe economic pressures, high prices, and hardship among the workers, although the landed classes and investors prospered and their way of life was hardly affected.

Britain emerged from the Napoleonic Wars with leadership of the allied European nations, control at sea and increasing imperial power. The loss of her American colonies was compensated for by the gain of Canada and a growing Eastern empire. At home her resources in coal and iron, combined with capitalist enterprise, put her in the lead in the Industrial Revolution which now began to transform the western world.

The large-scale application of scientific and technical discoveries made in the 18th century led to the use of steam power and increased mechanization, with a dramatic expansion of industry, not least in the manufacture of textiles. In England during the first half of the century cotton mills achieved a four-fold increase in output with a negligible increase in the labour force. Railways, steamships, macadamized roads and the telegraph were all being developed, with consequent improvements in communications and trade. Mechanization, however, caused unemployment among agricultural workers and hand-loom weavers who rose in revolt against the privations they suffered. A rise in the population from nine to fourteen million between 1801 and 1831 in England and Wales also brought increased unemployment and hardship to all the labouring classes. In America, where, by contrast, there was a shortage of manpower, the use of machinery was at first hailed as a release from drudgery but it brought similar problems of exploitation and unrest. The half-century from 1800 to 1850 presents a diversity between the growth of capitalist affluence and the desperate conditions of the workers, in spite of early moves towards social welfare and reform.

There is also a marked contrast between the women's fashions of the early years, still influenced by the revolutionary and neo-classical trends of the late 18th century (though to a less extreme degree in Britain and America than in France) and those of the sober and more settled respectability of the 1840s. For men, the ideal image of the Regency buck was to change to one of simple elegance epitomized by the upright Victorian gentleman and, in particular, by Prince Albert; but in the first decade of the century, one individual, 'Beau' Brummel, was to effect a lasting influence on men's clothes This arbiter of fashion ordained that a gentleman's dress should be distinguished by an inconspicuous propriety and that social superiority should be expressed not by colour and decoration but by perfection of line and proportion, quality of cloth and immaculate grooming. His dictum of restraint as the foremost principle of male sartorial elegance has lasted even till today in conservative circles.

The study of costume from this period onwards is facilitated by a greater quantity of contemporary evidence, including, from the 1840s, photography. Periodicals featuring articles on fashion, and fashion plates, although in existence during the late 18th century, increased prodigiously in the early 19th. Published in most of the major cities

American, 1800.
Black, low-crowned top hat and velvet collar. Dark grey coat, waistcoat and breeches. Child in white muslin dress, gold sash and shoes.

Danish, 1807. Lady carrying parasol, reticule and large shawl.

American, 1820.
White muslin gown with deep ruff Sleeves with small puff at upper arm and gather into wrist band Fob watch worn on sash; reticule with rigid top. Bonnet and shawl on table.

Italian, 1814-15. Simple muslin gowns, delicate embroidery around the hem.

(left) English, 1808.
Deep blue tailcoat, white waistcoat and trousers. Black top hat.

in Europe, many fashion plates were copies of French originals, copyright laws being only lightly observed; and according to Doris Langley Moore in *Fashion through Fashion Plates 1770–1970*, this practice continued in America for longer than in Europe, where local artists began to be used more often by the 1820s. Mrs Moore also comments that it is difficult to be precise as to the origin of the styles illustrated, as French editors legitimately sold plates to be bound into magazines produced in other countries. Wherever they originated, these charming, detailed drawings are an excellent source of information, bearing in mind that they represent advanced styles, so that with additional study of reliably dated original garments a balanced view of what was fairly general wear may be obtained.

MEN

The shirt became more fitted over the shoulders, with a yoke at the back and slimmer sleeves, and by about 1830 the front frilling was replaced by vertical pleats or tucks, except for evening wear. The neckband became a high 'standing' collar with stiffened points showing on the cheeks above the cravat. Around 1820 a separate collar was introduced, attached to the shirt by a button at the front and ties at the back; later these were replaced by studs, as were the three or four buttons fastening the shirt front, particularly after 1850 when starched shirt fronts were introduced.

Drawers might be short (knee-length or above), cut fairly full, tied in front with a ribbon and pulled in at the back by tapes; or long to the ankle, sometimes with a band under the instep, and supported by passing the braces through holes at the waist; after 1845 the holes were replaced by loops of tape. They were known as long pants or trousers – a name that may have evolved from 'trowsers', a wide-legged ankle-length garment buttoned in front without a fly, worn by sailors or soldiers in the 18th century; the actual source of the name is uncertain but from early in the 19th century it also referred to outer garments.

A cambric or linen stock with a stiffened frame continued to be worn until the middle of the century. A black military stock, adopted by civilian dandies, was considered correct wear at court from 1820, and the Royal George, a stock of black Genoa velvet and satin tied in a bow in front, was worn between 1820 and 1830.

The cravat, of lawn, muslin or silk folded to the required width, was swathed high around the neck over the shirt collar and tied in front in a bow or knot (a style associated with Beau Brummel). A variety of names were given to cravats and neckcloths, each being tied in a slightly different way – the Napoleon neckcloth (1818), the American or Yankee neckcloth and the mailcoach neckcloth (1818–30), and the Osbaldeston tie or barrel knot (1830s–40s). During the 1840s the shape of the cravat became lower at the neck with less emphasis on the high swathing and more on the bow which became larger; or it might completely cover the shirt above the waistcoat and be called a scarf; a smaller version was called a necktie, a term which came into use even in the 1830s and was partly to replace the name cravat. An unstarched collar worn unbuttoned at the throat and held casually in place by a loosely tied scarf, as worn by Lord Byron, was associated with the poetic image; later, in the 1840s–50s, the name Byron was given to a small, narrow necktie. Until 1810 cravats were either white (especially for evening) or black, but by 1828 fashion writers were suggesting coloured cravats such as plaid for sporting dress or sky blue with a riding habit, and by 1840 colour was usual for day wear.

The tail coat, introduced in the 18th century, was well-nigh universal wear between

1800 and 1815. Usually double-breasted, it was cut square across the front, often above the waistline to reveal the lower part of the waistcoat; the tails hung straight to knee level. The collar, at first standing high and turning over abruptly with a deep separation between it and the revers, gradually developed a slightly lower and longer roll separated from a smaller rever by a notch cut in the shape of an M. (This notch was not used on day coats after 1850, but continued in use on some evening coats until 1870.) The sleeves often had a little fullness at the top, then tapered down to the wrist or slightly beyond, with a buttoned opening often left undone to reveal the shirt cuff.

For formal, court or evening wear, the coat with curved-back fronts continued to be worn, especially in France, until about 1816; in silk or velvet and embroidered down the fronts, it was knee-length, with a 'stand' collar, and might be caught at breast level by a hook. It was succeeded by the dress coat, made of cloth and derived from the tail coat, with foreparts cut back and tails to knee level. The term 'dress clothes' was applied during the first half of the century to costume for formal social functions, day as well as evening; for evening, the dress coat was always single-breasted and rarely fastened, for day it was single- or double-breasted. After 1850 'dress clothes' usually referred to evening dress; but for riding in town a coat similar in cut to the dress coat but with shorter tails with rounded corners was known as a riding dress coat and worn until 1860.

A single-breasted coat with fronts sloping back from waist-level to the rounded corners of a thigh-length skirt and pockets in its back pleats was known in 1825 as a riding coat. The slope away from the mid-line in front steadily increased, starting above the waist, and flapped pockets were added at the hips; by 1830 it was called a morning walking coat, in 1838 a Newmarket coat, and in 1850 a cut-away coat. It was a forerunner of the morning coat of the 1870s – another example of an informal garment later attaining formal status.

From 1816 the frock coat (the name previously given to a coat with tails and turn-down collar) was a formal, waisted, close-fitting coat, at first single-breasted with a shawl collar, buttoned to waist level, with a fairly full skirt hanging vertically in front to just above the knee, a vent at the back, side pleats and hip buttons; by 1823 it was cut with a seam at the waist, a collar with revers, and flapped pockets on the hips, and, with slight variations, was to remain a basic style throughout the 19th century. A riding frock coat worn in the 1820s was similar but had a deep collar and large lapels. A frock greatcoat, again cut like the frock coat but double-breasted and somewhat longer, was fashionable in 1830 for outdoor wear and might also be known as a surtout greatcoat. The frock jacket of the 1840s was like the frock coat but shorter, just covering the crotch.

Between 1820 and 1840 men's coats were cut with a long sloping shoulder, a small waist above which the padded chest swelled out, and tails or skirts curved out over rounded hips – a surprisingly feminine silhouette, at a time of fairly aggressive progress. Long curved shawl collars helped to emphasize the outline, as did the habit of wearing the coat open and thrown back. Men's wear at this time also lost some of its earlier restraint and elegance, becoming somewhat flamboyant in the use of colour and pattern.

Waistcoats, to the waist or just below, were cut straight across or to a slight point, or in two points just overlapping the breeches or trousers. Early in the century, double-breasted waistcoats might be left partly open and turned back over the lapels of the coat; or, when single-breasted, often had a high standing collar visible inside the high

French, 1813. Cloth frock coat with nankeen pantaloons.

French, 1805. White dress with self stripe; very fine gauze tucker; narrow white satin sash. Gold coloured mittens, long white ermine boa.

French, 1810–11. Court suit, worn with dress sword; chapeau bras under arm.

French, 1805. Shirt collar points show above cravat, waistcoat collar outside it. Dark tail coat, light breeches with small fall. Fob watch.

English, 1811. Evening 'full dress' showing classical style. Dark green tunic with gold and white trimming, over white dress trimmed green and gold. Turban, green and gold/white stripes, trimmed with osprey feather.

French, 1803. Woman: white gown and capote trimmed pink ribbons; pale orange gloves, red bag, blue stockings and brown shoes.
Man: Yellowish-green coat, buff breeches, black boots with brown tops.
Child: long gown in peacock blue.

English, 1816.
Tail coat with double-notch lapels; pantaloons and Hessian boots.

French, 1818. Girl: hair coiled high; gown with ruffles at hem and wide neckline.
Woman: bonnet trimmed with flowers and lace veil; gown with wide collar and full sleeves; large shawl with patterned border.

Man and older boy are dressed alike, except for cravat. Small boy wears skeleton suit and shirt with ruffled collar.

coat collar. After 1830 single-breasted openings were more popular, varying in length but always low for evening. Between 1830 and 1850 waistcoats were laced at the back and might be collarless; deep curved lapels were gradually replaced by shorter pointed ones, but the styles overlapped.

Coat and waistcoat rarely matched; the waistcoat was often lighter in tone, usually but not always white for evening. As the century progressed brighter colours and patterns were used for waistcoats and, although frowned upon by those of refined taste, many men favoured floral or formalized patterns, stripes and checks, particularly in the 1840s–50s.

By about 1816, breeches were worn only for evening dress, for riding, or at court where they were obligatory. They were replaced by pantaloons, worn between 1795 and 1850, very close fitting, at first ending just below the calf and later at the ankle, usually with a slit at the side, and finally strapped under the foot in the 1840s; or by trousers, fashionable for day wear from 1807, first with a small fall fastening, then with a fly front closure becoming general from 1840, and replacing evening breeches by 1850. It is sometimes difficult to distinguish between pantaloons and trousers, particularly as both terms were used rather indiscriminately, much as 'pants' – an American abbreviation – and 'trousers' are used today. Cossacks were full trousers pleated into a waistband and tied around the ankles with a drawstring, said to have been inspired by the costume of the Czar's attendants at the peace celebrations of 1814. By 1840, having lost much of their bagginess and with double, then single, straps under the instep, they became known as pleated trousers.

Although hair powder was advertised in New York papers as late as 1800–10, only very old-fashioned men would have used it. The natural 'neo-classic' style of haircut, fairly well established by 1800, lasted until about 1825. During the 1830s a centre or side parting replaced the curls and fringe, and hair was worn smooth to about chin length. From the 1840s, perfumed macassar oil was used to subdue and give a shine to the hair – hence the use of antimacassars on chairbacks to protect the upholstery. Sideburns grew longer and by 1828 some men favoured small moustaches.

Apart from the chapeau bras worn or carried for full dress occasions (called an opera hat by the 1830s), the top hat or 'topper' was the principal male headgear throughout the 19th century. In the 1840s the opera hat was replaced by the gibus, a top hat with a collapsible crown, named after its inventor but, confusingly, more commonly also called an opera hat. The high-crowned top hat (which reached a height of 8 inches in the 1850s) had, at different times, tapering, waisted or vertical sides and a narrow brim usually slightly rolled but almost flat in the 1830s. It was correct wear with the frock coat, cut-away or morning coat, and by 1840 was acceptable with an evening dress coat. Made from the traditional beaver until 1830, it was subsequently rivalled by the silk hat, a topper with a glossy silk surface on a felting of rabbit fur.

From 1800 to 1820, high boots were general wear in both town and country. Some were adapted from military styles and named after military leaders. After 1830, high or 'over' boots were confined to country or sporting wear, but the short boot, worn under trousers, remained in fashion in various forms into the next century. Hessians (1790–1850) and hussars (1800–20) were both calf-length behind, rising to a point in front just below the knee, low-heeled, and of black leather. Hessians occasionally had a narrow border of contrasting coloured leather around the top and were always trimmed with a tassel at the point. Hussars might have a turn-over top. Wellingtons, from 1817, were like 18th-century top boots without the turnover; the name was later

America 1810–1835

1810. Cloak with cape and wide collar; top hat, high black cravat, trousers fastened under the foot.

1820. Hair coiled up at back of head and secured with a large comb, curls in front of ears and on forehead. Muslin yoke and ruffles.

1815. Beige dress, matching slippers. Large dark green parasol matches upper section of bag; lower section is scarlet, as is jewel in necklace.

Blue necklace and earrings

1845. Dress in light and dark satin. Pearl necklace arranged across bodice and over shoulders. Rather heavy, strange-shaped fan.

1830. Probably a wedding dress; pale blue with cream belt, hem trimming and small puffs on sleeves. Fine lace shawl and ruffles round neckline. Blue shoes, beige handbag.

1835. Dark grey tail coat, dark blue trousers, blue and white waistcoat, black cravat over pointed collar.

1820. Hair dressed high with ribbon band and elaborate curls.

to be used for rubber boots in the 20th century. Bluchers (1820–50) were close-fitting half-boots laced up the front over a tongue; metal eyelets, patented in the early 1820s, made lacing easier and more practical. Albert boots, from the 1840s, had cloth tops, patent leather toe-caps and side lacing; they might have a row of pearl buttons down the front, purely for decoration. Elastic-sided boots, with gussets of indiarubber material patented in 1837, were worn by women as well as men.

A fancy for wearing gaiters in the country early in the century was short-lived and they quickly became again part of the dress of rural or manual workers (and, curiously, of the costume of Anglican bishops and deans).

With knee-breeches and pantaloons men wore white, grey or transparent black stockings and low-heeled black pumps, short-vamped and round-toed, trimmed at first with a small buckle and later a small flat bow. Pumps with bows continued to be worn with trousers when these replaced pantaloons for evening.

Cloaks for outdoor wear over day and evening dress continued throughout the century, often with a contrasting coloured silk lining, velvet collar and cord fastening; but evening overcoats were also worn – the Polish greatcoat of 1810 was long and loose-fitting, with frog and loop fastening, its collar, lapels and cuffs faced with Russian lambskin. For day wear from mid/late 1820s, however, coats in a variety of styles were more popular than cloaks. The paletot, a French term rather loosely used towards the end of the century, denoted around 1830 a short greatcoat with a plain back or short vent and no waist seam. There was also a paletot cloak (1850s), short, double- or single-breasted, with slits for the arms; and a paletot-sac (1840–50), a short, straight, single- or double-breasted coat, often with a hood instead of a collar. A greatcoat with a flat, wide collar, wide lapels and cuffs faced with velvet or silk, waisted and full-skirted (no pleats, but a central back vent) and with slit pockets, was christened a Taglioni after the creator of the ballet *La Sylphide*. Probably the best known and longest lasting top coat at this time was the Chesterfield, named after the Earl of Chesterfield, a leader of fashion between 1830 and 1840. It was long (well below the knee), single- or double-breasted, slightly waisted with a centre-back seam and a vent, with flapped pockets on the hips, a smaller one on the left breast, and usually a velvet collar. In France during the 1840s a similar coat was called a twine.

The mackintosh, a short loose waterproof overcoat made from Mackintosh's patent indiarubber cloth, was worn from 1836, usually in a drab or dark green colour with proof straps over the seams.

WOMEN

Changes in women's costume during this half century may be traced to a number of sources. The influence of the French Revolution was understandably strongest in that country. In the early years of the century interest in ancient Greece and Rome was manifested in dress, and Parisian leaders of fashion might wear transparent muslin arranged in an 'antique' manner, their hair caught up in a 'Greek' knot, their feet in flat-heeled sandals. In England in 1809 the publication of Thomas Hope's *Costume of the Ancients* was welcomed not only for its historical interest but as a practical manual of dress. Henry Moses, at about the same time, produced a volume of drawings showing women's dress as classical in style as those of Hope, and English and French fashion journals published drawings and descriptions of similar designs, so it is reasonable to assume that some women in England consulted these sources, although no contemporary portraits of English women dressed in this manner apparently exist. Contemporary comments such as those of the Countess of Brownlow (*Reminiscence of a Septuagenarian*), writing of Madame Récamier's visit to England in 1802, also indicate that there was a marked difference between English and French feminine dress at that time and later, after the Napoleonic Wars in 1815, the periodical *Le Bon Genre* ridiculed English fashions; but this attitude was to change quickly. In America, although portraits of the First Ladies Mrs Dolly Payne Todd Madison (1809–17) and Mrs Elizabeth Kortright Monroe (1817–25) show a decidedly French influence, it is fairly obvious that opaque petticoats were worn under the thin muslin and that, as in England, the general effect was more muted than the extreme French fashions.

The Napoleonic Wars gave rise to military-style details in women's dress, and by 1820 the romantic/gothic influence already seen in literature and architecture in the 18th century showed itself also in women's costume.

The soft muslin dresses of the 1800s, clinging to the body, made superfluous any undergarments that might spoil the natural outline, and it seems fairly certain that some young girls and women with beautiful figures, in France, England and America, discarded their stays. Less fortunate ladies still required a little control under these very simple styles. The image often presented of the women of 1800–05 in dresses of sheer material clinging to a body clad only in pink tights is, therefore, probably true of only a few extremely fashionable, rather daring women with the necessary good looks, more likely in Paris than elsewhere.

The late 18th and early 19th century fashions, even if worn with stays and a single petticoat, were revolutionary and certainly more comfortable than whaleboned bodices and hooped petticoats, although the tight fit under the bust, and sleeves set in to an extremely narrow back, would seem highly restrictive today. Many of the simple early 19th-century dresses were mounted on a cotton lining with two separate pieces crossed over and fastened in front under the breasts to lift them like a brassière: this might well be the only form of support or control worn, but if more were needed to produce the slim, high-busted line there were whaleboned stays, extended to hip-level, with gussets replacing the former tabs. The French word 'corset' began to be used in England and America at the end of the 18th century as a refinement for 'stays', but for many years both terms were in common use. After about 1820 corsets or stays became an essential part of 19th-century costume, accepted universally in the west in spite of considerable outcry against them in French and English fashion journals. The new corsets, usually of strong twilled cotton, emphasized round curving lines flowing out from a small waist by the use of gussets at bust and hips and careful seaming. A basque-shaped piece over the hips was added to the rather long corset of the mid 1830s and early 1840s. As skirts widened, the corset shortened, reaching just below the waist by mid century. In the 1830s the French patented a woven corset made on a loom; lightly boned, without gussets, it became very popular and continued until late in the century. In the 1840s they also introduced a new cut, with seven to thirteen separate pieces, each shaped to the waist without gussets. The various types of corset are too numerous to list here, but it is important to realize, when making costume for period drama, that the shape of the outer garment relies on the foundation and that the correct corset will help the wearer to move correctly 'in period'.

Between about 1806 and 1820 a small padded roll, modified from the earlier 'rump' or bum roll, was worn at the back of the high waistline to prevent the skirt from falling into the waist. As the waistline was lowered and the skirt widened during the 1830s, this was replaced by a large pad stuffed with wool, worn across the back and on to the

French, 1802.
Gown of sheer white fabric with gold-coloured shawl. Hair held with decorative comb.

German, 1803.
Woman has large shawl draped over her arm. Man wears tail coat with white trousers and Hessians.

English, 1805-10
Gown of white sprigged muslin.

American 1812.
Gown of checked fabric with plain tucker.

English, 1807-10. Muslin dress, silk spencer and bonnet.

English, 1814. Dress and spencer in cream satin. White fur collar and muff.

English court dress, 1806
High-waisted gown over
large hoops which were
obligatory for full court dress
in England until 1820.

Bronze kid mule.

White kid slipper lined glazed
cotton, bound
and trimmed
with cream silk
ribbon.

White satin
slipper lined
with kid.

English, 1810. Corset with
gussets at hip and bust;
wearer is inserting a busk
down the front.

French, 1806 Bonnets
of straw and silk
decorated with ribbons
and ruching.

French, 1830. Corset with
more rounded curves.

English bonnet,
1804

English, 1827-9. Corset and bustle.

German, 1823.
Evening pelisse trimmed
with ermine, ruched
turban

Austrian, 1823.
Daytime pelisse
trimmed with
chinchilla.

French, 1823. Caped cloak.
Tail coat with velvet collar,
black cravat. Boots worn
under trousers.

English and French
cravats, 1812 and
c. 1825

French, 1826. Chestnut brown taffeta gown
with white gauze collar, gigot sleeves.
Gold bracelets and belt buckle.
'Apollo knot' hairstyle.

English, 1818-20.
Pelisse of figured
green silk; white
silk bonnet; cream
silk shawl with
patterned border.

English, 1823.
Bonnet in russet brown
silk trimmed with pink
roses.

hips and now called a bustle. This was superseded by stiffened petticoats; the most popular, appearing in 1839, was of crinoline, a stiff material made from horsehair and cotton or wool which was to give its name to the hooped petticoat of the 1850s and the later 'cage' petticoat of steel wires.

Women wore a chemise and drawers, the latter from approximately 1806, similar in cut to the men's but with the legs not joined at the crotch. From 1812 to 1840 long straight-legged drawers called pantaloons reached below the calf, trimmed with tucks and broderie anglaise or lace, visible under the shorter skirts of the 1820s. These went out of fashion before 1840, but children wore them until 1850 or so. They were usually made of cotton or fine wool, although a patent was issued in 1807 for elastic woollen stockinette drawers for riding.

The simple chemise-like dresses seen at the end of the 18th century, cut all in one and gathered at the neck and under the breasts and fastened at the back, gave way in the first decade of the 19th century to a bodice and skirt cut separately but stitched together. The basic garment until 1810 consisted of a narrow-backed, plain, brief bodice, cut low for evening, filled in with a tucker or cut high for day, the sleeves plain or puffed; the skirt, gathered at the centre back and only slightly, if at all, at the front, hung straight to instep or ground level, with a train for evening, with some variations such as a tunic or overdress and minor decoration.

Although the classical fashion had less influence in England, the romantic or gothic style spread quickly on both sides of the channel. As early as 1811, such unclassical details as vandyked ornament and Elizabethan ruffs were appearing; but the real sign of change was an increased use of flounces or decoration around the hemline, then spreading up the skirt which became shorter and wider, and more elaborate sleeves with a series of puffs from shoulder to wrist, a shorter puff above a long tight sleeve, or a puffed head tapering to a close-fitting lower arm and wrist. Short puffed sleeves were usual for evening, but between 1810 and 1820 long sleeves were often worn with full evening dress.

In England, between 1808 and 1814, the waistline tended to lengthen, but in 1815, with the return of peace and the French influence, bodices again became tiny. However, in the 1820s the waistline dropped steadily, reaching a more normal position by about 1825, tightly corseted, rounded and often emphasized by a wide belt and buckle or bow. The pointed bodice of the Victorian period was not to challenge the 'round' waist until the 1830s.

From approximately 1820 to the mid 1830s, bodices were close-fitting (darts being used for the first time), with long sloping shoulders and slightly dropped armholes; they were often plain with perhaps piped seams, but drapery gathered at the shoulder and drawn to the centre front, or a flat pleated trim from shoulder to waist, might be added. Necklines, low for evening and sometimes for day (perhaps filled in with a tucker), became wider and flatter to give an almost straight line across the shoulders, occasionally with a slight dip at the centre front. High necklines might be finished with a small ruff or fluted collar; or the width at the shoulder might be increased by a fichu pelerine, a cape-like collar made of cambric or muslin embroidered and trimmed with lace, also sometimes called a canezou in the 1850s.

Skirts were gored to give increasing width at the hem; gathering, at first concentrated at the back, later spread all round the waist. Decoration, placed below the kneeline though occasionally rising up the front, was in the form of appliquéd bands, shirred sections, ruchings or flounces. By the 1830s plain skirts were more common and

117

English, 1828. Dark brown coat, black waistcoat and cravat, soft collar. Fawn trousers. Purple cloak with deep black velvet collar.

English, 1826. Evening costume: white Chinese crape with satin rouleau above embroidered flounces, sash of watered silk, tulle oversleeves fastened at wrist with gold bracelets.

French, 1830. White silk gown sprigged with orange, pink and green. White gauze collar, sleeves and fichu-pelerine; pink silk bonnet; black pumps.

American, 1835. Man in sporting dress: light-coloured coat, dark trousers.

French, 1834. Top hats with straighter crowns

Woman wears dark silk apron over simple light-coloured gown with gigot sleeves.

French, 1839. 'Polish style' coat with interlaced braid embroidery; brown pantaloons.

Spanish, 1830. Court dress. Pale blue and silver brocade gown, white lace mantilla, dark orange and yellow feathers in hair. Elaborate diamond jewellery.

German, 1834. Frock coat with velvet collar.

English, 1830. Wedding dress, cream silk embroidered in white, with embroidered white muslin fichu-pelerine.

English, 1834. Morning dress: Dark frock coats, light trousers; striped waistcoat, patterned cravat.

American, 1835-7. Wide lace collar on low-necked silk gown.

English, 1839. Black satin cravat, pearl pin. Velvet collar on coat; trousers strapped under foot.

English, 1839. 'London promenade dress': lilac foulard figured in darker shade of same colour, trimmed with lace and ruching. White silk bonnet trimmed under brim with tulle and flowers, ostrich feathers on crown.

French, 1827-30. (left) White silk hat trimmed with pink or blue feathers, matching ruching on strings. (right) Pale grey silk trimmed with yellow or green ribbons.

English, 1836. Sleeve fullness becomes lower. Pale pink and yellow dresses, white collars. Black mittens, greenish-yellow and white striped apron.

French, 1830s. Shorter skirt reveals short boots.

Black square-toed pumps.

throughout this decade they were shorter, even above the ankle, but trains, added as a separate garment, were still obligatory for court. The dominant feature of dress between 1830 and 1835 was the enormous sleeves, set into a dropped armhole and cut to achieve width below the shoulder point. (The transition to large sleeves was foreshadowed during 1810–20 by the practice of placing a large transparent sleeve over an opaque small one in the old shape.) The gigot (1824–36), a daytime sleeve very full at the shoulder but tapering towards the elbow and tight at the wrist, was cut on the bias, set in smooth under the arm and pleated or gathered around the top; it required stiffening to hold it out some 12 inches or more beyond the shoulder, and some historians suggest further supports of whalebone, but this seems unlikely since a really stiff interlining or lining would be adequate to support most fabrics. The beret sleeve for evening (1829–35) was cut as a complete circle with a bound slit on one side for the arm to go through, the rest gathered into the arm scye but left flat under the arm; it might require a stiffened lining and was often surmounted by a frill or 'wing'. The imbecile or sleeve à la folle (1829–35) was a day sleeve, very full and gathered into a narrow cuff but with the fullness falling more softly to give width at the elbow or forearm.

The trend towards what we now think of as typically Victorian dress began in the late 1830s and was established during the 1840s – a tightly-fitted, boned bodice with a pointed waistline, sleeves (often surmounted by a mancheron or jockey – a kind of epaulette) set in so low that it must have been difficult to lift the arm, and a long, immensely full skirt over a crescent-shaped bustle and numerous petticoats. The style expressed bourgeois respectability and primness; even the seductive low décolleté of the ball dresses was offset by a deep bertha collar and the rigid bodice. It is difficult to imagine ladies of doubtful reputation wearing such fashions, although contemporary writings suggest that some impropriety existed.

Fashion journals of the 1840s indicate that the waist was not only extremely tight but also long, and although few of the available photographs confirm this impression, the seaming, decoration and pointed front were intended to emphasize length just as lines of trimming running from the lowered shoulder to the centre front of the waist and the angle of darts and seams emphasized the tiny waist. Necklines for day were high or medium, finished with stand or Peter Pan collars, tuckers or chemisettes; and for evening low and wide, almost off the shoulders, with berthas (deep falls of lace) encircling them. Daytime sleeves were set smoothly into the arm scye and close-fitting to the wrist, possibly finished off with a small cuff; gradually the lower edge was to widen again into a bell shape, and in the early 1850s sleeves were often three-quarter-length, with a detachable undersleeve of lawn or muslin gathered into the wrist. For evening the top of the arm was covered by either the deep bertha, short puff sleeves, ruffles or small drapes, or occasionally the whole arm was covered by full transparent sleeves.

The gored skirt went out of fashion during the 1830s. The immense new skirts were cartridge-pleated, pleated or gathered into a waistband, producing a domed silhouette. By the 1850s skirts might measure 10 yards round the hem, or more if in lightweight material; little decoration was added to day dresses, but for evening flounces or festoons gave an illusion of even greater width. The lined and boned bodice, often padded slightly between shoulder and breast to increase the rounded and curved shape, was put on over the skirt waistband and then either stitched permanently at the sides and back or fastened by hooks and bars at each wearing. For purposes of economy, an evening and a day bodice were often made to match one skirt.

Austrian, 1842. Woman's bonnet trimmed with veil and feathers. Sleeves and flounce of skirt cut on bias of checked fabric.
Man wears dark frock coat and light-coloured top hat.

English, 1847. Double-breasted coat buttoning high; narrow trousers. Black cravat, silk hat.

English, 1840.-50. Bonnet of shot silk on cane foundation.

Blue kid elastic-sided boots, probably English, 1830's.

English, 1841-3. Evening dress in blue and white striped silk, which has an alternative matching bodice for day wear. Headdress of Honiton lace.

French, 1845. Pink satin with black lace flounces, pink roses on bodice and in hair. Long black sheer 'scarf' shawl.

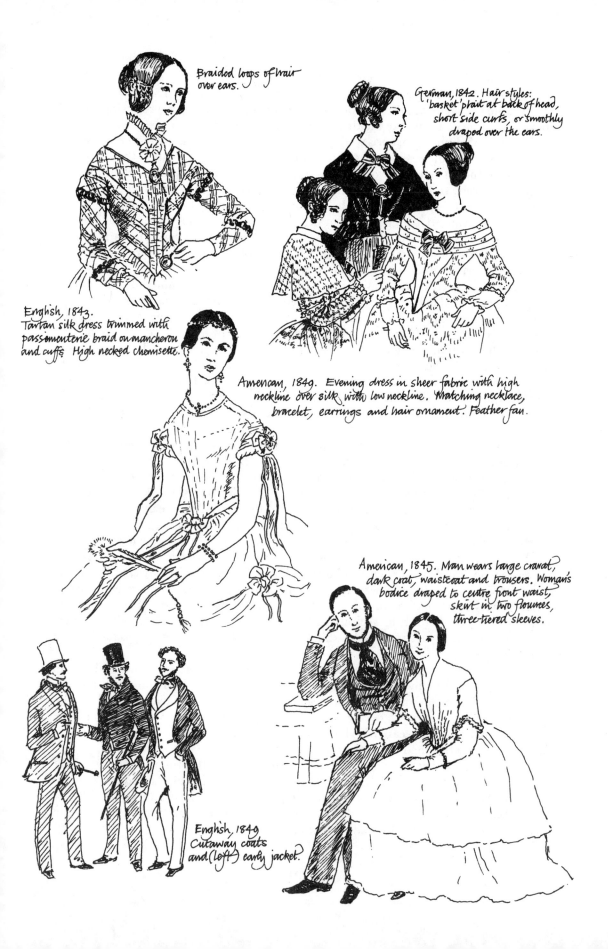

Braided loops of hair over ears.

German, 1842. Hair styles: 'basket' plait at back of head, short side curls, or smoothly draped over the ears.

English, 1843. Tartan silk dress trimmed with passementerie braid on mancheron and cuffs. High necked chemisette.

American, 1849. Evening dress in sheer fabric with high neckline over silk with low neckline. Matching necklace, bracelet, earrings and hair ornament. Feather fan.

American, 1845. Man wears large cravat, dark coat, waistcoat and trousers. Woman's bodice draped to centre front waist, skirt in two flounces, three-tiered sleeves.

English, 1849 Cutaway coats and (left) early jacket.

The hairstyle with tumbled curls on the forehead lasted only briefly after 1800. By 1815 a centre parting was generally accepted (and remained in fashion until the 1860s); the back hair was drawn into a knot fairly high on the head, producing a small, neat appearance. Then, like the dress, the hairstyle became more elaborate; between 1825 and 1835, bunches of curls were arranged over the temples, the rest being twisted up in loops and bunches high on the top of the head; false hair, plaited (braided) and wired to stand in one or two loops, was termed an Apollo knot, and trimmings, artificial flowers, ribbons and feathers were added, particularly for the evening.

In the demure 1840s the front hair was drawn down smoothly from the centre parting and arranged in long ringlets or in smooth loops over the ears, or brought down on to the cheeks, sometimes plaited, and looped back to expose the ears, a style associated with the young Queen Victoria. The knot of hair was lowered and by the 1850s was worn almost in the nape of the neck.

Hats with high crowns and small brims trimmed with feathers, and the 18th-century bergère, continued to be worn early in the century, but although hats were worn from time to time later, the bonnet, varying in shape over the years, dominated millinery fashions from about 1810 until almost the end of the century. A kind of poke bonnet with a soft crown and a rigid brim around the face, sometimes called a capote, later evolved into a similar shape with a firm crown, made of silk, velvet or straw (chip or strip) trimmed with ribbons, feathers and occasionally flowers. The crown then increased in height to accommodate the hairstyle, and the brim flared out to an increasing width; this style might be worn over a cap or have frills sewn inside. From roughly 1825 to 1835 hats were similar to bonnets but had brims of equal width all round, whereas bonnet brims were wider at the front; both might have ribbon ties, often left undone, and were elaborately trimmed with ribbons, lace, artificial flowers and fruit, or feathers. Veils of lace or gauze were draped over the brims. Large and elaborate hats were worn for evening functions such as dinner or the theatre. As the skirt widened, the bonnet decreased in size; the angle of the crown became flatter, the brim smaller, and by the late 1830s brim and crown formed a straight line, often with a bavolet (a kind of curtain to shade the neck) at the back, a ubiquitous style lasting for the next ten years.

At the beginning of the century caps were worn only by older ladies and servants; young women rarely wore them, and their hair was decorated with flowers or ribbon in the evening. By the 1820s, however, caps of net, muslin and lace for morning, lace and gauze for evening, had again become general wear; by the 1830s they were high-crowned with brims (or ruffles) rising up from the face and quite elaborately trimmed; in the 1840s they lay close to the head, following the bonnet line, but caps for evening wear declined.

Turbans worn for evening included the mameluke (1804) in white satin, the front rolled up like a brim over a domed crown, trimmed with an ostrich feather, and the Madras (1819) made from a blue and orange Indian handkerchief; through the 1830s they were twisted up from lace or gauze scarves. By the 1840s they were out of fashion. Between 1820 and 1835, caps with large flat halo crowns called berets, usually of velvet and extensively trimmed, were worn with evening dress.

Flat or very low-heeled pumps with toes pointed (1800–10), rounded (1810–30) or narrow and squared (1830–50) were made of silk, cloth or kid for day, silk or satin for evening, either in neutral colours or to match part of the ensemble until the mid 1820s, then black or white. Trimming, if any, would consist of a small bow on the low-cut vamp, or ribbons crossing over the instep in the 1830s.

Half-boots just covering the ankle, with very low heels, lacing down the front at first, then on the inside of the foot, were worn for walking. They were made of leather, cloth, cotton or silk, and after 1830 of cloth with toe-caps of kid, either matching in colour, such as fawn on fawn, or contrasting, such as black on drab. Silk half-boots were also worn on dress occasions. Elastic insets replaced lacing during the 1840s.

Fashionable stockings of silk, some with cotton tops, and everyday stockings of cotton and wool, were usually white, but pale pink stockings were occasionally worn during the 1830s.

For outdoor wear, the spencer (1790–1820), a short jacket ending at the fashionable waist level, usually in a contrasting colour to the dress, was revived between 1839 and 1840. During the earlier period a sleeveless and very ornamental version was also worn indoors for evening and referred to as a canezou (the name also used, confusingly, for the fichu pelerine in 1850). The pelisse (1800–10) was three-quarter-length with or without sleeves, and later ankle-length, sleeved and figure-fitting with possibly one or two shoulder capes. To accommodate the enlarged dress sleeves, the pelisse was supplanted by the pelisse-mantle (1838–45), a full-length cloak with a cape reaching the waist and draped around the arms to form open hanging sleeves; in the 1840s it was pulled in at the back waist. The pelisse-mantle or a cloak, often interlined or padded, with deep capes, were the outer garments most used in cold weather. It should be noted that the pelisse-robe, a day dress (1817–1850) fastened down the front with ribbon bows or concealed hooks and eyes, was, after 1848, called a redingote, the name previously used for an overcoat. The mantelet returned to favour in the late 1820s as a useful small wrap, shaped over the shoulders like a cape with long scarf ends reaching the knees in front; it was worn, in a wide variety of fabrics and colours, well into the 1840s.

Long fur boas, narrow scarves and wide shawls were popular from 1800 to the 1830s. During 1820 a factory in Paisley, Scotland, among others in Europe, began manufacturing fine woollen shawls woven with an oriental style of design based on shawls sent home by officers in Napoleon's army during the Egyptian campaign of 1795, and this type of pattern (still known as Paisley) was to become popular for the large square, triangularly folded shawls worn during the 1840s–50s.

CHILDREN

Early in the 19th century children retained the unrestricted clothes of the previous twenty years, but before long girls, in particular, were again forced into replicas of adult styles. Boys were more fortunate, since men's clothes were by now fairly comfortable; and girls were not laced into corsets as early as in previous centuries. Both sexes were still dressed alike until almost four years old, though boys' skirts were shorter. Both wore pantaloons or pantalettes, probably over under-drawers, which were visible below the boys' shorter skirts and, during the 1820s, those of the girls.

From the age of about four, boys wore skeleton suits, adding a short jacket when seven or eight years old. During the 1830s this outfit was replaced by a skirted tunic (a youthful version of the frock coat) and trousers. From the age of twelve, boys dressed like men but with a plain linen shirt collar folded down over the coat collar; for younger boys this would have a frilled edge. The short Eton jacket associated with the English public school originated during the early 19th century.

Girls' clothes followed women's fashions on the whole, though their skirts were shorter, except during the early 1800s when they might trail.

Spanish, 1784. Gauze collar with ruffled edging. Broad sash, shoes with rosettes.

French, 1808. Ruched cap, combination trouser suit.

English, c. 1800. White muslin with coloured sash and slippers.

English, c. 1800. Nankeen trousers buttoned high on to button-trimmed top.

French, c. 1800.

English, 1800. Girl in low-necked muslin frock, muslin cap. Boy in skeleton suit

English, 1814. White embroidered muslin

English, 1830. Gold-coloured woollen cloth dress decorated with smocking, appliqué and embroidery. Pantalettes gathered into bands.

Swedish, 1845. Tunic blouses laced across chest between rows of buttons.

American, 1840. Pleating on sleeves held in place by straps with narrow binding; narrow tucks decorate the pantalettes

American, 1837. Black wool broadcloth coat with velvet collar. White cotton sateen trousers and knitted cotton socks, black leather shoes with ribbon ties.

English, 1832. Boy's tunic and girls' dresses all have gigot sleeves. Note short hair for both sexes.

The habit of taking snuff now began to wane, and as the snuff-box passed out of use, beaux or dandies affected the quizzing glass; the most popular type was rectangular, about 2 × 1 inches, with a handle.

A gentleman was not considered well dressed without gloves, in kid or silk, usually white or very pale, for evening, or in doeskin or leather for day; during the 1830s the latter might be yellow or lilac-coloured for the ultra-fashionable, but the most usual colour was probably light beige or buff. Cotton and worsted wool were also used for gloves. With formal day or evening dress men also carried a cane or walking stick made of polished wood with probably a decorative handle or knob; a plainer, more sturdy type might be used in the country.

Jewelry worn by men during the 19th century consisted of little more than a ring and a heavy watch with fobs and seals hanging singly or in pairs from a waistcoat pocket. Gold or coral was used for the newly introduced shirt studs, and occasionally a diamond pin might be stuck in a cravat.

Ladies' gloves or mittens, also indispensable, were long to meet the short sleeves around 1800–10, three-quarter-length for evening by 1812, shorter still by 1830, ornamented with ruching in 1835 or so, and wrist-length during the 1840s and '50s as were those for day wear from the mid 1820s. Colours could be bright early in the period, but by the 1820s white or pale kid or silk was usual, or black for elderly ladies or for mourning.

Parasols were small and short, sometimes carried by a ring from the ferrule during the first decade or so, a little larger and taller through the 1830s, small again during the 1840s; they were made of shot silk or taffeta trimmed with lace or fringe, with beautiful bone or ivory handles which by 1838 were often made to fold in half.

The fan, usually a fairly small folding type, was a customary evening accessory, and in the 1820s–40s it also became fashionable to carry a small bouquet. For day, huge muffs of fur or shirred silk were carried until the 1830s, when they became smaller and rounder. Flat bags or reticules were a necessity with the slim, straight dresses, but as skirts increased in size pockets to hold small purses could be placed in their folds. Informally, in the privacy of their homes, ladies might wear a small muslin or silk apron to protect their dresses.

Jewelry, rarely worn in France during the period of austerity after the Revolution, returned with a flourish with Napoleon; women were festooned with glittering necklaces, earrings, Greek-style garland diadems, belts and bracelets. In Europe and America generally an increasing amount of jewelry was worn for evening, and even during the day, in the shape of lockets, crosses, gold chains, earrings, bracelets and mosaic and cameo brooches, and matching sets of jewelry became popular. In the 1840s the use of jewelry was more restrained, but even then it was usual to wear a brooch, a chain and locket or a bracelet. Throughout the period classical and gothic influences can be seen in jewelry design.

FABRICS AND COLOUR

The range of fabrics and colours in men's clothes was fairly restricted; satins and velvets for coat, waistcoat and breeches were retained for court or ceremonial dress, but woollen cloth became universally popular and fashionable for evening as well as day wear. Coats of fur broadcloth, a cloth made of fine merino yarns in plain twill weave, heavily milled with a dress face finish, might be black, brown, bottle or olive green,

American, 1847. Bonnets
with bavolets at back to
shade the neck.

Italian, 1845. Bold striped fabric
used on the bias to accentuate the
pointed bodice. Fringed shawl.

Scottish, 1845. Necktie of patterned silk
tied in a barrel knot. Fine checked
wool waistcoat. trousers in barger
check.

French, 1849. Evening dress. Sheer fabric over
silk with ruched trimming. Hair braided and
wreathed, with roses at side. Man's waisted
tail coat has wide
curving revers;
white waistcoat
and cravat
with small bow.

English, 1849. Bonnet
trimmed under brim
with cherries and lace;
wide patterned ribbons

Sleeves widen at wrist to reveal
white engageantes.

plum colour, a variety of browns or blue (favoured by Beau Brummel and popular for evening wear until overtaken by black). Some coats and overcoats had velvet collars and from the 1820s sable or other furs trimmed some coats for outdoor wear. Nankeen, a yellowish-brown cotton cloth at first imported from Nankin, China, was used for coats and trousers for tropical wear. Waistcoats until 1810 were made in white or pale shades of plain silk, satin, or fine cashmere; some pattern was then added and by the 1820s–30s figured or embroidered satin and flowered and striped silk joined the plain fabrics, in colours such as jonquil yellow, buff, sky blue and cream; similar colours also began to be used for cravats or neckties.

Pantaloons of stretchable wool or silk jersey, or trousers of firm material such as twill, were usually of a lighter colour than the coat early in the century; by the late 1820s dark grey or black was worn for evening, and cream, tan, fawn, buff, light or dark grey for day, rarely matching the coat. Plaid woollen fabrics for trousers in the 1840s demonstrated a general increase in the use of pattern such as stripes and checks for men's more informal clothes.

Influenced by Napoleon's court, satin and velvet returned to favour for women's evening dress, often combined with gossamer muslin or gauze over silk, still white or very pale in colour but frequently with metallic threads of gold or silver. For day, muslin was still popular, despite the wide choice of fashionable fabrics such as printed linen, chintz, cotton, calico, merino wool or cashmere, but by the 1820s silks, taffetas and velvets were more frequently used for dresses and spencers. Wool was used for riding habits and for shawls and cloaks intended for extra warmth, with maybe a fur trimming.

White predominated for women at first, with pastel colours added in sashes or hair ribbons; but stronger colours such as deep red or green, lilac or blue, began to be used for spencers and the early style of pelisse, and colour gradually spread to the whole outfit, although the lightweight fabrics were usually pale – pink, blue, green or lavender – and the stronger or darker colours such as brown, bottle green or purple were reserved for heavier fabrics. During the 1830s striking colour combinations such as red flounces on a black ground or a pea-green silk gown under a pelisse of lavender and pink shot taffeta appear to have been fashionable; but since vegetable dyes were still used, these colours would have been more harmonious than they sound.

Until around 1825 any pattern on fabrics was of small flower or leaf motifs, but then larger patterns such as the Paisley pattern on shawls appeared. Striped silk and cotton and woollen plaids were very popular from the 1820s.

During the 19th century women's clothes began to be designed for a specific purpose – a summer evening party, a walking or carriage dress, a dinner party dress, etc. Riding costumes, still based on men's coats, had increasingly voluminous skirts. A definite formula also began to be set for wedding dresses; the traditional white or cream wedding dress was becoming more firmly established and by 1844 took the form of a high-necked afternoon gown. Bridal veils were rare before 1800, but from then on a veil of white lace was attached to the head and hung almost to the ground at the back; an orange-blossom wreath was added in the 1830s.

For the very poor, fashion obviously did not exist, but those of modest means attempted to follow the trends as best they might by studying periodicals and using their dressmaking skills and cheaper materials. There was naturally a time lag in the taking up of fashion among the servant or poorer classes. Slow transatlantic communications also meant that new fashions reached America somewhat later than their appearance in Europe.

The period from 1800 to 1850 combined adventurous progress with an increasing and almost contradictory respect for established institutions. A remarkable contrast existed between the earlier revolutionary freedom of diaphanous shift-like dresses and the concealing mass of skirts, shawls and bonnets of the 1840s when prudery seems to have reigned supreme and legs, if referred to at all, were called 'limbs' and men's trousers were known as 'unmentionables'.

1850–1900

A belief in the sanctity of science and the inevitability of progress pervades western civilization during this period. Advances in technology and industrial processes in Europe and America were creating competition and great prosperity, and colonial expansion was encouraged by the need for imported raw materials and overseas markets. Britain's Great Exhibition of 1851, designed to demonstrate to an international audience her new technological and artistic achievements, was followed by similar exhibitions in Paris and Vienna. The luxury and splendour of the French court of Napoleon III and the Empress Eugénie established Paris more firmly as the centre of feminine fashion, and even after the Prussian invasion of 1870 and the fall of the Second Empire she was able to maintain this leadership, which lasted well into the 20th century. America, having survived the Civil War of 1861–5 and the assassination of President Lincoln, was establishing herself as a powerful and influential nation; gold, silver and oil were discovered, railroads were built and great fortunes were made, although increased immigration from Europe and Asia caused severe overcrowding and poverty in many city slums. Merchants from the old world were quick to appreciate the rapidly expanding market for clothes, textiles and works of art, and British aristocratic families were not backward in marrying their sons to a wealthy American heiress to help buttress the family fortunes.

Many of the material benefits and social advantages taken for granted today originated from this time. The transatlantic cable was laid in 1860; trams (the forerunner of the public motor-bus) appeared on city streets in the 1860s: the Union Pacific, first trans-continental railway, was established in 1869; Edison produced the phonograph in 1877 and exhibited his first electric lamp in 1879. The first patent for a horseless carriage was taken out in America, also in 1879, and Ford's first car appeared in 1893. By the end of the 1880s the telephone, if rare, was an accepted method of communication. The fight for higher education for women and women's suffrage gathered momentum (the State of Wyoming in America was first to give women the vote, in 1890). In the field of dress, the development of the sewing machine in the 1850s, the ever-increasing use of technology in the textile industries, and the spread of the department store all contributed to the wider availability of fashion.

Although there was much over-elaboration and ugliness in architecture, interior design and dress during this period, in England the Pre-Raphaelite painters and, later, the Arts and Crafts movement started by William Morris, and the 'artistic style' worn by their wives and admirers, began gradually to have an influence on dress. Dickens, George Eliot, Hardy, Zola, Balzac, Mark Twain, Checkov and Ibsen were among many writers who sought to affect thought and opinion about social matters, and Oscar Wilde was closely associated with the Aesthetic movement of the 1890s. It was a lively period in the theatre, and actors began to be accepted in respectable society; Irving was the first to be knighted, and Ellen Terry, Sarah Bernhardt and Eleonora Duse were admired for their style of dress as well as for their histrionic ability. Famous beauties who also graced the stage, such as Lily Langtry, had even more influence on fashion. The importance of stylish dress to an actress at this time is apparent from an American critique in *The Spirit of the Times*, October 1882, of a touring production of Charles Wyndham's: 'None of the ladies is a professional beauty, all are good looking and will become beautiful, after a few months' stay in America has taught them how to make up and how to dress. There is one thing in the performance, that could be advantageously cut, and that is the stay-laces, English women are too fond of the corset.' The American style of dress, easier and rather sporty, was typified in the 1890s by the illustrations of Charles Dana Gibson and known as the 'Gibson Girl' look; and it was during this period that the American fashion magazines *Harper's Bazaar* (1867) and *Vogue* (1893) were launched, both notable for their high standard of presentation, and extending into English and French editions during the next century. This period also saw the opening of fashion stores such as Macey's (1858) and Nieman Marcus (1897) in New York and Liberty's (1875) in London.

The growth of sporting activities, for women as well as men, was phenomenal, particularly between 1870 and 1900. For the wealthy, riding, shooting (rarely practised by women) and hunting were joined by yachting; other sports available to those with more modest incomes, in particular the growing middle classes, included croquet (often replaced by tennis, especially in America, during the 1870s), archery, golf, hockey, and cricket (women's teams were formed during the 1880s–90s). In America, inter-collegiate football was born around 1869 and baseball became the national sport in 1871. There was ice-skating in winter, roller-skating all the year round from the 1860s in America and from 1880 in England. The popularity of seaside and country holidays increased the practice of bathing, swimming and walking, and with the arrival of the bicycle in the 1880s–90s, cycle clubs were formed and phalanxes of men and girls, some on tandems, bowled away into the country on Sunday mornings.

All these activities required special clothing – riding habits, tailored suits for golf, shorter skirts for tennis; and from the late 1860s bathing costumes were featured in women's magazines. The English *What-not or Ladies' Handy Book* commented in 1861, 'The chief drawback to ladies swimming, is the bathing dress used in this country. The most commodious and at the same time, the most pleasant to the wearer, is a garment, consisting of a dress and drawers in one, made of grey serge, and having a band to confine the waist.'

The fact that women cycled in the long cumbersome skirts of the 1880s is almost as incredible as their going mountaineering in bustles. By the 1890s the need for some kind of bifurcated cycling garment was felt strongly enough for women to adopt divided or baggy knickerbockers called bloomers. The name came from a form of dress introduced around 1850 by an American, Amelia Bloomer, who was an active campaigner for the emancipation of women and reform in dress. Consisting of what she called 'baggy pantaloons' beneath a loose tunic reaching to or a little above the knee, this costume, adopted by other liberal-minded American ladies, was ridiculed by such papers as *Punch* and in music-hall songs which referred to women 'wearing the trousers'. The cycling costume of the 1890s received a similar response, including denouncements from the pulpit, but ladies of a dashing disposition continued to wear it.

Men's clothing became on the whole a little more comfortable, with a slightly easier fit and lower collars. However, like women, they were bound by the growth of rigid conventions stipulating the 'correct' dress for each and every occasion; in fashionable society a man might be required to change his outfit several times a day. Whereas in

Country and sports wear 1860s – 1880s

English, 1867.
Country suit in check tweed
with full knickerbockers,
matching waistcoat and
jacket. Thick socks and
laced shoes. Oxford tie.
Fringe beard and small
moustache.

English, early 1870s. Shooting
outfit; University (orange-fronted)
jackets, narrow knickerbockers,
thick socks with or without gaiters,
laced boots.
Square-crowned hard felt hats,
Ascot ties.

American, 1888. For
archery, striped blazer
with white flannel
trousers. Woman: long
bodice, draped
overskirt; hat with
feathers.

Dundreary
Whiskers.

Polish, 1878-9
Patrol jacket and
tight breeches,
thick socks,
laced boots,
worn for cycling.
Similar outfits
are illustrated
in English and
American
fashion plates.

English, 1889. Golfing suit
in fine check, short jacket,
slightly sloped back from
lowest button, has flapped
pockets. Small cap.
Short spats or
gaiters over
long socks.

American, 1887.
For tennis. White dress
with black banding,
tam-o'-shanter, black
stockings and shoes.
Dark jacket with
matching waistcoat
and trousers, high
collar, narrow tie,
bowler or Derby hat

Sporting wear for women 1860s–1890s.

French, 1864. Riding habit: close buttoned bodice with braided sleeves; silk hat with veil.

English 1878–80. Cycling costume with matching cap.

American, 1876. Boys riding suit in dark brown cloth trimmed with rows of stitching and buttons, linen collar and cuffs, felt hat.

American, 1876. Riding habit in black cloth, bodice and skirt cut in one, buttoned down front, pocket on right hip. Collar and cuffs of fine linen. Blue grosgrain cravat, black beaver hat with blue gauze veil.

Flat straw hat with brim wider than boater.

American, 1896. Shirt-waist blouse with leg-o'-mutton sleeves, and tweed skirt, for golf.

English, 1893. Tailor-made suit with three-quarter-length jacket; leg-o'-mutton sleeves.

American, 1887. Yachting or tennis dress based on Redfern original: blue and white striped serge or flannel with blouse of dark blue silk surah. White boater hat with blue ribbon band.

Bathing Costumes 1860s — 1890s

French, 1864. Blouse and pantaloons in fine white merino wool, trimmed black

English, 1883. Blouses and pantaloons for bathing.

American, 1871. Red Flannel trimmed with black braid, black ribbon sash. Child's bathing costume in light grey serge trimmed worsted braid.

American, 1881. Red flannel trimmed with white braid, hat trimmed to match.

American, 1881. Costume and hat in blue flannel.

English, 1898.-9. Navy blue serge trimmed with white braid; white serge sailor collar trimmed with navy; navy and white striped vest.

previous centuries a courtier or gentleman would be noted for his lavish and colourful style of dress in contrast to the modestly attired poorer classes, from around the 1850s good cloth in sober colours and immaculate tailoring and grooming became increasingly important. It was left to lively members of the working and lower-middle classes or the nouveau riche to indulge in a flashy tie or figured waistcoat. Both Charles Dickens and Benjamin Disraeli received derogatory comments during the 1840s on their somewhat flamboyant style of dress with brightly coloured and decorated waistcoats; but in later life they became more conventional, and during the 1870s they were included in the curious practice of sticking the heads of well-known people on to fashion plates.

An enormous variety of styles was worn by women during this half-century, many of them remarkably ugly. The invention of the sewing machine seems to have encouraged over-elaborate decoration, and the introduction of aniline dyes produced some garish colours.

The invention of the steel-framed crinoline in 1856 provided some relief from the enormous weight of stiffened petticoats and ever-widening skirts. By the 1860s the shape of the frame became flattened at the front, spreading and widening at the back and evolving into the bustle by the 1870s. This almost vanished during the fashion for the cuirass body during the mid 1870s, but returned in the 1880s in its most exaggerated form, looking, it has been suggested, like a camel with two legs. By the 1890s it had become once again a small pad.

In the 1860s Charles Frederick Worth, an Englishman, became chief dressmaker to the Empress Eugénie and was responsible for raising the status of the dressmaker or dress designer, opening the way for the eventual development of Parisian Haute Couture. Worth survived the Seige of Paris in 1871, the Commune, civil war, and the establishment of the new Republic, and the name Worth became synonymous with Paris fashion. Wealthy American ladies from Boston, according to Edith Wharton in *Age of Innocence*, bought their clothes from Worth but, being of a prudish nature, laid them down like port to mellow, waiting two years before wearing them in public. Although Worth had previously dismissed English women as parsimonious, Lily Langtry bought seventeen trunks full of new dresses from him in 1881. Wealthy and fashionable ladies deemed it necessary to have a different outfit for mornings at home, visiting, taking tea, dinner or garden parties, the opera or balls – not to mention special gowns for weddings, presentation at court, and sporting costumes. The amount of time spent in changing their clothes during weekend parties at grand country houses must have been prodigious.

The intensity of mid nineteenth-century fervour for social reform is exemplified in its attack on the whole concept of fashion; but demands for change only gave rise to new fashions. Though aware that fashion extended into other forms of expression, progressive thinkers felt the need for reform in dress, especially for women, to be the most urgent on hygienic, artistic and rational grounds. Dress reform for men came from such sources as William Morris, Walter Crane writing in his journal *Aglaia*, and Dr Jaeger, Professor of Zoology at Stuttgart University, and resulted in such outfits as the somewhat 18th-century style with silk knee-breeches worn by Oscar Wilde when touring America in 1882, and in the craze for wearing wool (from the skin outwards), considered by Dr Jaeger to be cooler than any other material and taken up by intellectual circles. George Bernard Shaw bought a complete Jaeger outfit of brown knitted wool and another of silver-grey woollen stockinette in the 1880s and continued to wear similar suits all through his life. G. K. Chesterton, writing of him in 1910, said, 'his costume has become part of his personality: one can come to think of the reddish-brown Jaeger suit as if it were a sort of reddish brown fur ... his brown woollen clothes, at once artistic and hygienic, completed the appeal for which he stood; which might be defined as an eccentric healthy-mindedness'. But few men had any desire to change their image, while for women the need to show their position in society was a spur.

The demand for rationalization in women's clothes came from those like Mrs Bloomer and other strong-minded women in Germany, England and America who were also working for their emancipation, but the growing popularity of sport added impetus to the movement, giving rise to tailored and 'masculine' styling. Since the 17th century women had adapted male garments for riding, and this inclination was now followed for golf, sailing, country walking and cycling.

The movement for artistic reform, started by the Pre-Raphaelites, was taken up by The Council of German Women and by such people as Walter Crane and Mrs Haweis (author of *The Art of Beauty*), and particularly by Arthur Lazenby Liberty, who opened his shop in Regent Street, London, on 17 May 1875. The name Liberty is inextricably interwoven with the Aesthetic Movement and its influence on interior design, clothes and manners; although particularly English, and restricted to a limited section of society, it carried a social cachet to which the Pre-Raphaelites had never aspired. 'Aesthetic' or 'artistic' dress was based on a liking for Greek drapery or other costumes of the past with a natural, flowing line and an interest in Japanese or Eastern art and colours in what W. S. Gilbert derisively called a 'greenery-yallery' range. But many of the oriental fabrics, at first imported and then manufactured by Liberty's, were in very beautiful colours, and their soft, easily-draped texture was an essential part of the Aesthetic style. Dresses illustrated in a Liberty catalogue of 1905 (a little later than the period covered by this chapter) are simple, charming garments in excellent colours. The movement had some ridiculous and unfortunate imitators and received much comment and ridicule from George du Maurier in *Punch* and from W. S. Gilbert in *Patience* (1881).

Alongside women's demands for greater intellectual and physical freedom and the desire for an 'artistic' style of dress came admiration for a new type of beauty: the tiny, frail creature with minute hands and feet, represented by Dickens' young heroines, gave way to the type painted by Watts and Leighton and described by Mrs Oliphant in her novel *At his Gates* in 1872 as 'a full-blown Rubens beauty, of the class that has superseded the gentler pensive heroine in these days'. But however strong these various feelings were, it was to be many years before easy, practical and beautiful clothes were generally accepted, and in fact this ideal has been very rarely achieved.

MEN

Even before 1850 doctors had been advocating flannel underclothing, and by mid century vests or undershirts were worn. Hand- or machine-knitted natural wool, recommended by Dr Jaeger, was endorsed at the International Health Exhibition held in London in 1882. The woollen vest and underpants worn next to the skin might also be joined to form combinations, patented in 1862 but not commonly worn until the 1880s, when another innovation for men, the sleeping suit, began to replace the nightshirt. Originally from India, pyjamas (pajamas in the US) were of silk or wool in various colours, often striped, and by the late 1890s *The Tailor and Cutter* noted that 'The doom of the sleeping shirt is written'; but country folk and elderly or conservative men continued to wear nightshirts for a decade or so into the 20th century.

Different Types of dress reform 1850-94

English, 1882. Style worn by Oscar Wilde on his American tour: velvet coat with silk facings, satin breeches and silk stockings.

American, 1850. A music hall version of Mrs Bloomer's revolutionary costume.

English, 1894. 'Improved' evening dress for gentlemen.

flat patent leather pumps with silk bows

English, 1894. Knee breeches, favoured by athletes aesthetes and followers of Dr Jaeger.

American, 1865. Tunic and trousers worn by Dr. Mary Walker while serving with the Federal Army during the Civil War.

English, 1866. 'Pre-Raphaelite style of dress - no crinoline, loose bodice of soft silk.

English, 1894. A design by Walter Crane reflecting classical ideals and depending for its effect on fine, soft fabric.

English, 1894. The Aesthetic style: evening dress in Liberty brocaded satin with hand-embroidered bands.

The shirt changed very little. The frilling for evening finally disappeared completely by the 1860s, the fronts being plain, stiffly starched and fastened with decorative studs. Collars, separate from the shirt, and cuffs were highly starched; cuffs showed an inch or so beyond the coat sleeve and for formal occasions were double, fastened with cuff-links. Collars were lower between the late 1850s and 1880, single and straight or winged on formal occasions, double – i.e. turned over – for informal. By the 1890s collars about $2\frac{1}{2}$–3 inches high were again in fashion, and many elderly men continued to wear the high collars with points projecting on to the cheeks which had been fashionable in their youth.

During the 1850s and early 1860s coloured shirts might be worn by working-class men, but gentlemen usually wore white. French printed cambrics in various coloured patterns were introduced for informal wear during the 1860s, and by the 1890s neat stripes in blue or pink were accepted as 'perfectly good form' even with frock coats, provided that the collar was white. Artistic, intellectual and unconventional gentlemen might wear shirts of solid colour; William Morris had one dyed indigo blue for him in his own workshops. The dickey (or dicky), a shirt-front with an attached collar of starched linen worn over a flannel shirt, was available throughout the period, though never worn by a gentleman; it was often a source of humour or ridicule.

The stock continued to be worn for sporting occasions, particularly for hunting. The cravat or necktie, now cut narrower in the centre where it went around the neck, then widening out, was tied in various ways. In the sailor's reef knot, from around 1870, the central knot had vertical borders at the sides with the ends flowing loosely; though very popular during the 1890s, it was rivalled by the four-in-hand (also known as a Derby) in which the knot presented a free edge above and below; this was worn informally under the turn-down shirt collar and was also adopted by women to wear with masculine-styled blouses. Also worn by both men and women in the 1890s was the Oxford tie, a narrow straight necktie of uniform width. The octagon, from the 1860s, and the Ascot, from 1876, were scarf-like: the former was a made-up tie with the front arranged with four tabs above a tie pin, fastening at the back with a hook and eyelet hole; the latter, though similar in appearance, was usually self-tied, and might be puffed out at the centre front and called a puffed Ascot. A broad necktie tied in a bow was worn during the 1850s and a small neat bow was particularly favoured during the 1890s, either tied by hand or ready-made; and the small white cambric bow tie was to become more or less obligatory for formal evening wear, although black might be seen until the end of the century.

The cut of men's coats through this period changed from long sloping shoulders, tight waist and rounded hip to a straighter, longer-waisted, more masculine shape, and by 1875 shoulders began to be padded much as they are today. They were called at first 'American' shoulders, and probably originated there, as a feeling for more casual and easier-fitting clothes certainly did, although this influence only gradually found its way into Europe. The coat was often double-breasted, cut with waist and side body seams and frequently an added section under the arm, giving five seams in all, which allowed for considerable graduations of fit. The frock coat continued as the basic coat style, correct for formal day wear. During the 1870s–80s morning frock coats and dress frock coats seem to have been very similar, except that the latter opened low, exposing more of the shirt front than the former, with long narrow lapels faced with silk to the edge and often a narrow velvet collar. Silk facings and braid binding on collars and revers were extensively used from the 1860s–80s.

During the 1870s–80s the morning coat, low-waisted, single-breasted, its skirt cut away from centre front, rivalled the frock coat; but the latter held its own, returning to high favour in the 1890s, and by the turn of the century these two coats, previously a riding coat and a casual country coat, were now correct for formal daytime wear.

The jacket, originally a garment worn by labourers, apprentices, postillions and the like and used by 18th-century gentlemen only when powdering, became acceptable in the 19th century as part of a gentleman's suit, replacing the coat for informal occasions. Already worn in the 1840s, it became increasingly popular from the 1850s on, varying a little in shape and known by various names. The lounging jacket from the very late 1840s was single-breasted and short-skirted, with rounded fronts, flapped pockets on the hips and a slit or welt pocket on the left breast; without the latter it might be referred to as an Albert jacket. During the 1860s the lounging jacket became part of the lounge suit – trousers, waistcoat and jacket all made of the same material and acceptable for informal wear. The Tweedside, from 1858, was a loose, single-breasted jacket reaching mid thigh, with slit or patch pockets, a small collar, often short lapels, and buttoned high; often only the top button was used. A knee-length version was worn as an overcoat.

The reefer was double-breasted, cut to crotch level and square at the front, with three or four pairs of buttons; it had no back seam but vents in the side seams. The collar was small and flat, the lapels short. It was worn from 1860, sometimes as an overcoat, and by the 1890s was only fashionable as such. A similar garment was adopted by women and both male and female garments in dark blue serge were considered suitable for seaside wear.

Popular in the 1880s and also adopted by women was the Norfolk jacket, reaching mid thigh, single-breasted, buttoned high, with box-pleats down each forepart and at the centre back, large patch or bellows pockets on the hips and a belt of self material, usually Harris tweed or a similar fabric. An earlier version with shirt-like cuffs called the Norfolk shirt was worn from the mid '60s. In the 1890s the jacket might have a yoke from which the pleats would start. Eventually, with matching knickerbockers, it became the Norfolk suit and was much in evidence for shooting and informal country occasions. About 1888 it replaced the patrol jacket, hip-length, single-breasted, fastened high with a small or Prussian collar, worn with matching tight breeches for cycling during the 1870s. The university or angle-fronted jacket, also worn for sport between 1870 and 1880 or so, was single- or double-breasted, its fronts cut to form an opening exposing the waistcoat and the bottom of the front skirts cut into obtuse angles. By the 1890s cricketing and boating were enlivened by the blazer; originally a scarlet jacket, it was later also made of other brightly-coloured cloth.

The tail or dress coat cut away across the waist, in fine black cloth with silk or velvet collar and facings, was worn on formal evening occasions only after 1860. The day coat of previous years was now relegated to the costume of indoor upper servants. By the late 1880s, following the daytime trend, a less formal evening coat was introduced; called at first a dress lounge, then a dinner jacket (or in America a tuxedo), it had a continuous roll collar turning low to waist level and faced with silk or satin, and one or two buttons (by the late 1890s only one), usually left open; it was fairly easy-fitting, the back cut whole, the sleeves often cuffed, with slit pockets on hips and left breast. It was increasingly worn at home or for dining at 'one's club'. If ladies were not present or had 'retired', a smoking jacket (introduced in the 1850s) was often worn; single- or double-breasted, usually made of velvet (though cashmere and plush were also used), it was ornamented with braid frogging and tassels in a military style and might be quilted for extra warmth.

Waistcoats were cut as earlier in the century, although during the 1870s they were hardly visible under the high-buttoned coats. As coats, trousers and waistcoats in matching cloth became more popular the fashion for patterned or embroidered silk waistcoats declined, though checked, striped or tartan woollen, often with wide lapels, continued for some time. During the first half of the 1850s waistcoats might match the trousers, the coat fabric being different; from 1855–60 coat and trousers matched, and the waistcoat was different; but there seems to have been no very hard and fast rule, and there is still evidence in the 1870s of all three garments in different material as well as all of the same. For formal wear waistcoats were usually black; checked fabrics became associated with country and sporting activities. About 1895 a sporting waistcoat of fancy check, single-breasted with four flapped pockets and no collar, was called a Tattersall. Single- and double-breasted waistcoats fluctuated in popularity throughout the period for day wear and by the 1890s a double-breasted style was considered permissible for evening dress.

In the 1890s knitted sweaters, fairly long with a crew neckline, might be worn in place of a waistcoat over knickerbockers, and a polo-necked style was introduced, particularly for golf, around 1894.

Trousers during the 1850s might widen somewhat at the ankle but on the whole a tubular shape prevailed, and both styles, if in plain material, were often braided down the side. In 1857 trousers gathered into a narrow waistband with a strap and buckle at the back were introduced; known as American trousers, they could be worn without braces, and led to the waistcoat being discarded for informal wear in the 1890s, particularly in America, and to the wearing of belts with trousers. Trouser length varied from the ankle to over the instep, but by the 1860s the strap under the foot was uncommon. Peg-top or zouave trousers for day wear between 1857 and 1865 were cut wide at the hips, tapering to a close fit at the ankles; these never became a universal fashion, although a modified version was re-introduced in the 1890s with more success.

Between 1865 and 1890 variations in the cut of trousers were slight; during the 1870s they were of equal width at knee and ankle; in 1881 'tight slacks' were tight at the knee and loose at the ankle, and around 1884 eelskin masher trousers were excessively tight, probably favoured by 'mashers', the 1880–90 name for a dandy. The invention of the trouser-press in the 1890s facilitated the fashion for a crease down the front and back of trousers, and the turn-up at the ankle and hip pockets at the back, sometimes called 'caddies', also appeared at this time.

During the 1860s trousers in plaids and checks were often worn with dark coats, and grey striped fabric found increasing favour for wear with formal day coats, while white flannel became correct for cricket and boating.

Cloth breeches were still used for riding, often retaining until the end of the century the fall fastening, and close-fitting breeches were worn with the patrol jacket, but in the 1860s easy-fitting knickerbockers were introduced, worn with socks and gaiters, for many country pursuits and sports and even, in light colours, for tennis in England until replaced by white flannels.

Men wore their hair fairly short throughout this half century, from just over the top of the ears at the start to a moderately close cut in the 1890s. A centre parting running from forehead to nape was fashionable in the 1870s, but there was considerable individual choice in the way the hair was combed – parted slightly off-centre, at the side or brushed straight back.

142

From the late 1860s to the 1890s the majority of men presented a hirsute appearance, with the exception of aesthetes who believed that a clean-shaven face gave them a more fastidious and aesthetic appearance. Sideburns, allowed to grow further down the face, developed into a variety of side-whiskers – broad and bushy 'mutton-chop' whiskers, or long and combed out, known as Piccadilly weepers or Dundrearys (from the character of Lord Dundreary in Tom Taylor's play *Our American Cousin*) during the 1870s. Side whiskers might be worn with or without a moustache, as might the fringe beard running round under the chin, in the late 1850s and early 1860s. (It is interesting to observe that the men of the Annish People, a religious sect in the Pennsylvanian Dutch Country, continue to wear a type of fringe beard without a moustache, with a broad-brimmed felt hat similar to the 19th-century wide-awake hat but probably descended from earlier 17th-century hats.) Full beards covering the chin, combined with a moustache, were cut in many different ways – full and very bushy, rounded and neat like General Grant's in America, or slightly more pointed like that of the Prince of Wales in England. A narrow pointed beard from just under the lower lip to an inch or so below the chin, known as a goatee, was worn by Napoleon III with a long moustache waxed out straight at the sides. A waxed moustache turned up at the ends was associated with Kaiser Wilhelm II of Germany and might be referred to as a 'Kaiser' moustache. By the late 1880s and the 1890s the clean-shaven face was coming back into fashion; Charles Dana Gibson's illustrations of the 1890s show the dashing escorts of his 'Gibson girls' as clean-shaven. But many older men continued to wear a beard or moustache well into the new century.

The tall silk or top hat continued for formal day and evening wear; the opera hat (gibus), covered in corded silk, also continued for visiting the theatre, as it could be folded flat and put under the seat. A light grey top hat was worn in the late 1860s for coaching or racing parties (and is still worn for Ascot Week in England). The bowler (Derby) named after its designer, the hatter William Bowler, worn from 1860, was a hard felt hat with a domed crown, varying in height over the years, and a narrow brim rolled up at the sides. At first, when worn with the lounge jacket, it was black, but as its popularity increased it was also made in brown or fawn and teamed with the Norfolk jacket. A similar hat with a hard square crown was worn in the 1890s and much favoured by Winston Churchill, who continued to wear it into the 20th century.

From the 1870s an increasing number of hats were considered suitable for informal wear. The Homburg, made fashionable by the Prince of Wales, was a stiff felt hat with a dent in the crown running from back to front, its brim bound with ribbon and curving up at the sides. The trilby, worn in the 1890s, had a similar dent in the crown but was softer with a wider, unbound brim. The wide-awake, a broad-brimmed felt hat with a lowish crown, was a countryman's hat, but there are photographs of Alfred Tennyson looking extremely impressive in one in the 1850s. The boater, a stiff straw hat with a moderately deep, flat-topped crown encircled by a petersham ribbon and a flat narrow brim, was universally popular with men and women for the country, the seaside and boating; also worn by the seaside was the helmet, made of cloth with a small brim and a helmet-shaped sectional crown. Caps of tweed or firmly woven wool had small peaks and were quite close-fitting; the deer-stalker had a peak fore and aft and ear-flaps worn tied together on the top of the crown.

Half-boots (calf-length) or knee-length boots were now rare, worn if at all only for riding, but the short ankle boot continued throughout the period, the elastic-sided variety holding its own against the laced fastening until the 1890s. Dandies favoured a

French, 1856.
'Cinnamon-brown silk, the flounces on sleeves and skirt edged with black velvet and lace; white lace collar and undersleeves. White bonnet trimmed with pink roses, white ribbon strings. Deep red shawl with broad patterned edge in dark and light yellow.

1855. White silk-lined kid boot with pink rosette on toe.

1851. Woman's boot in blue wool with patent leather toe-cap

American, 1854
Cutaway coat and straight trousers in dark grey cloth, lighter grey waistcoat. Large tophat.

English, 1858. Dark frock coat over pale trousers and waistcoat of different fabrics; old-fashioned shirt collar.

American, 1854. Wedding dress of cream taffeta trimmed with flat pleating, deep fringe and large ribbon bows.

Man's half-boot in tan morocco leather and black patent with elasticated slit front.

German, 1857. Gown of purple wool with flounces and pagoda sleeves edged with deeper purple check fabric and narrow silk fringe. White undersleeves of sheer wool; collar of notched lace.

English, 1852. Frock coat, top hat and side whiskers.

French, 1864 (left) Gown, with jacket-style bodice in mid blue silk moiré, small pattern binding and embroidery in navy. Lace bonnet with amber-coloured ribbons, trimmed with spray of wheat. (Right) Black velvet Zouave jacket, trimmed braid, over white blouse with black trimming; black belt with gold buckle. Emerald green silk skirt trimmed black braid and tassels.

American, 1867. Bonnets trimmed with feathers, flowers and embroidered gauze.

Bowler or Derby hat

1865. Boot in ivory silk with silk-covered bobble.

1860, Boot in emerald green satin laced at front, with braid bow and buckle trimming

English, 1865. Matching braid-edged frock coat and waistcoat; check trousers and cravat.

Italian, 1863. (from the French). Lounge suit with stitching on flapped pockets, collar and front edges.

American, 1868. Dress of grey silk with double skirt, pleating and rosettes of same material, grey satin banding and belt, silk tassels.

pointed toe during the 1850s–60s and again in the 1890s, and a long, blunt, square-toed shape was worn during the 1880s. Buttoned boots with cloth tops, another vogue of the 1880s, corresponded with the fashion for wearing short gaiters with knickerbockers and spats with more formal clothes. Spats, in white, light grey or fawn, were buttoned at the sides and fastened under the foot with a buckled strap. Boots with contrasting tops, particularly patent leather with kid or cloth tops, continued in fashion until about 1920, as did spats. Boots and shoes were black or brown until the 1890s when white was introduced for summer wear. Laced shoes might be worn from the 1880s, particularly for summer, occasionally with fancy socks. Normally socks were black, even with light shoes. From the mid 1890s they were supported by sock-suspenders, bands of elastic worn below the knee with a pendent clip to hold the top of the sock. Rubber and canvas shoes, forerunners of the American sneaker, were worn for tennis from the late 1870s.

Until the 1890s some men liked to wear thinner-soled elastic-sided boots for evening in place of pumps, but the low-cut pump in patent leather with a large flat bow of grosgrain ribbon was worn more or less universally from the 1890s until the 1920s.

Evening cloaks gradually declined in favour during this period although the Talma cloak, knee-length with a wide turnover collar (which might be quilted), was worn during the 1850s. By the 1870s–80s evening coats were considered smarter but they might have a cape and frequently a velvet collar.

In the 1850s–60s a single-breasted loose coat reaching the knees, with wide sleeves and buttoning higher as the period proceeded, was known as a 'sac' overcoat, a term also applied to other loose coats in the 1850s such as the double-breasted, thigh-length Wellesley, often bordered with fur and fastened with frogging, or the single-breasted Palmerston with wide cuffless sleeves, broad collar and lapels and flapped pockets. The popular Chesterfield was joined in the late 1850s by the equally popular Inverness, a large single-breasted knee-length loose overcoat with a deep cape, fairly formal in smooth dark-coloured cloth, or countrified and suitable for travelling in plaid wool or tweed. Also for travelling was the Ulster, double- or single-breasted, with a cape in the 1870s, and reaching almost to the ankles; the double-breasted Gladstone of the same date also had a cape but was shorter and edged with astrakhan. The raglan overcoat, which appeared in the 1890s, was full and long with a fly-front fastening and raglan sleeves; a version in waterproofed material replaced the earlier mackintosh.

The covert overcoat was very popular from the 1880s with the younger 'sporty' set; only a few inches longer than a jacket, it was cut straight with side vents, fly-front fastening closing high, top-stitched seams, flapped hip pockets and welted breast and ticket pocket; it might also be cut with raglan sleeves in the 1890s and was then called a raglan covert.

WOMEN

Throughout this period women's underwear became more elaborately trimmed and progressively prettier and more alluring, culminating in the 1890s with 'frou-frou' petticoats. The chemise continued, and drawers reached to just below the knee with a frill; a fashion for drawers of scarlet flannel occurred around 1855–60. Drawers and chemises were combined in 1877 as combinations, sometimes high-necked and long-sleeved for day wear in linen, merino, calico or nainsook, but by the 1890s sleeveless and more glamorous with frills, tucks, lace trimmings and ribbons. Undervests of coloured washable silk with shaped gussets for the breasts were worn by 1875, and knickers made of flannel, similar to men's knickerbockers, might occasionally replace drawers in the 1890s.

'Petticoat' in the 19th century referred only to an undergarment, whereas previously it might be the name for a visible underskirt or the actual skirt of a gown. In the 1850s, as in the 1840s, numerous petticoats decorated with broderie anglaise, tucking and lace, some stiffened to support the widening skirts, were worn; but with the advent of the crinoline frame in 1856, only one or two petticoats were necessary – one reason, perhaps, for the crinoline being considered somewhat immodest, although this opinion probably stemmed more from the fact that, in spite of its solid appearance, it was liable to sway and occasionally tip to reveal a tantalizing glimpse of an ankle or, in a high wind, even a little more. Petticoats followed the shape of the outer skirt, cut with a shaped band to give a smooth line over the hips during the 1870s and very much like a second or third skirt in the following decades.

Stays or corsets in the 1850s–60s were short, lightly boned but often stiffened by cording or quilting. White was considered ladylike, but they were also made in grey, putty, red or black, always lined with white. In the 1870s the corset grew longer, moulding the hips, and more rigid. This decade also saw the introduction of elastic suspenders attached to the border of the corset to support the stockings, previously held up by garters. Corsets remained extremely rigid until the end of the century, but the front gradually straightened over the stomach, pushing the surplus flesh out over the hips and bottom, evolving into the S-bend of the 1900s.

Although not intended to be visible, as were many 18th-century corsets, those of the 1880s–90s were elegant and beautifully made; black sateen was machined with yellow, blue, pink or green and embroidered, or a wedding corset might be of white satin embroidered with orange blossom motifs. A short-sleeved or sleeveless under-bodice called a camisole or, in the 1890s, a corset cover or petticoat bodice, was worn over the corset to protect the tight-fitting dress. Towards the end of the century, petticoat and bodice might be combined.

From 1850 to 1866 the dress bodice remained very close fitting, the shoulder a little less sloping, the waist pointed, although some early-1850 bodices had a basque giving a jacket effect, and might even be in jacket form, opening over a chemisette (a white muslin or cambric fill-in often trimmed with broderie anglaise). During the late 1850s the 'princess' dress, cut without a waist seam, appeared, and in the 1860s the round waist was slightly raised. Any seaming and decoration still emphasized the small waist. The neckline was high except for evenings: as C. W. Cunnington remarks, 'The high water mark of modesty would ebb after sunset some six inches!' (*A Handbook of English Costume in the 19th Century*).

Garibaldi's visit to England in 1863 gave enormous appeal to anything named after him. The Garibaldi blouse or shirt, worn for day during the 1860s in place of a bodice, was of scarlet merino trimmed with black braid; it had epaulettes, full or plain sleeves, and usually overhung the skirt, confined by a belt; so began the fashion of blouse and skirt, which has lasted with varying popularity for over a hundred years. The Garibaldi jacket for outer wear was short and made of scarlet cashmere with military braiding; a Garibaldi sleeve of thin material was full and gathered into a band at the wrist, worn for morning or afternoon occasions.

Blouses were often worn under a zouave jacket, based on the costume of the Algerian zouave troops in the Italian wars of 1859. Made of silk, velvet or cloth, it reached just to or slightly above the waist, the fronts rounded off and fastened at the neck only; it was

German, 1857.
Cotton crinoline.

English, 1866. Corset in
scarlet drill (strong twilled linen)
and cage crinoline

German, 1862.
Crinoline with
horsehair flounce

English, 1872. The Alexandra
tournure, made of 'brillanté'
(cotton with a small lustrous fleck)
with narrow steels, cord and elastic.

English, 1887. The Cranfield
or Langtry bustle.

American, 1872. A tournure
made from horsehair mounted
on calico.

English, 1870–1875. Horsehair bustle.

American, 1869.

Corset in white coutil (a twilled cotton cloth)

French, 1878. Chemise in cambric trimmed with tucking, lace insertion and edging.

English, 1880. Petticoat with detachable train, in cambric and broderie anglaise.

French, 1867. Nightcaps in fine percale cotton.

French, 1867. Drawers in cambric and broderie anglaise.

American, 1872. Petticoat in jaconet (a fine cotton similar to nainsook) trimmed with tucks, lace insertion and edging.

American, 1891, House slippers.

American, 1892. (Left) cambric nightcap, (right) muslin breakfast cap.

American, 1892. Lace trimmed corset and high-necked corset cover.

American, 1892. Combinations in fine cotton with broderie anglaise edging and insertion.

one of many bolero-type jackets worn between 1860 and the 1900s. The tendency for the sleeve to widen below the elbow in the 1850s led to the pagoda sleeve, seamed on the inner side and cut to expand widely at the elbow, caught up at the bend of the arm and falling almost to the wrist at the outer edge. During the late 1850s it was slit open almost the whole length in front, hanging away at the back like an oversleeve and worn with detachable white undersleeves edged with lace or embroidery, sometimes with a matching chemisette. For evening dress, sleeves were short, puffed, ruffled or looped up, or the bodice could be sleeveless with a deep bertha collar covering the upper arm.

The typical skirt of the 1850s was still dome-shaped; its slight reduction in size was concealed by the addition of flounces, on average three to five, edged with embroidery, a printed or woven pattern or velvet bands. As the decade progressed evening dresses were trimmed with more and more ruches, puffs, ribbons, flounces and lace. Max von Boehm, the social and costume historian, records that the Empress Eugénie appeared at a ball wearing 'white satin with one hundred and three "flounces" of tulle' (*Die Mode 1843–1878*). Tulle, net and tarlatan (a thin gauze-like muslin, much stiffened) were chosen for these vast flounced gowns which were subject to severe creasing during the evening's festivities and a considerable fire hazard.

The late 1850s saw the skirt changing shape from a dome to a bell, the top hoops of the crinoline frame being reduced in diameter and the skirt gored so that it flowed out gradually from the tiny waist to the immensely wide hemline. The 1860s skirt was cut to flow and spread out at the back, the front hanging fairly straight over a crinoline frame adjusted to give this silhouette. Somewhat heavier materials were used in the 1860s and decoration was confined to the lower part of the skirt.

Skirts were long, often trailing, but as early as 1857 they might be looped up for convenience when walking in the country or on the beach, and this led to an arrangement of cords and rings which enabled the skirt to be drawn up in festoons. Both methods revealed a petticoat which might be of a bright colour with applied bands of contrasting colour and stockings striped to match. By the mid-1860s this fashion was general in Paris for outdoor wear, and accepted by other countries for such activities as archery and croquet. A definite distinction was thus made between 'walking' and 'visiting' dresses, the latter remaining very long, and coloured petticoats were for informal wear only; otherwise they were white, as were the stockings. The years 1865–70 saw the decline of the crinoline, not without some resistance; its popularity had permeated all classes and it was regarded by many as indispensable. It was worn by peasant girls in the fields, maidservants and factory workers, as well as by the wealthy and fashionable; even actresses playing classical roles would not part with their crinolines, and guests at fancy dress balls happily appeared in what they thought of as medieval dress over crinolines!

With the round and higher-waisted bodice of 1866–69 the crinoline became small and cone-shaped for day, worn under a dress cut shorter than a matching underskirt for walking – or this effect might be simulated by bands of ribbon in a contrasting colour. A short tunic or overskirt called a peplum, cut away at the front and back and hanging in points at the sides, was fashionable between 1866 and 1868; if worn with evening dress it might be called a peplum basque, being shorter and attached to a waist-belt. Evening skirts swept the ground and required a larger crinoline projecting at the back to support the train, though of modest size compared to those of the late 1850s and early 1860s. Sleeves were long and slim, neck-lines high for day or, if cut lower, filled in with a chemisette; the low décolletage was retained for evening without

American, 1868. High-waisted street dress with fichu, the skirt caught up over petticoat with double flounce.

English, 1865 Early style of morning coat with matching trousers; bow tie.

English, 1866. Walking dress with skirt drawn up over a striped petticoat, hem trimmed with broad pleating divided by tabs. Matching jacket bound with braid.

French, 1867. Straw bonnet bound with red grosgrain, Ivy trim, white ribbon strings.

French, 1868. Princess dress with 'pinafore' look, emerald green over paler green, the bodice ruched between narrow lace bands.

English, 1869. Casquette or pill-box hat trimmed with small beads.

Italian, 1869. Black lace overskirt, fichu and flounces over blue taffeta. Black waistband set high with fringed loops and bow at centre back. Cream hat trimmed blue ribbon and feathers, cream gloves

French, 1872. Bonnets trimmed with ribbons, feathers lace and ruching.

Bronze silk hat trimmed coral ribbon and flowers.

English, 1872. Ball dress of striped pink and white satin; bodice has a basque jutting out at the back. White gauze overskirt with gathered flounce is looped at the side and back, decorated with spray of roses. Headdress of roses arranged in a bunch at the front and trailing at the back. Slippers of pink satin and white lace.

English, 1870. Man in early Homburg hat and reefer jacket, broad knotted tie. Woman in fur-trimmed jacket with matching hat.

American, 1872. Skirt of black faille with pleated flounce and rows of puffed ruching. Polonaise of bronze faille, with black velvet bands on bodice and sleeves embroidered in bright colours.

English, 1871. Breakfast caps in Swiss muslin and lace trimmed with ribbon.

a bertha, and sleeves were short and puffed or simply little draped sections of gauze or lace.

When, earlier in the century, such women as Florence Nightingale or Mrs William Morris in England and Mrs Bloomer or Doctor Mary Walker in America discarded their crinolines for ascetic or practical reasons, they were considered eccentric, but in the late 1860s it was considered somewhat distinguished, if a little daring, to do so.

Between 1868 and 1870 fashion wavered between straight and rounded lines. The high-waisted bodice and cone-shaped skirt were challenged by an outbreak of historically-inspired fashions. The Antoinette fichu, usually of muslin or lace, covered the shoulders, wrapped across the breasts and tied in a long-ended bow behind; wide sashes were tied at the back with big puffed-out bows (wearing these styles women stood leaning slightly forward in an attitude called obscurely the Grecian Bend). There were suggestions of 17th-century lace collars and 18th-century *paniers*, and these concoctions were not confined to the ball-room; an outfit for the beach in emerald green and white shot silk trimmed with black velvet ribbon was described as 'in Louis XV style'. Rounded and more voluptuous curves finally triumphed over the vertical. The upper skirts were drawn up and back, the underskirt becoming the main skirt, and were supported by a kind of decadent crinoline called a crinolette, with hoops at the back only. The age of the crinoline had given way to that of the bustle.

The decade of the 1870s is one of the most complex periods of women's fashion. The style of the early 1870s (indications of which had been seen in the late 1860s) relied on the revival of the polonaise, drawn back, bunched and puffed up into an elaborate arrangement at the rear, over a supporting bustle or tournure; the tight-fitting bodice was still short-waisted, the sleeves plain, easy-fitting and finished with a ruffle or cuff, tending to widen slightly at the wrist. The underskirt, trimmed with pleated or gathered flounces, gauged sections, tucking and/or ribbon bands, was trained. The earlier bid for simplicity and freedom was overwhelmed by a profusion of puffs, ruchings, fringes, ribbons, drapery, flounces with additional headings and edgings, and strange combinations of materials and colours.

Around 1874 rather plain masculine-style jackets were introduced, paving the way for a new fashion typical of the second half of the 1870s, the cuirass bodice; extremely tight-fitting, long-waisted, boned and descending over the hips, it moulded the body like a corset. This and the princess sheath dress or polonaise which had a similar line with bodice and skirt cut in one (popular between 1878 and 1880), were associated with the Princess of Wales, later Queen Alexandra. Although Paris was fashion's focal point, the gay, sociable and well-dressed Edward and Alexandra had their followers; in America the activities of the English Court and developments in English fashion, particularly for sport, were of great interest after the Prince of Wales's visit in the 1860s. Both the cuirass bodice and the princess sheath were worn without a bustle but possibly with a small pad. The skirt narrowed, fitting the figure almost to the knees and tied back tightly with ribbons inside to flatten the front which might be draped symmetrically or asymmetrically, trimmed with fringes, flounces, etc. The back skirt was draped and decorated even more elaborately and finished, except for active sport, with a train reminiscent of a peacock trailing his closed tail.

Sleeves, set into a normal shoulder, were slim fitting; on evening and dinner dresses they might be elbow-length but on ball gowns they were tiny, and the neckline was low in front, narrow and fairly high at the back. Frequently sleeves were of a different fabric to the bodice, the latter matching the underskirt, the former the overskirt, but in

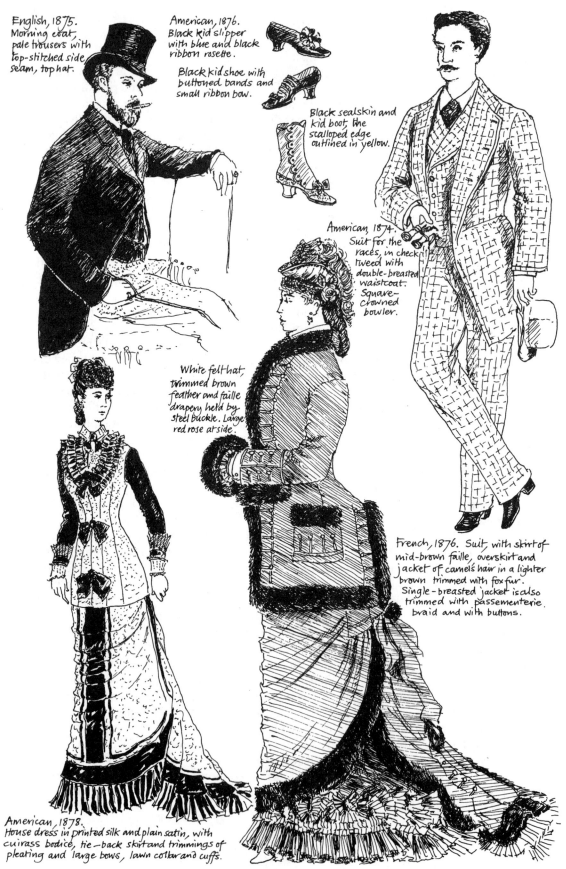

English, 1875.
Morning coat,
pale trousers with
top-stitched side
seam, top hat.

American, 1876.
Black kid slipper
with blue and black
ribbon rosette.

Black kid shoe with
buttoned bands and
small ribbon bow.

Black sealskin and
kid boot, the
scalloped edge
outlined in yellow.

American, 1874.
Suit for the
races, in check
tweed with
double-breasted
waistcoat.
Square-
crowned
bowler.

White felt hat,
trimmed brown
feather and faille
drapery held by
steel buckle. Large
red rose at side.

French, 1876. Suit, with skirt of
mid-brown faille, overskirt and
jacket of camel's hair in a lighter
brown trimmed with fox fur.
Single-breasted jacket is also
trimmed with passementerie,
braid and with buttons.

American, 1878.
House dress in printed silk and plain satin, with
cuirass bodice, tie-back skirt and trimmings of
pleating and large bows, lawn collar and cuffs.

French, 1888. An evening dress combining white spotted gauze with pale and dark green satin. A cascade of roses and foliage falls from shoulder to back and down the side. Long pale cream gloves. Large pale green fan decorated with painted roses.

American, 1884-5. Hat in velvet with ruched silk under brim, trimmed ribbon, curled ostrich feather and feather wing.

Bonnet of lace straw trimmed bouquet of mixed flowers and ribbon.

German, 1885. Morning coat and wing collar.

English, 1884. (left) Chesterfield with silk hat. (right) Lounge jacket with bowler.

American, 1887. Costume in pearl-grey cloth trimmed with bands of gold embroidery on bodice and sleeves. The bodice front is gathered pearl-grey crape; the skirt is bordered with chinchilla. Red felt hat trimmed red velvet, feather and grey ribbon.

the late 1870s the combination of colour and fabric became less patchy, often using two fabrics of the same colour, one matt, the other shiny, or fabrics in two shades of the same colour, or a striped fabric with a matching plain one. Horizontal trimming or drapery seen on skirts of 1878–9 intensified in the early 1880s and the fashion for a long train declined for day wear.

From about 1882 the plain, high-necked, tight-fitting day bodice grew shorter, cut to a point at the centre front and often, until the middle of the decade, at the centre back also. Sleeves were plain and tight. Interest was centred on the skirt, with pleats, flounces, draped *panier* or apron effects, kilting, braiding, etc. Trains, no longer worn by day, persisted for evening wear, often as a separate attachment which could be fastened under drapery at the back. Formal ball gowns were often sleeveless and the décolletage was cut slightly wider and to a point at both front and back.

The return of the bustle, confidently announced in Paris in 1880, was not completely accepted elsewhere until 1885. Very different to the 1870s bustle, it was now worn jutting out horizontally from the hollow of the back, its supporting structure more rigid as in the Cranfield or Langtrey bustle where an arrangement of metal bands, working on a pivot, could be raised when sitting and sprang back automatically when the lady stood up. This large protuberance naturally required a wider skirt. A certain aggressiveness and rigidity about the erect, square-shouldered female figure during the mid to late 1880s (the sleeve head was raised and slightly gathered by 1888), appears to reflect the increasing demand for the emancipation of women. Notable at this time was a liking for military dresses, and the tailor-made became high fashion, largely owing to the couture house of Redfern in Paris. Redfern's designer at that time was an Englishman, Charles Poynter, and English tailor-mades were eagerly bought by American and European women. Only the bodice or jacket was tailored, the skirt remaining elaborately draped to emphasize the tiny corseted waist.

The bustle, gradually diminishing in size, became a mere pad by about 1893, and the silhouette changed to an hour-glass figure; but simultaneously the small gathered sleeve-head of the late 1880s began to grow in earnest by 1892. Expanding each season, sleeves reached an enormous size by 1895–6, each requiring something like $2\frac{1}{2}$ yards of material. Close-fitting from wrist to elbow, they swelled out to reach such proportions that women must have had to turn sideways in order to pass through doorways of moderate width. Like those of the 1830s, they were called leg-of-mutton or gigot sleeves, but they were now set into a high or normal armhole with the width at shoulder level, rather than swelling from the low dropped armhole of the 1830s; as in the earlier period, evening dresses often had a lace flounce added above the sleeve to increase the impression of width.

The width at the shoulder was balanced by added width at the hemline. Skirts were gored to give a fairly close-fitting effect over the hips, widening in a straight line to the hem; some pleating from the waist-band was retained at the back and a certain amount of padding was added when necessary to round out the hips. As skirts became plainer, the tight, high-necked, high-busted and long-waisted bodice became more ornate, with lace jabots or frills, cross-overs or epaulettes. Designs from the French couture houses of extravagantly expensive, elaborate gowns in velvet or satin, richly embroidered or trimmed, might dominate the fashion pages of English and American periodicals, undoubtedly appealing to the wealthy and influencing many, but a preference for the tailor-made suit, and in particular the image of the American Gibson girl, elevated the combination of blouse or 'shirt-waist' and skirt into the realm

English, 1893-4.
(A) Double-breasted morning coat worn with striped trousers, wing collar and top hat.
(B) Chesterfield overcoat with fur collar and cuffs.
(C) Back of frock coat, showing seaming.

(D) Evening dress with single-breasted waistcoat, stiff shirt-front with studs, small white bow tie.

American, 1893.
Graduation dresses

French, 1889.
Dress in shot silk striped rose pink, green and brown, trimmed with black velvet bands and white guipure lace. Natural straw hat trimmed with roses and striped fabric of dress.
Parasol of guipure lace with pink and green shot silk ribbon loops.

White crêpe de chine and satin dotted with spangles

White surah silk with lace; bands of satin ribbon on bodice are edged with opalescent beads.

American, 1898-9.
The 'Gibson Girl' look: shirt-waist blouse and skirt.

English, 1896. Covert overcoat worn with bowler hat

American, 1894.
Blouse in spotted silk.

American, 1898.
Blouse in striped cotton for young girl.

French, 1896.
Gown of shot silk moiré in grey and mauve with collar and draped belt of white satin. Bodice trimming and parasol of white gauze appliquéd with lace.
Hat of fancy straw trimmed flowers, ostrich plume and stiff lace aigrette.

A

B

C

D

English footwear 1890s
(A) 1890 Black patent leather court shoe with white grosgrain ribbon stripes and satin bow.
(B) 1897. Gold and ivory brocade court shoe with small buckle trim and gold satin lining.
(C) 1897. Man's button boot.
(D) 1890. Woman's front-laced boot in rust satin overlaid with black chantilly lace.

of fashion. Ready-made blouses could now be bought in great variety, high-necked and masculine or dressy enough to wear with a plain skirt on informal evening occasions. The tailor-made suit of the 1890s had a three-quarter-length jacket, wide revers and enormous sleeves, a plain skirt to instep or ground level, and might also sport a waistcoat. These somewhat masculine styles often have a certain provocative charm and indicate not only the working woman's desire to look smart but also the increase in active sports for women, and it was during this decade that cycling became the rage. Amelia Bloomer died in 1894, and although the rational dress she devised in 1849–50 never attained popularity in her lifetime, a year after her death a form of knickerbockers called bloomers, very full and extending to below the knee, became a popular cycling costume for women.

From 1896 the size of the sleeve decreased and the next fashion cycle began to take shape, heralding the S-bend typical of the early 1900s; with the bosom appearing fuller and lower, an exaggerated fullness was gathered at the front of the bodice overhanging the straightened front of the skirt.

Women's hair styles tended to reflect the lines of their gowns. As skirts were drawn back in the mid to late 1860s, so the hair was also drawn up and back to reveal the ears, for so long covered, but kept flat on top, with curls or a small twist at the back of the head reflecting the back interest on the dress. With the first bustles in the early 1870s the hair was lifted higher, sloping upward from forehead to occiput, then cascading to the shoulders in lavish twisted plaits (braids) or curls, or both, or occasionally worn in a chignon. During this period enormous quantities of false hair were used by the very fashionable, obtained, in Catholic countries, from novices entering convents, and everywhere from prisoners or paupers in workhouses; hair might fetch a good price, and peasant girls in Germany, Italy and France whose traditional headdresses hid the absence of hair found its sale a source of income; even middle-class girls in England or America, in need of cash, might sell their hair, as Jo March did in *Little Women*.

In 1876 *The Englishwoman's Domestic Magazine* announced that the use of false hair was a thing of the past; the slim straight line of the cuirass body was enhanced by hair dressed to give a smaller, neat appearance, close and high on the head. A few curls might be arranged to fall from the back of the head to the shoulders in the evening, and the increasingly fashionable, closely-curled fringe favoured by the Princess of Wales might often be false; a false fringe would avoid cutting the front hair. These fringes were thick enough to support a diamond clip in the shape of a star or crescent for evening. The small neat hairstyle remained in fashion through the late 1870s and into the 1880s, when the hair was scraped up into a bun on top of the head. The curled fringe was reduced to small tendrils on the forehead. By the 1890s it had disappeared altogether, and the hair was again dressed back from the forehead but fuller and softer, possibly over pads to give a more bouffant style, still with the twist or bun on top of the head.

Throughout the half century, bonnets and hats, apart from sporting styles, were lavishly trimmed, and hair was invariably decorated with flowers, jewels or feathers for evening. Indoor caps were gradually discontinued, by the 1870s worn only, perhaps, with a tea-gown or breakfast jacket and by elderly ladies; servants and country folk wore them well into the 20th century. The variety of millinery styles throughout this period was enormous, and it is only possible to indicate the main shapes, which were dictated by the hairstyles. During the 1850s bonnets became shallower and set further back on the head, developing in the early 1860s into the spoon bonnet, which had a narrow brim close to the ears, rising vertically above the forehead in a spoon-shaped curve and sloping down behind to a very small crown, edged with a bavolet at the back. Bonnet strings (or ribbons) were wide, and often not tied but held by a brooch or pin under the chin, occasionally with a tiny bunch of artificial flowers. A curious addition to the bonnet between 1848 and 1864, appropriately called an ugly, was an extra brim resembling the front of a calash, made of half hoops of cane covered with silk and worn round the front as a protection against the sun; when not in use it could be folded flat. The most romantic-looking hat of the 1850s was a leghorn straw with a very wide brim dipping down at the back and slightly at the front and a high or low crown, trimmed with a lace or tulle veil, ribbons or flowers, or possibly all three; it appears to have been more popular in France and Germany, but was certainly adopted with slight variations in England and America for children's wear.

With the massive arrangement of hair at the back of the head in the late 1860s and early 1870s, bonnets had to be worn further forward, the front curving from just above the hair-line to behind the ears where the ribbons were attached, the back cut away to allow the hair to flow freely. At this time hats were also perched on the forehead; a pill-box shape is sometimes referred to as a casquette, a name also applied to a hat following the lines of the Scotch glengarry cap. The Lamballe bonnet or plateau (named after the Princesse de Lamballe) might be classified as a bonnet or hat – worn in the same way as the pill-box, it closely resembled it but was more oval in shape and tied on by strings under the back hair or chignon or, when curved down slightly at the sides, would have ribbons tied in a large bow under the chin.

Small-brimmed hats, slightly wider in summer, toques and tiny bonnets set on top of the head above the close, high-dressed hair and fringe, helped to increase height in the late 1870s and 1880s; crowns rose, with a flower-pot shape appearing in the late 1880s. Trimmings, arranged to give a vertical line, could be elaborate and even bizarre: small birds, feathers, feather wings, aigrettes, beetles, flowers, fruit and vegetables intermingled with loops of fancy ribbon, velvet and/or tulle. Fur decorated some winter hats, and toques made of sealskin became very popular. At the same time, for country and sporting activities, plainer and rather masculine hats were in vogue. Boaters, introduced as early as the 1860s, continued to be worn, straight or tilted, into the 20th century. The Fedora felt hat, similar to a Homburg, was named after the heroine in a play by Sardou in which Sarah Bernhardt scored a success. Yachting caps were worn for sailing or at the sea-side. The tam-o'-shanter, for country wear, was a soft, round, flat cap or hat with no brim and a bobble in the centre of the crown; in the 1880s it might be made of velvet, plush, cloth or crochet; a knitted version became usual later.

During the 1890s, bonnets lost favour with the fashionable although still worn by some elderly ladies, even after 1900, and for mourning with a long crape veil. Hats became wider-brimmed, worn high on the head over the fuller hairstyle; even toques were often quite large, draped or ruched in velvet, silk or tulle. Trimmings, ribbons, flowers and feathers still emphasized a vertical line.

Heels were added to boots in the late 1840s and the 1850s and to slippers between 1860 and 1865; on both they were small, $1-1\frac{1}{2}$ inches high, straight on the inner side and curved in from the back; the toe might be squared at the tip, rounded or pointed. Coloured satin or fine kid was used for formal slippers and boots, and kid, sometimes combined with cloth uppers in white, black or bronze for informal. Elastic-sided boots continued, but lacing on the inner side of the boot increased. The tops of boots might be decorated with bows or tassels, enchantingly glimpsed under the spreading skirts.

Heels increased in height during the 1870s and 1880s, now curved on the inner side and the back to a small base, often termed a Louis, Pompadour or French heel. Boots might be laced down the front or buttoned slightly towards the outer side. By the 1890s heels could be very high and toes long and pointed; close-fitting boots rose to calf-length and shoes and slippers might be ornamented with buckles and high tongues or small bows. Footwear in the 1890s could be very dashing: boots in rust satin overlaid with black chantilly lace, green morocco leather shoes with high tongues and steel buckles, black patent leather slippers or court shoes striped with white grosgrain ribbons and with black and white satin bows. For cycling, skating, golfing and rough walking, low-heeled laced boots, or shoes with leather or cloth leggings which might reach the knee, were worn. During the summer, shoes laced over the instep called Oxfords were in white for the seaside, brown or black for the country.

Silk stockings were considered a luxury, for evening or special occasions only; fine lisle, heavier cotton or wool was more usual. Until the 1880s they were mostly white or a pale shade, apart from the striped stockings worn in the 1860s, but by the early 1880s black was also worn, by children as well as women. During this decade, too, stockings became more fancy, in black and white stripes or with embroidered clocks, and by the late 1890s embroidery and/or lace insertion might decorate the instep of evening stockings.

Women's outdoor garments, like men's, became more varied during this period. The large shawl held its own until the late 1860s and cloaks were worn occasionally throughout the period for evening or travelling, and by the poorer members of society – but an increasing number of capes, wraps or jackets were fashionable. The casaque jacket (1855–60) was close-fitting, buttoned up to the neck, with a deep basque. The term paletot, though used rather loosely, was generally applied to short jackets with set-in sleeves; and the mantelet had now become a kind of half shawl, fitted at the front and back with the sides hanging like sleeves over the arms. The paletot mantle of the late 1860s was a three-quarter-length cloak with hanging sleeves and the paletot redingote of the same date was a long coat cut to fit the figure without a waist seam and buttoned right down the front.

During the 1870s–80s the cut of jackets and coats had to allow for the bustle. The carmago jacket (late 1870s) had a rounded basque draped up at the sides on the hips; the dolman was a favourite short wrap, the sleeve cut in one with the side of the garment and hanging loose, and might have mantelet ends hanging in front and a full basque at the back forming a puff over the bustle, or sometimes the centre back seam was left open at the back below the waist. Three-quarter and full-length mantles might also have dolman sleeves or a style of sleeve called a 'sling', like a cape looped at the bottom at waist level to support the arm. It is impossible to particularize the great variety of short and long wraps worn throughout the last few decades of the 19th century and some names can be misleading – garments are often called cloaks or mantles when they appear to be coats with fitted sleeves; but photographs, fashion plates and original garments of the period demonstrate the ingenuity of cut and dress-making skills practised at that time.

In the 1890s women adapted masculine jacket and coat styles for driving, travelling or sporting activities, including the Norfolk jacket, the reefer, the Ulster, and even the morning coat in 1895. But for formal occasions they still demanded more feminine styles: capes, short and high-shouldered, then bigger to fit over the huge sleeves, in fur, cloth, taffeta, satin, faille or even pleated chiffon, often elaborately trimmed with

French, 1864. Paletot in violet-coloured wool velours trimmed with black passementerie braid and large buttons. Hair drawn into a snood decorated with ribbon.

English, 1876. Double-breasted Ulster overcoat.

Wraps and Coats — 1860s—1890s

English, 1885. Dolman coat in dark red cloth trimmed with narrow metallic braid and matching buttons.

American, 1871. Mantelet in fine cashmere trimmed with braid and fringe.

English, 1891. Inverness top coat with fly front on cape.

English, 1893. Coat in Alaska sealskin trimmed with Russian sable. Velvet-covered tricorne trimmed ostrich and osprey feathers.

American, 1882. Opera cloak, white camel's hair trimmed with pearls and small beads.

American, 1892. Travelling or walking boots.

passementerie braid, ribbon or lace; for winter, little jackets of fur, fur and velvet, or sealskin, and full-length coats in broadcloth and moiré or velvet trimmed with Russian sable; for evening, coats with dolman or loose sleeves in rich fabrics richly trimmed, or sweeping full-length cloaks with shoulders adapted to contain the huge sleeves of the dresses and collars flaring out around the face. The restraint shown in men's dress was certainly not practised by fashionable and wealthy women, who had no hesitation in flaunting their wealth, both in lavish fabric and trimmings and in the extraordinary number of garments they required for different occasions and activities.

CHILDREN

The practice of dressing children in adult styles gradually declined during the second half of the 19th century. Boys benefited from more convenient and comfortable clothes earlier than girls, who had to wait until the late 1880s before enjoying clothes as easy as their grandmothers' had been or which began to resemble boys' styles rather than women's, although there was a considerable current of feeling against squeezing girls into corsets during the 1860s.

Boys still wore frocks with pleated skirts, or tunics and blouses over pleated skirts, until the age of three or four. Winterhalter's portrait of the Prince of Wales in a Scottish kilt in 1849 gave rise to a considerable vogue for pleated skirts; 'The costume worn by the Prince of Wales when at Balmoral has set the fashion of adapting the complete Highland costume', stated the *Lady's Newspaper* in 1852. 'Scotch' suits were worn from 1850 to the 1870s, but less frequently after that. In the 1860s a boy's suit might reflect the true Scottish costume: 'a waistcoat and jacket of velvet with a kilt of tartan poplin, plus scarf, brooch, sporran and Glengarry cap, if the jacket is of cloth, then woollen plaid is used for the kilt.' (*Englishwoman's Domestic Magazine*, 1867). But some very quaint travesties of Scottish dress were considered ideal for boys, and there was a profusion of 'Young Highlanders' wherever European fashion was followed, especially in America.

Boys between the age of three and seven had their sartorial problems solved during the 1860s by the knickerbocker suit, probably first developed in America, consisting of full knickerbockers closed under the knee and a short collarless jacket fastening at the neck only (resembling the women's zouave jacket) over a white frilled shirt. In the 1870s the knickerbocker suit was worn until the age of ten or so, with a waistcoat and jacket in serge, cloth, melton or washable materials such as drill, the edges braided. The knickerbockers were narrower by the 1880s, and by the end of the century they might hang loose like trousers cut off below the knee.

Along with the popularity of the knickerbocker suit came a naval influence, again starting with the young Prince of Wales being dressed in naval uniform, and later encouraged when his two young sons appeared in similar outfits. 'Sailor suits are always popular, and ever since the Prince of Wales' two sons have adopted the naval uniform the preference has increased', said the *Queen Magazine* in 1879 – and the fashion lasted into the early 20th century. The 1860s sailor suit consisted of a blouse with square collar worn with knickerbockers and a hat with a straight, narrow brim and low flat crown trimmed with black ribbon with bow ends. By the late 1870s the suit had many variations, with blouse or jacket, knickerbockers open or closed below the knee, or bell-bottomed trousers. The middy suit had a jacket and the Jack Tar suit a blouse, both worn with long trousers, in blue serge for winter and white drill for summer. These suits 'sold in their thousands' in the 1880s according to *The Lady's*

World, and were now worn with either a hat with a wide upcurving brim or a round flat cap, both with a band bearing the name of a ship. In the 1890s the man's reefer jacket, another somewhat naval style, the Norfolk suit and the blazer were also adapted for boys.

During the 1880s, Frances Hodgson Burnett's popular book, *Little Lord Fauntleroy*, led to another fashion for small boys, the Fauntleroy suit - a velvet tunic and knickerbockers, with a white lace collar over the shoulders and a wide sash with a bow and hanging ends on one hip, worn preferably with long hair in ringlets. As Mrs Burnett was American the vogue started there, but it quickly spread, better loved by artistically-inclined mothers than by the wearer.

The knitted jersey introduced for boys around the 1860s, at first for the seaside with knickerbockers and a tam-o'-shanter or a kind of stocking cap, was a great advance in comfort and became very popular in the 1880s. It was soon to be worn by girls also.

Girls' clothes followed adult styles fairly closely at first, even including the crinoline and bustle, but with shorter skirts from below the knee to near the ankle. The dress and hair-style immortalized by Tenniel in Lewis Carroll's *Alice in Wonderland* represents the simplest dress of 1860–65, worn with a pinafore. Pinafores in white muslin, checked gingham, black silk or sateen, were an accepted part of girls' dress throughout the century, and were also worn by small boys. The long hair, brushed back straight and smooth under a band, was typical if curls could not be achieved, but some girls' hair was braided, or occasionally even cropped, although this was rare; for hygienic reasons certain school authorities decreed cropping, but the practice met with considerable resistance and had died out by the late 1860s.

The over-elaboration of women's dress was extended to girls' wear during the 1870s, but from about 1880 the influence of Kate Greenaway's illustrations, which began to appear in 1872, led to the return of high-waisted dresses with simple ribbon sashes and other versions of 'Empire' fashion, though still encumbered by huge bonnets trimmed with feathers, beribboned 'baby' caps and muffs, etc. By the end of the decade girls were wearing sailor blouses like their brothers, with a pleated skirt which was also worn in the 1890s with a knitted jersey and tam-o'-shanter. Fairly simple smocked dresses, based on the smock frocks of English rural workers, were adapted for women's tennis dresses, then for girls' everyday or party dresses. 'How pretty are these old English smock frocks that have of late years become so fashionable for girls of all ages', said *Women's World* in 1888. Smocking remained popular for children's clothes into the 20th century and is still used occasionally.

Cotton or woollen stockings were worn by boys and girls, brightly coloured for boys wearing knickerbocker suits in the 1860s or plaid to match Scottish outfits, or striped in red, blue or magenta on white for boys and girls. By the 1880s ribbed wool was more popular than cotton, in plain dark colours, black, brown or grey. On special occasions girls might wear silk, over a second pair of fine lisle if extra warmth was required. Boys under the age of six wore socks, and when trousers became the fashion older boys wore them also.

Elastic-sided and buttoned boots were general wear for children until shoes buttoned or laced over the instep were introduced in 1880; these became more popular in the 1890s, when a shoe with a bar over the instep was also available, or older girls might wear a low-fronted shoe with a small buckle for parties. Heels were flat or low until the 1870s when girls' and even some boys' fashionable shoes and boots were made with moderately high heels.

Children's wear 1860-95

American, 1860-5. Boy's suit: jacket, kilt and short trousers in red, blue and green tartan wool with black velvet appliqué. White cotton shirt with broderie anglaise trimming.

French, 1864. Girl's dress in fine wool trimmed with velvet and braid appliqué; lawn chemisette and undersleeves. Boy's woollen tunic and trousers trimmed braid.

English, 1885. Girl's dresses: (left) green plush and white guipure lace; (right) cream cashmere embroidered in red.

American, 1895. Boy's three-piece sailor suit in mid blue broadcloth stitched and embroidered in navy; brass buttons. Broad-brimmed straw sailor hat.

American, 1871. Girl's dresses: (left) overdress and skirt in taffeta trimmed with self pleating and braid; (right) jacket and double skirt in silk and fine wool trimmed with braid and buttons.

Socks and buttoned boots.

As with men and women, the amount of complicated clothing worn by children during the late 19th century seems astonishing today. Eleanor Acland in *Goodbye for the Present* recalls wearing underwear around 1880 that included a vest, a calico chemise reaching the knees, stays of wadded piqué buttoned down the back with additional buttons at varying levels around the waist to support drawers, stocking suspenders and a flannel petticoat, long black wool or thick cotton stockings, and over all a white petticoat with a bodice.

ACCESSORIES AND JEWELRY

Gloves were still considered essential for both men and women. Men's gloves might be fairly heavy for driving but were otherwise made from fine kid in grey, brown or black, joined by natural chamois in the 1890s. White gloves with evening dress were obligatory; extra pairs might even be carried to a ball to ensure an immaculate appearance throughout the festivity. Women's gloves were short, to the wrist or a little above, until the 1880s when long gloves to the elbow and beyond were worn for evening and some three-quarter-length for day, all very snugly fitting. Light colours were usual, but black became rather fashionable in the 1880s. Mittens were rarely worn after the 1870s.

Umbrellas were used by men and women but were more utilitarian than fashionable until the last two decades of the century, when a tightly-rolled umbrella might be carried by men in place of a cane; both sexes took pride in owning an expensive silk-covered umbrella.

Men's canes or walking sticks were lightweight with silver knobs, or might be heavier with crooked handles during the 1880s; in the 1890s it was often considered dandified or affected for a young man to carry a cane, but the custom continued until World War I. Accessories associated with cigar smoking were carried. Jewelry consisted of scarf pins, gold or jewelled cufflinks and heavy gold watch-chains worn across the front of the waistcoat between the pockets, passing through a buttonhole or, after 1888, a special chain-hole. The monocle, associated by the Americans, Australians and others with the English 'dude', was worn around this period and into the next century, though rather rarely; pince-nez were also worn towards the end of the century.

Parasols in the 1860s were tiny, about 12 inches across, trimmed with lace and fringe, often with a folding handle; they varied in size between 1870 and the 1890s when they were large and long-handled, light-coloured and ruffled, or more dashing with, for instance, black lace over brilliant pink silk. Muffs, rather small and rounded in wool, velvet, sealskin and Persian lamb, were used by women throughout the period, becoming a little larger in the 1890s when fur such as sable or chinchilla might be used. Reticules of various sizes and shapes, silk, netted or beaded, were carried during the 1850s–60s and continued for evening and occasionally for day until the 1890s. Small, pretty aprons were worn for sewing or similar ladylike pursuits until the mid-1860s, but after that they became practical articles, worn by housewives, or by cooks in gingham or white linen, by parlour maids in fine cambric or linen with bibs, and by teachers, governesses or shop assistants in black sateen. Bouquet holders in gold or silver were carried at evening parties, chatelaines and chatelaine bags were hung from the waist in the 1890s, when decorative buckles or clasps often fastened the belt. Brooches were large and heavy and varied in design; gold and pinchbeck, garnets and turquoise set with seed pearls were popular from 1865. By the 1890s they were smaller and lighter in design, as were rings which previously had been broad and rather heavy. Sets of jewelry – bracelets, brooches and earrings, plus possibly lockets, large or small – were worn; earrings, increasingly popular as the hair was drawn back off the ears, were large from 1865 to 1875, then smaller. Cameos were worn throughout the period, gold chains between 1865 and 1890, and in the 1890s broad 'dog collars' of diamonds or brilliants (a style highly favoured by the Princess of Wales), bangle bracelets, watches attached to an ornamented brooch and decorative hair combs or hair pins set with pearls could all form part of the fashionable woman's ensemble.

FABRICS AND COLOUR
Men's clothes became even more sober in colour; the darkish blues, light fawns and plaids for trousers of the 1850s and early 1860s faded by the 1870s into a general range of grey and black, with broadcloth as the favourite fabric, perhaps slightly relieved by a rare flash of colour in a necktie, and by check tweeds for country suits or plaid for an Inverness caped coat. Silk was still used occasionally, in a ribbed form for waistcoats, and for linings and some facings. Variations during the 1890s included fabrics such as linen, duck, pongee or seersucker in lighter fawns, beige or white for summer wear, and white flannels and brightly coloured wool blazers for sport, but for town or formal wear dark grey or black in woollen cloth remained correct.

Conversely, the range of fabrics and colours widened for women, but it is important to appreciate how different the pure silks, cottons and woollens were from those of today, which so often have synthetic threads or crease-resistant agents added. Taffeta, for instance, had a beautifully crisp, light quality which made it particularly suitable for bouffant styles; satin, backed with silk or cotton, was almost firm enough to stand on its own, unlike many of the soft, rather limp satins today.

Throughout the period light colours were fairly general for evening wear and were considered more suitable for young ladies, as were cottons like muslin or tarlatan, but by the 1860s cotton had lost ground as a high-fashion fabric, and silk, satin, taffeta, faille, moiré, silk poplin from Ireland, and velvet for more mature ladies, were used for formal dresses. Many of the softer colours, both pale and dark, of vegetable dyes gave way to those produced by the new aniline dyes – strident magenta, electric blue or vivid yellow, often contrasting harshly in one outfit during the 1870s–80s; but softer, more muted colours also appeared in the fine soft woollens such as delaine, a cloth resembling cashmere but with a silk warp or weft, and in the more mannish serge or tweeds used for tailored suits and dresses. Liberty silks and the Eastern influence were gradually shifting the vogue towards subtle colours, but in general the 1890s presented an image of fairly bold colour and pattern with broad stripes, guipure lace, and passementerie braid with jet, although an increasing use of sheer fabrics such as mousselaine de soie (a fine chiffon) hinted at the softer style to come in the 1900s. Furs used for trimming, short jackets, hats and muffs were usually short-haired, such as Persian lamb, sealskin, beaver, sable and mink.

Except for the very poor who relied heavily on cast-offs from the well-to-do, the desire to be well and fashionably dressed increased considerably during this half-century. The sewing machine and the introduction of the commercial paper pattern, originally intended for dressmakers and tailors but quickly selling to the home dressmaker, the increasing number of magazines reporting and illustrating fashion from Paris, Vienna, London or New york, and a growing ready-to-wear trade, enabled a shop assistant or a maid-servant at the end of the 19th century on her occasional afternoon off to have quite an air of fashion about her, and her male escort took pride in being as fashionable as his pocket would allow and at least well brushed and with immaculate collars and cuffs. Unlike today, Sundays and Bank Holidays were regarded as an opportunity for dressing up and giving as great an impression of prosperity and wealth as possible.

1900–1939

The period 1900–39, beginning with the Edwardian era and covering the years between the two world wars, was one of sensational change, during which traditions were challenged, class barriers broken down, and exciting new styles in art, literature and music emerged. Fashion, as always in the mainstream of human activity, reflected these changes.

Already, by the early 1900s, electric light, the telephone, the cinema and the motor-car were practical realities, and in 1903 the successful flights of the Wright Brothers demonstrated the possibility of air travel. In the continuing fight for social change, women were prepared to suffer imprisonment in their demand for the vote, leaders and supporters of labour movements were shot in riots and strikes, and behind the sunset glow of Edwardian England and the lively and picturesque presidency of Theodore Roosevelt in America, rumblings of future trouble were becoming audible. For the privileged few, however, it was an age of extravagance and ostentation, lavish country house parties, balls, dinners, race meetings and sailing parties. As Virginia Cowles comments in *Edward VII and his Circle*, 'more money was spent on clothes, more food was consumed, more infidelities were committed, more birds were shot, more yachts were commissioned, more late hours were kept than ever before.' Edward VII's love of France and his incognito visits to Paris, then at the height of the legendary *belle époque*, reinforced that city's reputation.

It was to Paris that the women of America and Europe looked for fashion, buying their clothes there if they could afford to or reading of the latest trends in such magazines as *Harper's Bazaar* and *Vogue*. The fashion houses of Worth, Callot Soeurs, Paquin, Redfern, Lucille and Doucet flourished, now showing their outfits on live models in the salon and also sending mannequins dressed in the latest style to fashionable race meetings and society functions as a form of publicity. Actresses, too, modelled couturiers' clothes for magazine photographs as well as wearing them on stage. Worth sold some models to America, but the fashion industry was still in its infancy.

Female clothing at this time favoured the mature woman, with a corseted waist, full bosom, ample hips and posterior. The fashionable woman's wardrobe consisted of a vast array of gowns, coats, suits, blouses, hats, furs, feather boas, parasols, fans and gloves, outfits for morning, for afternoon visiting, for travelling by car or carriage, for dinner, for afternoon or evening receptions, for the opera or balls, not to mention hunting and sailing. This required the constant attention of a personal servant or lady's maid, responsible for assembling and caring for her mistress's clothes, accessories and jewels, and often for dressing her hair, all for a wage of about £30 ($60) a year plus her keep. Country house guests would usually bring with them their own lady's maid or valet: men also changed their outfits frequently and a 'gentleman's gentleman' was considered essential for perfect grooming and sartorial elegance.

Even before the end of the Edwardian era in 1910, radical changes were occurring in the intellectual and artistic field: the theories of Sigmund Freud, the Cubist movement

1902. Frock coat with silk facings. Double-breasted waistcoat, striped trousers. High single collar silk top hat.

1905. Princess gown in lace-trimmed cream silk muslin over silk; deep collar gives a bolero effect. Matching parasol, fine straw hat trimmed oyster ribbon bow and ostrich feathers.

1906. Morning coat, single-breasted waistcoat, striped trousers, silk top hat. Handkerchief in breast pocket.

Pink silk hat trimmed with bow and white ostrich feathers

1902. Two-piece dress, pale grey and white sheer fabric over pink silk; bodice, front, belt,

pink silk belt

slits on outer side of sleeves and skirt trimming all in pink silk.

Pink parasol lined pale grey.

1905. Hat of dark brown straw trimmed with ostrich plumes and ribbon in autumn shades

1905. Motoring toque and veil of deep-cream-coloured gauze and white feather wings.

1905. White satin bar shoe with bead embroidery, and court style in black box calf.

1906. Afternoon dress: chestnut-brown cloth with matching velvet collar, cuffs, buttons and draped belt, dull gold buckle and button-edges. Bodice has a bolero effect and elbow-length sleeves with close-fitting undersleeves. Vest of ivory silk embroidered in shades of mauve, gold and brown.

Hat of golden brown taffeta, drape and knot of mauve velvet, ostrich feathers in shades of brown.

1906. Tailored costume in purple frieze wool has double-breasted three-quarter-length coat with purple velvet collar and cuffs. Fox fur muff and stole.

1907. Chesterfield overcoat in overchecked tweed.

Single-breasted lounge suit

Black bowler or Derby.

Double shirt collar.

1906. Blouse in pale blue Japanese silk trimmed with tucks, white lace and insertions.

1905-10. White buckskin brogue Oxford

1910. White satin wedding shoe, bar-strap trimmed crystal beads.
Court shoe in dark brown velvet and brown, beige and red brocade with paste buckle.

1910. Tailored costume or suit with chinchilla fur collar and cuffs.

Wide hat with upstanding white feathers.

1910. Single-breasted lounge suit. Single shirt collar, bow tie. Light brown bowler or Derby.

Men's collars, 1905

Single   Wing   Double.

led by Braque and Picasso, the music of Mahler, Debussy, Stravinsky and Ravel, Isadora Duncan's revolutionary style of dance and costume, and Diaghilev's Ballets Russes first seen in Paris in 1909 and in London in 1911. The vigorous dancing and brilliance of colour and design of ballets such as *Firebird* and *Petrushka* with music by Stravinsky and *Shéhérezade* with music by Rimsky-Korsakov caused an overwhelming sensation.

In fashion the essence of the period was most clearly presented by one of the greatest of the French couturiers, Paul Poiret. After working with Doucet and with Worth, he opened his own establishment in 1903 and by 1905–7 had produced a revolutionary style. He claimed to have been the first to abolish the corset, a claim contested by Vionnet (who was working for Doucet in 1907) and by Lucille; but he certainly sponsored the brassière, to separate and round the breasts. He designed for the tall woman with a young, slim and pliant figure which was to become the ideal of the twentieth century. Extremely sensitive to trends in painting and design, Poiret was the first dress designer to break away from the soft shades of the late Edwardian period, introducing the vibrant primary colours used by the Fauve painters; and the exoticism and orientalism of designs by Bakst and Benois for the Ballets Russes is also reflected in his tunics, turbans, harem skirts, Turkish trousers and evening wear shimmering with gold and silver and glittering with beads. Poiret surrounded himself with artists such as Erté and Dufy and had an enormous influence not only on dress but on textile and interior design and on the presentation and illustration of fashion. Sadly, his unique individuality and outstanding ability as a designer could not adapt to the demands of the mid-1920s; his house was closed in 1929, and he died in poverty in 1944.

Although the creation of women's fashion was so strongly centred on the Paris couturiers, influences came from elsewhere and not least, around 1910, from the United States of America, where society was less rigid and stratified, greater emphasis was placed on wealth than heredity, and the younger generation was quick to take up a new craze such as the mania for dancing, no longer restricted to balls, but starting at tea-time in restaurants and continuing until the small hours in night-clubs and also in private houses to the 'player-piano' and phonograph. The Tango, imported from South America, gave rise to tango skirts slit up the front and tango slippers laced up the leg for women, and a Latin look with long side-burns and greased black hair for men, and was soon followed by rag-time. The craze quickly spread to Europe, aided by the success of the dance team of Irene and Vernon Castle; Vernon's elegant English tailoring and Irene's lithe figure, simple flowing dresses and short hair (which she had bobbed as early as 1918) were much admired. The film industry was already having a considerable impact as early as 1910; silent films attracted up to five million spectators a day throughout America and Europe, and it was not long before movie stars began to attract a following.

The assassination of the Archduke Ferdinand of Austria in June 1914 was to precipitate almost the whole of Europe into the four-year conflict of World War I, affecting also Canada, Australia, India, New Zealand, Turkey, Greece and the United States. It was not a time for fashion to flourish, but it is never static; many women were in uniform, and those who were not began to dress in tailored suits, easier-fitting dresses and shorter skirts, in the move towards greater simplicity.

The changes brought about by the war were probably greater than any before or since. With over six million fatal casualties in all, women, of necessity if not by choice, had to manage without male support; the old social structures were undermined, the

From Poiret designs 1909-17

1911. Grey velvet afternoon dress trimmed with braid.

1912. Turban made from a large square of brocaded satin

1910. Fur-trimmed brocade evening coat with smaller pattern on lower section of sleeve.

1912. Evening 'lampshade' tunic and skirt, pale pink and black satin, with bead embroidery in pistachio pink and mauve on sleeves and wired tunic skirt; pistachio pink sash, black fur round tunic hem.

1913. Grey velvet suit with matching hat. Pink scarf matches knee-length boots.

1909. Summer dress in printed Liberty fabric, predominantly carrot red.

1911. Bodice and pantaloons in white chiffon over ochre. Hoop skirt in gold cloth edged with gold fringe. Gold and white turban with white aigrette, large turquoise jewel.

1917. Grey dress and cape worn with violet boots. Cape is lined with velvet and edged with fur; collar forms a scarf crossing at front and fastened at back.

working class became more fully aware of their contribution to society and began to demand improvement in their life-style and conditions, revolution in Russia had swept aside the old aristocracy and many were to place their hopes in socialist and communist ideologies. Fashion, too, would never be quite the same; although Paris retained its lead in Haute Couture, fashion was to become less the prerogative of the few and available to an increasingly wide public.

In 1914, Gabrielle 'Coco' Chanel, successful as a modiste, opened premises in Deauville and later in the Rue Cambon in Paris to become a leading couturier and to epitomize the spirit of the 1920s. Her little jersey dresses, straight to the knee, worn with cardigans, short skirts, short hair and small hats, gave women's dress a sense of independence and emancipation. Aware of the changing way of life and its economic and social requirements, she produced clothes as smart, uncluttered and functional as the new architecture; but having removed all but the bare essentials she covered her outfits with jewelry, real or fake, and it was she who popularized 'costume jewelry'.

To call the period from 1919–29 the Jazz Age suggests the dominant flavour of that time; the original Dixieland Jazz Band, formed in New Orleans in 1916, was the first to tour Europe and intensified the craze for dancing which had started before the war. The Charleston became the rage. Dance halls and night-clubs provided the background for a new style of young woman who drank cocktails, smoked cigarettes, had bobbed hair and pencilled eyebrows and used lipstick, rouge and nail varnish, to the horror of the older generation who dubbed them 'good-time girls' and 'flappers'. Clara Bow, a film star of the early to mid 1920s, was the blueprint for this type of girl, impulsive, modern and wild; her film make-up was undertaken by Max Factor, a Pole who had been chief make-up artist for the Moscow State Theatre, emigrating to Hollywood in 1908; he shrewdly put his cosmetics on the market and became a household name.

A link between the fine arts and dress has probably never been more apparent than during the first three decades of the 20th century, and many leading couturiers were patrons and friends of artists. Art Nouveau and Art Deco styles influenced embroidery and textile design and particularly jewelry, and the combined influences of Cubism, African art and the Bauhaus were evident in the Exhibition of Decorative Arts in Paris in 1925 where, in addition to glass panels by Lalique, chromed furniture, etc., clothes designed by the painter Sonia Delaunay were shown in abstract, cubist-inspired patterned fabrics, often using patchwork (she also painted motor-cars to match!). In the thirties Elsa Schiaparelli, an Italian from a cultivated Roman family (dismissed by Chanel as 'that Italian artist who makes dresses'), linked fine art even more closely to dress. Christian Bérard designed a Medusa head for her to be embroidered in sequins for the back of an evening cape and she commissioned Cocteau, Drian and Vertès to design fabrics and buttons for her. Her association with Salvador Dali and the Surrealist movement resulted in pockets like a set of drawers or outlined like red lips, and hats in the shape of a shoe or a chicken. No dress designer has used artists, even minor ones, to such advantage since. She was also the first designer to feature the zip fastener in the 1930s, although it had been invented as early as 1919. She was accused of using gimmicks, and was well aware of their publicity value; but her basic design was. so good and her colour sense so superb (the startling 'shocking pink' which Diana Vreeland of the Metropolitan Museum of Art called 'the pink of the Incas' was to become her symbol), that she stands out as one of the finest designers of her day. As Chanel represents the 1920s, so Schiaparelli represents the escapist mood of the 1930s. Mrs Vreeland said Schiaparelli brought to fashion 'daring, playfulness and fun', to which Ernestine Carter added 'audacity, originality and the courage of her most outrageous convictions'. With the squared, broad military shoulders featured in her outfits of the late 1930s she may also have foreseen the uniformed years of World War II.

The samba, rumba and conga rhythms replaced the jazzy Charleston in the 1930s, suggesting a certain romantic fantasy, a façade behind which lay a world of considerable misery and potential horror. Germany's economic crisis in 1921, leading to a massive level of inflation, paved the way for Hitler's rise to power in 1933. The year 1929 also saw an economic collapse in America which shook the world. Britain's mass unemployment in the 1930s brought hunger marches and demonstrations. The West's fear of Communism tended to obscure the rising tide of facism, and although some politicians, artists and writers might draw attention to the problems of the day, the wealthy international set sought escape from reality, skiing at St Moritz in winter, spending the summer on the French Riviera and the 'season' in Paris or London. The less wealthy escaped to the cinema, where, for a few cents or pennies, an hour or so might be spent in a make-believe world populated by goddesses of the screen such as Garbo, Dietrich, Jean Harlow or Joan Crawford, wearing low-backed slinky dresses in a setting of languorous sensuality. This desire for escapism may have led fashion in the late 1930s to produce some nostalgically romantic crinoline gowns, such as those designed by Norman Hartnell for Queen Elizabeth (now the Queen Mother) for her state visit to Paris in 1938. But for all the nostalgia and escapism, by 1939 it was obvious to most that war was imminent.

These links between social, political and artistic movements and fashion reflect the growth of the fashion trade (France's second-largest export as early as 1927) and its need to please a far wider public. Diana Vreeland observes that 'Fashion in the final analysis is a social contract. It is a group agreement as to what the new ideal should be. There is always a degree of trial and error. Designers keep proposing something new, but whether their ideas come to fruition depends ultimately on whether the society that counts accepts them or rejects them.' As the fashion trade grew, Haute Couture had the problem of keeping some exclusivity for its wealthy clientele while widening its influence and increasing its income. The simple styles of the 1920s led to some copying, to the fury of many designers – although the masterly cut of a Vionnet model defied imitation, and Chanel's view was that 'If there is no copying, how are you going to have fashion?' Aware, therefore, that the future of fashion was in the ready-to-wear market, Patou, Lelong and Chanel opened in 1929 small departments selling ready-made clothes; and with technical advance and increasing efficiency in the ready-to-wear trade, a model or 'toile' from a famous couture house could be sold to a manufacturer, who would simplify the cut or detail and make it up in a range of sizes in cheaper material to provide a passable imitation of the original which the woman in the street might buy off the peg or by mail order at a price she could afford. To extend their influence and sales world-wide, couturiers encouraged the promotion of their designs in fashion magazines, especially those of the calibre of *Vogue* and *Harper's Bazaar*; *Vogue* launched an English edition in 1916, *Harper's* in 1926, and the reporting and illustration of fashion was to produce journalists, photographers and illustrators of outstanding ability.

MEN

Changes in men's clothes during this period consisted of minor alterations rather than any fundamental change in cut; A.A. Whife, Technical Editor of *The Tailor and Cutter*,

175

recorded in 1968 that the lounge jacket had remained unaltered in construction, although not in detail, for a ·hundred years. The main change in men's clothes, particularly after 1918, was in their increasing informality, and American unconventionality was beginning to have some influence on style.

Underwear and night attire continued much as before, but tended to become lighter in weight. Short underpants became more popular and pyjamas completely ousted the nightshirt; dashing silk pyjamas and dressing gowns were a feature of the 1920s young-man-about-town's *déshabillé*, popularized by Noël Coward.

Shirts buttoned through the front like a jacket to avoid pulling them over the head were introduced in America quite early in the century but were not accepted generally for some time, and in England not until the late 1930s. The stiffened shirt-front continued to be worn for formal day wear until the 1920s, even later by die-hard conservatives, and was considered essential for full evening dress well into the 1930s, though a soft-fronted style might be worn with a dinner jacket (tuxedo).

Separate collars of starched white linen up to about 3ins high were the accepted wear in 1900, but gradually the height decreased to about $1\frac{1}{2}$ins and unstarched collars became acceptable; the double (stand-fall) collar superseded the single, but single collars were worn with evening dress (and formal day dress until the 1920s), the wing style becoming generally accepted. Coloured collars attached to flannel sports shirts were worn from around 1910. The 'four-in-hand' method of tying the long necktie was almost universal and has continued to be so; this type of necktie and the bow-tie of medium size with square corners were the most popular forms, although the Ascot was worn with a morning coat on formal occasions. Neckties were made of plain small-patterned, woven or knitted silk in black and fairly neutral colours, and red, white or blue were very popular at the beginning of the century. Regimental, club and school ties, introduced at the end of the 19th century, became particularly popular after World War I. White cambric or piqué bow-ties were worn with evening dress or tail-coats, and black or white with a dinner jacket (tuxedo) until about 1914, but after that date a black silk bow was correct with the less formal style. Around 1910–12 some young men attempted to revive the fashion for wearing a black stock with a dress suit, but it never attained universal popularity. During the 1930s intellectuals or 'arty' types wore open-necked shirts.

The frock-coat continued for formal occasions, generally worn by older men and, by the 1930s, rarely seen except on some European elder statesmen; usually worn unfastened, it was fairly low-waisted and longer than the 19th-century version, usually double-breasted with two or three buttons each side and two buttonholes continuing up the lapels above the line of the buttons. The lapels were mostly rolled to the waist and faced with silk as far as the buttonholes. Two buttons were stitched at the back, above the tail-pleats which followed the line of the side body seams either side of the centre back vent; pockets were inserted under the pleats, and an inside or outside breast pocket might be added. The sleeves were finished at the wrist with either a round cuff trimmed with buttons on the outer side or with a buttoned slit. Made from a firm cloth such as vicuna, usually black or dark grey, the frock coat was worn with a matching or lighter-coloured waistcoat fastening high, double- or single-breasted, with lapels (occasionally a collar), and slightly tapered trousers in narrow grey stripes, small black and white checks or matching material.

The single-breasted morning coat in black with striped trousers and differing waistcoat gradually replaced the frock coat as correct wear for formal occasions (after

World War I mainly for weddings) and has continued to do so with minor alterations in width of lapel, etc. At first fastening fairly high with two or three buttons, a long rolled lapel was then introduced, and by 1906 a single button fastening became general. The cut-away at the front was swept further back, narrowing the tails, which reached the bend of the knee in the early 1920s. Later the lapels were widened and the tails somewhat shortened. Buttons, pleats and pockets at the back were arranged in a similar manner to the frock coat. The waistcoat was single-breasted and, after the 1920s, almost universally light grey. If coat, waistcoat and trousers were made of the same material, such as tweed or checked worsted, they were referred to as a 'morning coat suit' and would be worn on rather less formal occasions; in a light grey suiting they were worn during the 1930s to smart race meetings and occasionally to weddings.

The single- or double-breasted lounge jacket and lounge suit gradually became the predominant style of dress for men, and has lasted with slight variations throughout the 20th century. The double-breasted version merged with the reefer jacket, descriptions early in the century referring to 'a double-breasted lounge or reefer jacket'. Lounge jackets were at first buttoned high, slightly low-waisted and fairly long with a centre back seam and vent, sleeves finished at the wrist with a slit and buttons, flapped pockets at hip level and a welted breast pocket. American influence around 1910 produced broader shoulders and looser fit with lower fastening and longer revers. The centre back seam and vent also tended to disappear by 1918. By 1925 the jacket was shorter, more closely fitted to the waist, and had more normal shoulders, changing yet again in the 1930s to broad shoulders, a loose fit across the chest and close over the hips. In the late 1930s there were some two-piece suits worn either with just a shirt or with a sweater or pullover. Single-breasted lounge jackets had rounded fronts, double-breasted were cut square. Jacket, waistcoat and trousers usually matched, but variations could include a black jacket worn with a white waistcoat and fine-checked trousers. In the 1920s–30s the black jacket and striped trousers became *de rigueur* for the English business or professional man at work but was not considered suitable for social occasions. Colours remained sober and patterns generally small.

The adoption of the lounge suit for formal wear encouraged the popularity of the sports jacket, worn with matching or flannel trousers for holidays or weekends, walking or golf and most informal occasions. The Norfolk jacket with knickerbockers continued, now often cut with a shoulder yoke, and although rather unfashionable by the 1920s many countrymen, particularly in Britain, continued to wear it, and occasionally it makes a come-back. Tweed jackets with a half-belt at the back and sometimes shoulder yokes were popular from about 1905 until the 1930s. Sports jackets might be cut like the lounge jacket, the material and perhaps patch pockets giving the necessary casual appearance; Harrods of London advertised in 1922 'a sports lounge model with slit back, three buttons and patch pockets'. Blazers, single- and double-breasted, or flannel jackets were worn for tennis and also for the increasingly popular seaside holiday. Knitted cardigans could by the 1920s take the place of a casual jacket, especially for golf, worn with matching stockings or socks.

For day, the double-breasted waistcoat was strictly only correct if worn with the frock coat, but might be worn with a morning coat or lounge suit; buttoning high with four or five pairs of buttons, collar and revers or lapels, it was cut square across the front and had three or four pockets; it steadily declined in popularity, with a slight revival in 1923. The more usual single-breasted waistcoat, with about five buttons and often an extra vertical buttonhole to accommodate a watch-chain, lost its collar and revers,

1912.
Tailor-made
costume in
striped suiting;
Huge black velvet hat
trimmed feathers

Large sable muff

Black
straw hat
trimmed
with ribbon

1913. Formal afternoon
tunic-dress in soft grey
silk; upper bodice of
sheer grey fabric reveals
pink underbodice.
White undersleeves, narrow
fur trimming round neckline
and hem of tunic, fox fur muff.

1914: Suit with
jacket cut like
morning coat,
hobble skirt.

Boater hat

1904.
Motoring coat in
large check wool
with detachable
lining; matching cap.
Double-breasted
suit in fine check.

1913, Single-breasted lounge suit,
shirt with wing collar, bowler hat.

1912.
Long double-
breasted reefer,
trousers with turn-ups.

Dress and cutaway jacket in plain
and printed fine wool.
Hat trimmed with jacket fabric and
feather pom-poms. Long necklace with tassel,
handbag with fringe.

1911. Evening dress: pink and blue shot watered silk with tunic of same coloured gauze trimmed with embroidered net and appliquéd Honiton lace. The back section of the skirt overlaps the tunic and forms a square train.

1911. Evening dress in black chiffon over satin, embroidered with gold beads. Soft orange-pink sash, train lined with gold satin.

1912. Evening dress suit; single-breasted white waistcoat, wing collar, small bow tie; braid down side of trousers. Black patent leather pumps.

1917. Evening dress, dark grey satin embroidered in gold over lighter grey georgette.

1913. Morning coat and tunic dress for a 'tango tea'.

1912. Dinner Jacket (tuxedo) with long roll collar; high single shirt collar; black tie and waistcoat.

1912. Evening dress suit. Dress with low 'V' back for evening dance.

having a fairly high V opening and an acute angle between the front points. From 1908 the bottom button of the waistcoat was left alone, a fashion said to have been started by King Edward VII that lingered long after his death. The foreparts of the waistcoat contrasted with or increasingly matched the jacket, the back was made of lining material and had a strap and buckle to adjust the fitting. Knitted waistcoats became popular before World War I and knitted pullovers, sleeved or sleeveless with a V neck, took the place of waistcoats with sports jackets during the 1920s; colourful fair-isle patterns were much favoured, as worn by the then Prince of Wales who did his best to encourage more colourful and lively dress for men.

Early in the century trousers were fairly narrow, and by the 1920s the turn-up, considered avant-garde in 1910, was accepted generally, as was the sharp crease down the front and back, although less universal than in later years. Trousers without turn-ups 'broke' slightly over the front of the foot; with turn-ups they were shorter, even showing a little of the sock in the early 1920s. America revived French peg-top trousers around 1912 with front pleating into a waistband. Casual self-supporting trousers on a waistband without braces (suspenders) were becoming more popular, and straps and loops were added to carry a belt or, for cricket, a scarf or tie in the 1920s. The early 1920s also saw trouser legs increasing in width, reaching a maximum by 1924–5 of some 24ins (63cm) at the bottom, almost, if not completely, covering the foot and flapping around the legs like a couple of skirts; they were called Oxford bags, possibly after the baggy towelling trousers worn by undergraduates over rowing shorts, and certainly popularized by young undergraduates. However, like many exaggerated trends, they were soon out of fashion, although trousers stayed fairly wide throughout the 1930s.

Knickerbockers also grew baggier and wider at the knee and in the 1920s were ousted by plus-fours, some of which reached ridiculous proportions, very full and pouching well over the calf of the leg; but usually they were a slightly fuller and longer version of knickerbockers and remained fairly popular into the 1930s. For hunting or riding, special breeches were now worn, curving out on the thighs and close-fitting over the knee, reinforced with extra material or leather on the inner side. They were worn with riding boots or gaiters and jackets with fairly long flared skirts.

Full evening dress consisted of a black double-breasted tail-coat worn open, matching trousers without turn-ups, usually braided down the outside seams, and a white waistcoat over a starched shirt front. In 1900 the coat had a square-cut front, rolled lapels to a step collar or a continuous rolled collar faced with silk, and tails reaching the bend of the knee; during the second decade of the century the tails were cut further back and higher at the side. The width of lapels, shoulder padding, and the cut of the trousers followed more or less that for day wear, and by the late 1930s the tails were very long, reaching the middle of the calf. The dinner jacket or tuxedo continued to be correct for minor evening functions, but after 1918 was worn increasingly for all but the most formal occasions. It followed the cut of the lounge jacket with either a long roll collar or pointed revers and a step collar, and a link-button fastening was introduced during the 1920s. A double-breasted version, adopted by the Prince of Wales in the mid-1920s, became the most fashionable and popular style throughout the late 1920s and the 1930s, usually with four buttons and jetted hip pockets. Attempts were made during the 1930s to popularize navy or midnight blue as a colour for evening wear but black held its own, apart from the smoking jacket, similar in form to that of the late 19th century, for informal wear which, although frequently black, might be dark blue, brown or burgundy.

White waistcoats, considered correct with a tail-coat after 1910, were single- or double-breasted, and at first cut straight across the front; by around 1915 short points were introduced on the single-breasted style and later on the double-breasted. Black or white waistcoats were worn with the dinner jacket until the late 1920s, after which they were always black.

Men's hair was short throughout the period, with a centre or side parting or, during the 1930s, often brushed straight back. Beards were worn only by elderly men and some artists after 1920 and moustaches also declined in favour, although a narrow 'tooth-brush' moustache as worn by the film star Ronald Colman and by the young Laurence Olivier in the late 1920s and early 1930s achieved a certain popularity. The 'look' in general between the wars was clean-shaven with very short hair slicked down with hair cream or brilliantine.

All the hats worn at the end of the 19th century continued in the early 20th century and all men covered their heads out-of-doors. As the frock coat and morning coat declined in favour, the top or silk hat worn with them also gradually disappeared from the daytime scene, though grey toppers were worn for smart race-meetings and weddings. The bowler or Derby, with a flat or slightly curved brim, was worn throughout the period and replaced the top hat for formal city wear. During the 1930s the Homburg and the bowler tended to be replaced by the trilby, made popular by Sir Anthony Eden (Lord Avon); in black felt it was often referred to as an 'Anthony Eden' and was worn with a dinner jacket in the late 1930s, although the opera hat was still correct with full evening dress. The straw boater became progressively less fashionable, though its popularity lasted longer in America than in Europe; a slight revival in the mid-1930s was probably influenced by the international fame of Maurice Chevalier who often wore one. Panama straw hats were popular for country and seaside, and a variety of tweed or cloth caps were worn in the country and by young schoolboys in England and by many working-class men. In the 1920s a larger, looser type of cap, pouched over the sides and front and fastened to the peak with a press stud, was worn.

Slim fitting, narrow-toed black boots, some cloth-topped, for town, and broader-fitting, rounder-toed brown boots for the country, were general wear until around 1910–12 when shoes began to become more popular; and in 1910 a blunt round toe with an upward bulge called a Boston, bull-dog or American was introduced, and brown began to be accepted for town wear with a lounge suit. After World War I, except for elderly, very conservative or working-class men, shoes predominated. Brogued shoes (brogues), at first worn only for sports, became acceptable for informal wear; the Prince of Wales liked them with fringed tongues; also made fashionable by him were two-toned shoes (known as co-respondents) and suede shoes, previously considered not quite in good taste and the sign of a bounder or cad (and the prejudice lingered). In general, the Oxford shoe laced at the front was the most popular, but in the 1930s a shoe made in suede and leather with a high tongue and strap-and-buckle fastening, known as a monk shoe, gained favour. Patent leather remained usual for evening wear but pumps were replaced by laced shoes during the late 1920s–30s when shoes replaced boots for day wear. Plimsolls or sneakers, of canvas with rubber soles, and sandals were worn at the seaside by the late 1930s. Rubber Wellington boots and galoshes (overshoes) were used in bad weather.

Socks were of silk, wool or cotton in dark colours until the early 1920s when shorter trousers encouraged gayer colours and striped and checked patterns; they were supported by sock-suspenders. Knee-length socks (or stockings) with turnover tops were worn with knickerbockers or plus-fours. Spats continued to be worn with formal dress but by the mid to late 1930s were completely out of fashion.

The Chesterfield, Inverness, Ulster, covert and raglan overcoats continued for outdoor wear. The Chesterfield, probably still the most popular, could be single- or double-breasted or have a fly-front fastening, its length varying from just above the ankle to just above the knee, and it usually had two hip pockets with a ticket pocket above the right-hand one, and a welted breast pocket. It might have a velvet collar until the late 1920s, when the length became more settled at just below the knee or to the calf and the coat might be cut straight or, more formally, slightly fitted. The Ulster, belted and double-breasted with inset or patch pockets, enjoyed considerable popularity during the mid 1920s. In America around 1915–25 the 'coonskin' coat, made from racoon fur with a leather lining, was a craze among the younger generation, but on the whole any fur used on men's overcoats was for trimming only. Mackintoshes or raincoats with double shoulder yokes and belts became very popular during and after World War I, reflecting a military style, and were referred to as trench coats.

WOMEN

In the first decade of the century there was little obvious change in women's dress from that of the late 1890s, but a closer look reveals hints of the enormous changes which were to take place: a less rigid outline, lighter fabrics, a lower daytime neckline (often filled in with a high-necked lace or muslin chemisette) and skirts fitting closer over the hips, allowing for less underwear. The diminution in the amount of clothes worn by most women is a particular feature of the 20th century.

The basis of the fashionable S-bend, at its peak in 1904–5, was a corset, either long or short, lined or unlined, with a straight-fronted busk which started a little below the bust and continued down over the stomach without dipping into the waist. Suspenders between the bottom of the busk and the top of the stockings helped to maintain a straight line from the top of the corset to just above the knees at the front, and as the waist was pulled in, the hips were thrust back and the bosom forward. By 1907, a long svelt line was achieved by a straight corset starting just above the waist and fitting well down over the hips; less boning was used and elastic gussets were often inserted at the base to allow for some ease of movement. These corsets cannot have been much more comfortable than earlier styles and by 1912 they might be so long and tight over the hips that sitting down was difficult. For sport or negligée between 1900 and 1910 a short corset made of ribbon or knitted fabric with a slight stretch was worn, and in 1911 the first elastic belts were introduced, lightly boned, sometimes fastened at the side without the front busk, precursors of the corset adopted by young active women during World War I.

Early in the century, as the corset was cut lower, the fuller bust was supported by a bust bodice, a tight-fitting, lightly-boned bodice which evolved from the corset cover or petticoat bodice; but when the slimmer line and raised waistline came into fashion around 1910, demanding a high, more rounded bust and less underwear, the bust bodice became even more essential. Following the trend for lighter material and construction in other underwear, a French illustration of 1914 shows a simple darted band worn under the breast, just reaching the nipples and supported by shoulder straps; originally called a bust bodice, by the 1930s it became known as a brassière (the name, although French, originated in America: the French call it a *soutien-gorge*).

The ideal female figure of the mid 1920s was young and immature; all curves had to

1907. Corset in white coutil to give the 'S-bend' shape, worn over lace- and ribbon-trimmed camisole.

1900-10. Corset in printed cotton satin with light boning and cording, worn for sport or when relaxing.

1911. White cotton chemise embroidered and threaded with blue silk ribbon, and lace. Matching knickers; this open style was discontinued by c. 1913.

1913. Brassière developed from the camisole.

1912. Long corset belt made of elastic.

1907-09. White muslin combinations embroidered and threaded with pink silk ribbon.

French, 1914. Evening brassière, possibly not worn elsewhere at this early date.

1936. Brassière with semi-circular stitching under breasts.

1928. Petticoat in orange-pink silk crêpe, embroidered; gathered sections over hips.

1925. White lawn knickers with drawn thread and appliqué lace edging, elastic at waist.

1923. Brassière, pink white or black satin: silk elastic pull-on belt.

1937. Handkerchief brassière in chiffon and black lace.

1935-9 Suspender belts.

1937. Cami-knickers in pink or peach crêpe or satin black lace.

1933. Corselet in Lastex; fancy lace finish on brassière section, low back laced at waist, six suspenders.

be eliminated, so a corset was devised to keep the hips narrow and the bust flat, using panels of elastic to dispense with lacing, and later an all-elastic 'roll-on'; these were worn with a brassière made of a straight piece of material, seamed and very slightly darted at the sides, or of elastic, to flatten rather than to support the breasts. On a plump figure a roll of fat might appear between belt and brassière, so the two were joined to form a combination garment (corselet or corselette), cut straight and held firmly down by suspenders attached to the stockings to produce the required uniform flatness. Many young women, now accustomed to more physical training and exercise, needed no more than a suspender belt to support their stockings, and corset sales declined by two-thirds between 1920 and 1928.

The 1930s saw a return to a more feminine figure. For the first time the breasts were raised and separated and it was realized that women with the same overall bust measurement needed different-sized cups. This revolutionized brassière design and doubled sales. Although the waist was back in its normal position the hips were closely fitted; skirts cut on the bias revealed every curve, and the development of Lastex, a thin elastic webbing that stretched two ways, made possible light-weight belts or girdles and pantie-girdles that moulded the body like a second skin. In the summer of 1939 *Vogue* reported that the variety of models shown in the Paris Collections all had a very tiny waist, requiring a small boned and laced corset.

Other underwear followed the line of the outer garments. Around 1910 chemise, camisole, long frilled drawers (joined through the crotch from 1913) and layers of flounced petticoats gave way to the straight line. The camisole was replaced by the brassière, and only one petticoat was needed (and as most skirts were lined, even this might be dispensed with). Under the short skirts of the 1920s, directoire knickers with elastic at the lower thigh or 'French' knickers, cut circular to fit over the hips and then flare out, were worn, with maybe a vest-like chemise with shoulder-straps or a petticoat cut straight from above the bust to just above the knee. Combined garments – cami-bockers (chemise and directoire knickers) and cami-knickers – were worn in the late 1920s, the latter lasting well into the 1930s, their only claim to be called knickers being a narrow strip of material passing betwen the legs, catching the hem together at back and front. Lightweight woollen vests and knickers were worn by some, and even woollen combinations by older women and children; but during the late 1920s and the 1930s a brassière, a girdle, pantie-girdle or suspender belt, cami-knickers or knickers and a petticoat were all that the fashionable young woman wore under her dress. From 1920 on, lingerie was made of the sheerest materials – lightweight silk such as crêpe-de-chine, or fine cotton or voile, delicately ornamented with lace insertion or embroidery – and, for the best quality, all hand-sewn. Pink was the favourite colour, a fashion which spread to brassière and corset.

Until about 1907–8 most dresses were still made in two pieces. The bodice was elaborately constructed with a fitted lining, often lightly boned, fastening independently from the dress with hooks and eyes or, by 1901 in America and 1905 in Europe, press fasteners (poppers), over which the dress material was arranged, gathered from a yoke with a group of tucks to give the fullness necessary for a deep pouch at the front. Cascades of lace, boleros or zouave effects also helped to emphasize the low, full bust line. Collars were high, supported by a silk-covered wire. Sleeves were very long and plain at first, then fullness increased below the elbows and was gathered into a wrist band. About 1905 there was a brief revival of the full upper sleeve, finishing at the elbow with, in winter, a light-fitting undersleeve, or in summer added ruffles. Skirts were cut to fall straight to the ground in front and to flow out at the back, trailing for a few inches on the ground. They might have between five and nine gores or panels cut straight on the front edge and flared at the back, pushing the fullness backwards, or pleats stitched down to knee level, then flowing free, or a moderately deep flounce around the hem; but the straight front and flowing back line was always the same, until straighter skirts came into fashion around 1909–10. Skirts were usually mounted or lined. Tucks, braiding, flouncing, etc., around the lower part of the skirt declined in popularity towards the end of the decade, and some practical daytime skirts just touched the ground all round by 1905 and might only reach the instep by 1907. The join between bodice and skirt was usually covered by a belt or a shaped and draped waistband, cut to a point at the front and sloping up to a narrow band at the back, emphasizing the S-bend. This line was retained when shirts were extended above the waist around 1906, the back raised higher than the front and boned to stay in position.

Dresses made in one piece between 1900 and 1907 were most frequently in the princess style, the bodice and skirt being cut in one with panel seams, or the Empire style in which the bodice was joined to the skirt with a high waistline. From 1907 the one-piece increased in popularity as the use of lighter-weight fabrics facilitated its construction.

Evening dresses followed the lines of those for day. The neckline, cut low, square, round or V-shaped, was softened with a bertha collar or fichu in sheer fabric, or the shoulders might be exposed, with only a strap to support the bodice, and although some might be sleeveless it was more usual for the upper arm to be covered by flounced, ruffled or puffed sleeves, often of transparent material as was normally the case with the angel sleeve, a square panel hanging from the armhole almost to the ground. Flimsy materials were used over silk or satin for skirts, which frequently trailed with a frilled and flounced hemline, often with an added frill of lace or chiffon on the underside.

Between 1906 and 1908 considerable changes began to take place in both day and evening dresses; the waistline was raised, the skirt width much reduced, and by 1910 the line of the skirt had become straight and narrow and a tunic line began to appear, influenced by Poiret.

The blouse or shirt-waist (the latter name more commonly used for summer garments) was one of the smartest and most popular garments during the early 1900s. Worn either with or without a jacket, it followed the same lines as the dress bodice, usually made of muslin, net or lace (a camisole was essential under these transparent fabrics). Embellished with tucks, insertions, silk trellis work, faggoting, appliqué and embroidery, these blouses were a triumph of the seamstress's art. White was considered the most suitable colour, but some might match the skirt. A simpler type of blouse worn with a plain woollen skirt or suit was to become general wear for the growing number of women employed in business and the professions by 1910.

The tailored costume or suit, consisting of a jacket or coat and skirt, became established as an essential part of most women's wardrobe whatever their social status, and has remained so, fluctuating in popularity, throughout the 20th century. Between 1900 and 1910 the style varied widely: coats might be double- or single-breasted, cut away at the front or straight, bolero-shaped reaching just to the waist, basqued or shaped to the hip, or three-quarter-length. With the straighter skirts of 1910, jackets were usually long, often with long rolled lapels buttoning over below the waistline.

As early as 1906 Poiret was showing clothes of admirable simplicity; his high-waisted

1914-1918 Wartime Uniforms and more Practical Fashion for Women.

1915. British Women's Land Army uniform: Overall, breeches and gaiters.

1914-18. British women's war work uniform: Cap, overall, trousers and heavy clogs

peaked cap with badge.

webbing belt.

1918. U.S. Soldier: steel helmet, puttees over breeches, gas mask.

1914. British army, infantryman; puttees over trousers.

1914-18. Pilot's flying boot in tan leather and suede, lined with sheepskin

1917. Black leather dispatch-rider's boot.

1914. French army boot.

1918. British army boot, black and brown leather with iron toe-plate and nails

1915-18. Dress in fine, soft wool; fine chains worn round neck; gaiters over shoes.

1918-20. Cardigan coat in brown and fawn knitted wool and rayon.

1916. Jumper suit (skirt, blouse and jumper) in jersey fabric – an early Chanel design

1914-18. British army, lieutenant's uniform.

dresses with magyar sleeves and slim, straight skirts caused a sensation, as did his 'sack' dresses hanging almost straight from shoulder to hem, and his tunics and hobble skirts (having freed women from the corset he then bound their ankles). In 1911 he gave a Persian party to promote his Oriental mode, short hooped tunics over a variety of draped trousers, anticipating the lounging pyjamas of the 1930s.

Although at first only a select number in the forefront of fashion wore Poiret-style outfits, society was ready to accept change and by 1910 the influence of these new lines was apparent generally. The one-piece dress on the whole superseded that made in two-pieces, although bodice linings or foundations lingered on until the early 1920s and skirts in light-weight fabrics were frequently mounted or lined. Muslin dresses were popular for afternoon wear between 1910 and 1914, charmingly simple in form but with elaborate embroidery and insertions of lace, white on white; they were known as lingerie dresses. The waistline was high for daytime until 1915 when it dropped to normal, and for evening until about 1918. Daytime necklines were lowered, the most popular being a fairly high V-shape. The tunic, short or long, was much in evidence; skirts narrowed, often with a draped effect and shortened to instep level. The hobble skirt of 1910–14 often had a wrap or slit and was not as restricting as legend would suggest, although a long stride was impossible; a film clip from a newsreel of the period shows women how to move and sit gracefully when wearing it. The basic line between roughly 1911 and 1914 was high-waisted, widening at the hips by means of a tunic or drapery and narrow at the ankle, giving a peg-top effect; within this framework an enormous number of variations could be made, some charming and graceful, some exaggerated and ridiculous.

Evening dresses from 1910 were usually one-piece or with a tunic or overdress; skirts touched the ground until 1915, then shortened to the ankle; trains, cut square or pointed at the end, hung in a kind of fish-tail, and were less in evidence during the war, although long sashes with their ends trailing on the ground gave a similar appearance. As for day, skirts widened during the war but narrowed again in 1919, though they might be split up the front, side or back and to obtain the fashionable peg-top look elastic was sometimes inserted in the hem. Contrasting fabrics were frequently used in one gown – for example, pink and blue shot and watered silk combined with pink and blue gauze, embroidered net and Honiton appliquéd lace (a dress in the Gallery of English Costume, Manchester). Suits achieved the peg-top form between 1912 and 1914 by cutting the jacket slightly high-waisted and sloping the fronts away like the man's morning coat from around waist-level in front to thigh length at the back, and placing it over a skirt that narrowed to the ankles and might wrap over or be buttoned at the front.

By 1915 the influence of the war on fashion was apparent. Many women were in uniform, or undertaking work previously done by men, so for ease of movement skirts became wider at the hem, flared or with soft pleats, and as much as 6 inches from the ground. Military styling appeared in braiding, large patch pockets, buckled belts and long basques on tailored suits, and even some dressed or 'coat frocks' were rather tailored, with collar and revers, buttoned to a fairly high waist, and full pleated or flared skirts, in cotton or shantung for summer, wool for winter. The jumper-blouse, belted or unbelted, straight from shoulder to hip, replaced the tunic; often hand-crocheted or knitted and pulled over the head without fastenings, it was worn in place of a blouse. A jumper-dress was a jumper worn with a matching skirt. Photographs of Gabrielle Chanel in 1911 and 1913 show her wearing informal knitted jumpers with deep pockets, and an early illustration of Chanel models in 1916–17 shows jersey jumpers cut to hip level and open to a deep V at the front, worn with matching full skirts and matching or contrasting blouses. This casual and comfortable style clearly indicates Chanel's attitude to dress, and it influenced the adoption for everyday wear in 1918 of long knitted coats or cardigans, previously only worn for sport.

The period immediately following the 1914–18 war gave rise to a number of bizarre shapes and combinations of fabric among the fashionable set, before the straight simple lines associated with the 1920s became established. During the early 1920s, although the bust was flattened, draperies, long sashes, soft fabrics and skirts to the ankle or just above produced a very feminine appearance. It was not until around 1925, when skirts rose to 14 or 16 inches above the ground and 'waistlines' descended to the hips, that the typical twenties look arrived, and in fact it was a short-lived fashion. By 1928 flared and uneven hemlines were suggesting an easy transition to the longer skirts of the 1930s.

Bodices were straight and shapeless and by 1925 the waistline was low on the hips, indicated by a belt or band. The straight skirt, often with pressed pleats, reached a few inches below the knee, although afternoon dresses might have skirts with godets or a slight flare to give a flattering movement. Necklines were modestly high for day, V-shaped, round or square or with rather flat collars and scarf effects. Sleeves were long and plain or to the elbow, often cuffed, and many afternoon and summer dresses were sleeveless.

By 1928 the return to a normal waistline was often indicated by a loose belt worn around the waist over the low-waisted bodice, giving the appearance of a hip yoke, a feature of many dresses in the early 1930s. Circular and bias-cut skirts, some in sheer fabric and longer than the short underskirt, heralded the return of longer skirts and a more feminine appearance.

The jumper-blouse, loose-fitting to the hips, was eminently suitable for the low-waisted straight look of the mid 1920s, but as time went on the term 'jumper' or 'jumper suit' was applied more to knitted garments, which increased in popularity. Early 1920s suits had slightly fitted, three-quarter or knee-length jackets, but by the middle of the decade the most typical shape hung straight from the shoulders, single- or double-breasted to wrist length, with slim set-in sleeves. The low waist was indicated either by a belt or the position of the buttoned fastening. Skirts often hung from a silk underbodice, covered by the blouse or jumper; others were mounted on a petersham waistband; they were frequently pleated, the pleats stitched down as far as the hips to give a close fit, then pressed to hang straight. Plaid, striped and checked fabric skirts with plain fabric jackets were fashionable until the middle of the decade; by 1927 three-piece suits with an overcoat of heavier but teamed material were not uncommon, and the ensemble of dress and matching full-length coat appeared around 1926.

The basis of the 1920s evening dress was a slim straight tube, varying in length between ankle and calf, sleeveless or with shoulder straps, with a low V-shaped décolletage back and front; over this various arrangements of (usually) sheer fabric might be draped or hung, forming hip bows, trailing side panels and, in particular, uneven hem-lines. Thus, by placing sheer fabric over opaque, designers were able to lead their clients gently back to long skirts by the end of the decade. As with day wear, evening dresses were at their shortest and long-waisted in 1925–6 and some magnificent bead embroidery covering the whole dress was produced; luckily some of these dresses still survive. In 1929 evening dresses fitted closely not only at the hips but also down the

Chanel designs.
1926-1936

1929.
Jersey suit with striped pullover, typical of Chanel. Deep pockets; side pleats on skirt, braided edges. Rows of pearls, bracelets, and two-toned shoes.

1927.
Silk dress and jacket. The 'easy' pleated skirt and the flower on the lapel are typical!

1936. The well-established Chanel suit, with turn-back cuffs and collar to match blouse.

1926.
The 'little black dress' in crêpe-de-chine, with tiny tucks arranged across bodice and skirt.

1933. Dress and bolero with broad-shouldered accordian-pleated sleeves.

1928-9.
Hand-knitted sweater with trompe-l'oeil bow and collar, an early success of Elsa Schiaparelli.

1938.
Evening bolero embroidered with circus motifs.

Shiaparelli designs, 1928-38

1938. Evening suit: jacket and long skirt in dark green velvet with embroidered and beaded decoration.

Large black hat, matching gloves and shoes. Extremely long pearl necklace.

1926. Morning coat in dark grey cheviot cloth, lighter grey double-breasted waistcoat, striped grey trousers. Black Ascot tie wing collar, black silk hat.

1926. Double-breasted suit in grey flannel; broad lapels, welted pockets; full-cut trousers with pleats below waistband, Trilby hat, striped tie.

1923. Formal afternoon dress by Vionnet in gradated tones of beige georgette; long pearl necklace and drop earrings. T-strapped shoes tone with dress

1923. Formal afternoon dress in boldly printed chiffon with matching plain chiffon hanging from left hip

1928-9. Cloche hats. Make-up with heart-shaped lips, mascara, plucked eyebrows.

1920's. Shoes in puce leather with cream leather decoration.

1926. Cubist-inspired knitted jumpers and printed skirts, one with matching scarf. Fancy handbags.

1926. Silk two-piece 'Jumper' with pleated skirt, belt passing through pockets, long tie of same fabric. Black court shoes; elaborate bracelets, diamanté brooches on tie and hat.

1923. Low-waisted evening dress in beaded and plain Georgette, trimmed with fur.

1925. Double-breasted dinner jacket with jetted pockets on hips and welted breast-pocket. Trousers have braid down outer leg seam. Wing shirt collar, black bow tie.

jewelled bracelets.

1927. Low-waisted evening dress in pale orange georgette with orange and yellow beaded fringe. Shoes in silver tinsel.

1923. Tunic-style evening dress, flesh-coloured net over cream satin under-dress; orange moiré ribbons hang from the shoulders and edge tunic and hemline; bead fringes. Cream satin shoes, orange feather fan.

1925-6 Evening dress made from fringe mounted on silk base.

1926. Formal evening wear; tail coat, trousers pleated from waist, double-breasted waistcoat, stiff shirt front.

1926-8 'Charleston' girl wears fringed afternoon dress. Man wears 'Oxford bags' and sports jacket.

1929. Satin and chiffon embroidered with beads; satin skirt cut straight to knees, flared chiffon dips to one side and forms trailing bow on right hip.

thighs, and the back décolletage sometimes reached the waist, now returning to a more natural position. Poiret's pantaloons or harem trousers had a limited following, but in the late 1920s designers were again suggesting pyjamas or Turkish trouser suits in brocade or other rich fabrics for wear at home in the evening as 'hostess pyjamas'.

With the passing of the post-war decade there was a return to femininity and a more natural silhouette, mainly in formal and evening dress, and in the latter a more alluring style reflected the influence of Hollywood movies. Costume designers in the film industry were required to consider glamour and sex appeal when presenting designs for the 'stars of the silver screen', and may also have been influenced by the physical characteristics of certain actresses; for instance, Adrian, who designed frequently for Garbo and Joan Crawford, both broad-shouldered, made a feature of the broad-shouldered look which became so typical of the late 1930s and early 1940s. A balanced impression of women's dress during the 1930s must include the various influences of, on the one hand, the sexually alluring gowns worn by stars such as Jean Harlow, and on the other the sophisticated wit of Elsa Schiaparelli's designs and the impeccable taste and elegance represented by the American Mainbocher and the English Molyneux, who were chosen, respectively, to design the wedding dresses of Mrs Wallis Simpson in 1937 and Princess Marina in 1934.

The main silhouette of the 1930s may be summarized briefly as tall and slim, with a small, high bust, the waist indicated but not restricted, the skirt fitting closely over the hips and thighs then hanging straight or slightly flared to about 12 inches from the ground for day and 6 inches for the afternoon in 1931, longer mid-way through the decade and shorter by the end. For evening and very formal afternoon occasions such as garden parties, skirts reached the ankle or the ground. Width at the shoulder was achieved fairly early in the decade by the use of ruffles or gathered and darted sleeve heads, and by the late thirties shoulders were padded, becoming really square and aggressive by 1940. One-piece dresses were usual, although tunics reaching the knee or below over a slim skirt were seen during 1935 and 1936. Basques, boleros, cape collars, cowl necklines, full bell-shaped, bishop, magyar and raglan sleeves helped to give a softer, more feminine effect, and shirring or gathering over the front of the bodice and an upcurved waist seam or corselette waistline indicated the return to more emphasis on the bust. Tailored suit jackets reaching the upper hip or three-quarter-length, square-shouldered and moderately close-fitting at the waist, double- or single-breasted or link-buttoned, were teamed with slim skirts slightly flared from the knee, or straight and plain, or straight with various types of box or inverted pleats; skirt and jacket in either matching or different colours and materials were popular. Boxy jackets hanging straight from shoulder to thigh and three-quarter loose 'swagger' coats varied the silhouette from the middle of the decade, and three-piece outfits of skirt, jacket and long top coat or cape, and dress and coat ensembles, were still fashionable.

The typical early to mid 1930s evening dresses were sheath-like, skilfully cut, often on the bias, to fit closely to the hips, thigh or knees, and then flow out to a fairly wide hemline. The deep back décolletage of 1929 continued and might be halter-necked, leaving the back completely bare. Boleros and coatees were used as 'cover-ups', especially if the evening dress was to double as a dinner dress, which would have sleeves and a more decorous décolletage. As economic pressures eased a little and political pressures increased, the whole fashion trend became escapist, either into fantasy or romantic nostalgia. Schiaparelli's fantasies in 1937–8 included decorating her admirably neat and trim evening suits, straight long skirts and crisp little jackets or boleros

1933. Striped silk dress cut to form chevrons. Double silver fox fur.

1937. Grey Flannel double-breasted suit; straw boater with vertically striped band; two-colour slip-on shoes.

1937. Single-breasted blazer, flannel trousers; panama hat with striped band.

Clutch handbags

1936. Printed silk afternoon dress with cowl neckline from gauging on shoulder; 'bishop' sleeves.

1931. Beige/cream printed silk afternoon dress, with fan belt, attached scarf and sleeve finish.

1934 'Tip-tilted' hats.

1938 late 1930s wedge-heeled sandal in suede of various colours and gold kid.

1937. Suit consisting of double-breasted check wool jacket and plain narrow skirt.

1938. Court shoe made in black, brown, or white crêpe-de-chine.

1938. Lady's suit in striped flannel; fitted jacket with padded shoulders, skirt with panels cut the reverse way of the cloth. Two flowers of contrasting colours worn on lapel.

1939. Suit in red, black and grey check wool; single-breasted, two buttoned jacket fastens high. Bowler (Derby) hat has squarish crown.

1935. Evening gown in gold lamé reflecting Hollywood emphasis on sex appeal; long white fox stole.

1931 Evening dress with back interest.

1934. Garden party dress in white muslin with black spots and belt. White straw hat trimmed with cherries.

1934. Outfit for Ascot: printed silk dress, taffeta jacket with ruffled neckline and huge puffed sleeves.

1935. Exhibition dance dress made of ostrich feathers

1939. Evening dress in white satin with black appliqué; small waist, rounded hips, an ultra-fashionable shape for the time.

Headdress of black feathers.

1935. Hat in baku straw with lace appliqué on brim.

1935. Evening ensemble in soft violet dull crêpe and metallic sequined fabric.

1935. Formal hat with stitched tulle crown, trimmed with ostrich feathers.

1935. Evening suit in black ciré satin, white blouse with five silver stripes with bravura embroideries representing such themes as the planets, the circus or even *trompe l'oeil* tears. Nostalgia was represented in 1937 by a short-lived fashion for Austrian-peasant-inspired dirndl skirts and even aprons, little-girl 'petticoat' dresses with an inch or so of broderie anglaise or lace showing below a fullish skirt, Hartnell's crinoline dresses for Queen Elizabeth in 1938, Mainbocher's frilly petticoats and tight-waisted corset in 1939 and, also in that year and combining nationalism with nostalgia, Balenciaga's designs such as his Infanta dress with tight waist, rounded bust and extended hipline, exuding an essentially formal, Spanish quality.

Until about 1910 women's hair was dressed full and wide, with a bun or coil high on the head, padding and/or false hair often being used as previously. After that date styles became simpler, with the bun or coil lower at the back and the sides puffed out over the ears. Permanent waving had been introduced early in the century. Young girls wore their hair loose or in plaits or braids (a large black ribbon bow to hold it back was popular in the United States) until they 'came out', an occasion celebrated by putting up their hair and wearing skirts to the ankle or the ground. Bobbed hair, cut to about ear level, waved or curling, came into fashion at the end of World War I, and clearly reflected women's greater emancipation in the post-war years. In the 1920s hair was cut even shorter – shingle close at the back with the front softly waved and covering the ears by 1924, and Eton-cropped almost like a man's by 1925.

With longer skirts and softer lines, hair was allowed to grow longer. By 1928 it was worn in flat waves over the top of the head with curls in the nape of the neck; a few curls or a small half-fringe might be arranged on the forehead, a fashion influenced by the Duchess of York in England. Between 1930 and 1940 the Hollywood influence was strong; longer hair was brushed back with curls in the nape almost to the shoulders, Garbo's long hair was copied, and the page-boy bob became fashionable around 1936, cut to chin level and turned under at the ends. Nostalgia was also evident in hair styles in 1937–8, with hair swept up at the sides and back into curls on the crown of the head a style somewhat inaccurately called Edwardian; under skilled hands this style could be attractive, but in many cases a mass of clips and combs spoilt the line. In contrast, from Hollywood came the Veronica Lake peek-a-boo style, long and loose to the shoulders with a lock falling over one side of the face; at the beginning of World War II this style caused accidents among her many young fans working in the factories, and Miss Lake was persuaded to make a film showing how attractive she could look with her hair drawn back.

Early 20th-century milliners showed astonishing versatility, skill and expertise in producing hats varying from brimless toques to those with huge cartwheel brims in straw, crinoline velvet, lace, ruched tulle or chiffon, trimmed with gauze veiling, ribbon, roses, osprey and ostrich feathers. Until about 1905 hats with medium-size brims were worn tilted forward, often with trimming under the brim at the back, while toques were worn well back off the face. At the end of the decade enormous hats, at times curiously out of proportion with the body, were worn by the ultra-fashionable. Straight, tilted back, or towards one side, strikingly trimmed with flowers, ribbons or feathers, they required voluminous padded hairstyles to support them and long hat-pins to hold them in place. Poiret's draped turbans led to smaller 'heads', and from about 1913 the size of hats diminished, with toques, tam-o'-shanters and berets in beaver, plush or velvet, deeper and closer-fitting crowns and brims, if any, small and flat. By the early to mid 1920s the cloche style with a domed crown and small drooping or turned-back brim, sometimes dipping to one side with a feather trim, was fairly universal, though for garden parties or smart race meetings hats might have wide brims, drooping at the side and usually a little narrower at the front. Towards the end of the decade the crown became shallower and brims lifted at the front.

Between 1930 and 1940 hats were fairly small, apart from the formal afternoon kind, and included various styles such as the fez, pill-box, Breton sailor, fur toque, tricorne, beret (large and small), turban and Homburg. With the swept-up hair-styles, hats were perched forward on the head; the Duchess of Kent launched some attractive versions of this style designed by Aage Thaarup for Ascot in 1938. The page-boy hair-style gave rise to Juliet caps, also worn with the hair drawn up around them in a roll. Scarves tied peasant-fashion began to appear for casual wear in 1938–9 even in wealthy, aristocratic or fashionable circles, and the habit of tying a scarf turban-fashion around the head was to become general during the war.

With evening dress, tulle bows were sometimes worn in the United States around 1908, and turbans there and in Europe by the ultra-fashionable between 1911 and 1914. From 1910 to the 1920s bandeaux or forehead bands were worn, and occasionally feathers, but after the mid 1920s the only evening headdresses were occasional flowers or a turban or small hat worn with a cocktail dress or suit during the 1930s.

Heels on boots and shoes were $2-2\frac{1}{2}$ inches high, usually waisted until the late 1920s and into the 1930s when the straighter Cuban shape became more popular, and slightly lower, for day. Wedge heels were introduced by the Italian shoe designer Ferragamo in 1936 and were the forerunners of the platform soles and rather heavy-looking shoes worn at the end of the 1930s and during the 1940s. The toes on shoes and boots were cut fairly long and pointed until the 1920s when the bull-dog toe, like the men's, was used on some day shoes. By the 1930s toes were rounded, and the cut-away 'peep-toe' was favoured for formal wear at the end of the decade. Between 1900 and 1910, and less fashionably later, calf-length close-fitting boots, either laced or buttoned (particularly when the uppers were made of cloth) at the side, were worn with tailored suits, coats or dresses, and gaiters were worn over Oxford shoes in the country. Boots were revived for fashionable wear between 1924 and 1926 with the introduction of the Russian boot, reaching the top half of the calf and leaving a few inches of stocking exposed between the boot and knee-length skirts; it either had no opening, wrinkling at the ankle, or was zip-fastened. The fashion was short-lived however – possibly because boots suggested that the wearer lacked the means to travel by car; fashion is frequently very snobbish. Ankle boots were worn during the 1930s and the rubber Wellington boot was now common for rough country wear.

Court shoes, some with buckles, were worn throughout the period, gradually being cut lower as the century advanced; and the bar and button fastening on shoes was joined in the 1920s by the T-strap. Oxfords were laced, as were brogues worn in the country. In 1900 black was the most usual colour for day, although some shoes might have cloth tops in grey or beige. White shoes were worn for summer with light or white dresses and later, in the 1920s–30s, brown, grey and some coloured shoes became more usual; sometimes two colours, or suede and leather in the same colour, were combined. Evening shoes in brocade or satin often matched the dress, or could be glacé kid, preferably bronze. As with day shoes, two different fabrics might be combined and in the late 1920s and the 1930s heels were sometimes decorated with jewels. Court shoes with ribbons criss-crossed up the ankles were associated with the Tango between 1910 and 1916 and fairly-low heeled shoes with a bar strap with the Charleston about 1927.

Fine lisle, silk and woollen stockings were worn throughout the period, with artificial silk or rayon for the mass market from 1912; at the end of the 1930s the United States began to manufacture nylon stockings but they did not reach Europe until after the war. Between 1900 and 1910 black and white were the most usual colours but coloured stockings to tone with or match either dress or shoes were available with coloured clocks or lace insertions on the instep for the more daring and some quite bright colours were worn towards the end of the decade. The short skirts of the 1920s promoted the fashion for flesh-coloured or light beige stockings with fawn or grey as alternatives, and evening stockings might be pink or interwoven with gold or silver tinsel. The 1930s colours were darker shades of the beige or flesh-coloured range.

Women's top coats during this period might vary in length from just covering the skirt of a dress or suit to a few inches above it or at any point between hip and knee, but they usually covered the short skirts of the 1920s. Some full-length capes and cloaks were worn until 1910, but after that they were rare for day. Dust coats made of silk or alpaca were worn in summer for motoring in the early, open automobiles. Straight, narrow coats with long collars or revers rolling to a low fastening were worn around 1912–14, often embroidered or braided on the collars and cuffs or even on the upper part of a garment for formal wear. During the war they became fuller and looser, often with patch pockets and a military air, and by 1920 were quite voluminous, some very like coats worn later in the 1950s.

By the mid 1920s coats had narrowed once again, evolving into the style typical of the period with high fur collar and short skirt wrapped across at the hip which lasted, with lengthened skirt and more fitted waist, into the early 1930s. But collarless coats or neat tailored collars and revers were also fashionable, as were lace or satin coats for summer, and the fashion for matching the coat lining to the dress was introduced at this time.

The three-quarter swagger coat hanging loose from shoulder to hem became fashionable about 1932, but both fitted or loose styles were equally popular. By the mid to late 1930s the choice widened to include a raglan-sleeved, belted coat with deep pockets, a boxy three-quarter or hip-length shape later to be called a jigger, the swagger, a buttoned, fitted shape, or an 'edge-to-edge' caught at the waist by a loop or hook and favoured for summer wear teamed to the dress. All had increasing width and height at the shoulder, obtained by pleating, darting and/or padding.

Evening wraps at the beginning of the century were elaborate, with trimmings of fur, feathers, embroidery, appliqué and lace flouncing. In the 1920s circular capes were gathered into a high fur collar, or coats with fur collars and cuffs and wide sleeves might be made of the same material as the dress beneath. The 1930s long evening dresses flaring from the knee were covered by long coats fitted at the waist and swirling out to the hem, or by short wraps, scarves or shawls.

SPORTSWEAR

The steadily growing popularity of sport and the increase in paid holidays for workers gave rise to more specialization in clothes for leisure and active sports. Seaside holidays, whether in the South of France or at a local resort, created a demand for swimwear and, during the 1920s–30s when sunbathing became the craze, for beachwear generally. Bathing costumes for both men and women gradually grew smaller; in 1909 a woman wearing a one-piece figure-fitting costume would cause quite an outcry, and even as late as 1922 girls on a Chicago beach were arrested and charged with 'offending decency' for appearing in one-piece suits; but by the end of the 1920s these were

1905–10. Dust coat for motoring, in fawn silk and alpaca. Brown straw hat, green silk muslin veil.

1935 Three-quarter-length coat.

1933. Formal coat with fox fur collar; bag and gloves in matching fabric.

1938. Belted raincoat with raglan sleeves.

1910. Long overcoat for motoring.

1920. Top coat cut very full, worn with turban hat and laced boots.

1936. Three-quarter-length astrakhan coat with leg-o'-mutton sleeves.

1915–20. Coonskin coat.

1925. Afternoon ensemble: dress in beige georgette with navy piping and embroidery; blue silk coat with antelope fur collar.

1928. Straight-cut single-breasted top coat.

1939. Brown wool coat with metal buttons, wide padded shoulders, deep armholes; turban hat.

Overcoats 1900 –1940.

accepted as normal, although a built-in half-skirt across the front lingered into the 1930s. Backless costumes and two-piece bra and shorts were usual by 1935 and Lastex stretch fabric was used for swimwear by 1940. Until 1912 men's one-piece swimming costumes, often woven with horizontal stripes, might have half-sleeves and legs to mid thigh. The sleeves disappeared first, then the legs were shortened; by the 1920s the armhole had deepened, and by 1935 the sides were cut away to give a Y-shape at the back and there were also some two-piece styles for men which might have an over-skirt. By the end of the 1930s short trunks had become normal male wear for swimming and sunbathing.

Beach pyjamas were worn by fashionable women during the mid 1920s. In the 1930s they were replaced by shorts, divided skirts, flannel slacks, and play-suits consisting of shorts or divided skirts joined to or with a matching but separate shirt or bodice. Men continued to choose flannel trousers and blazer for resort wear right through the period, but in the 1920s–30s a scarf tucked, cravat-style, into the open-necked shirt made the outfit more casual and comfortable; shorts and casual shirt without a jacket was an even more informal alternative.

The amount of clothing worn for tennis also diminished gradually. Men shed their jackets first, and by the 1930s were beginning to wear shorts in place of trousers, and short-sleeved shirts. For women, necklines were lowered and skirts shortened to the ankle by 1903 and just below the knee by 1925; then, ignoring the return to longer skirts for everyday wear, the tennis skirt eventually reached thigh-level. Trousers for tennis were tried by women around 1927 but never really caught on, though masculine styling did: Helen Jacobs wore shorts and shirt in 1933 with short socks. Bare legs at first caused some raised eyebrows, particularly at Wimbledon after the long white stockings of previous years. Masculine styling held its own for a year or so but during the later 1930s the flared or pleated skirt over tight panties was more popular and certainly more becoming to the female shape. From the late 1920s sport changed from being 'just a game', played for fun, to a form of entertainment involving considerable spectator participation, and leading tennis players, like film or stage stars, introduced or influenced fashions – for example, Suzanne Lenglen's bandeau and Helen Moody's peaked eyeshade on a band. From time to time efforts were made to introduce colour into tennis costume, but from early in the century white remained firmly established, as it did for cricket.

For shooting, golf and cycling in the early 1920s, men wore knickerbockers and plus-fours and women needed fairly short skirts with flares or pleats to give the required width at the hemline; both sexes wore similar jackets, such as the Norfolk or sports jackets with back yoke and pleats. Later the increased use of jersey fabric and knitted sweaters gave greater ease of movement. Changing patterns of leisure and travel in the 1920s included a new interest in winter sports, requiring specialized clothing. Women wore short pleated skirts for skating and both sexes wore trousers tucked into socks for skiing (earlier, men had worn breeches) with long thick sweaters, jackets of waterproof fabric, and knitted scarves, caps and gloves.

The practical advantages of riding astride, known to pioneering women in the USA, were discovered by European women working on the land during World War I; and by the mid 1920s many women had discarded the side-saddle and the voluminous riding habit in favour of breeches (previously worn beneath the habit) and a jacket cut like a man's or, informally, a long sweater – although, owing perhaps to its undoubted elegance, the skirted habit and side-saddle were retained by some.

199

Bathing and resort wear 1920s and 1930s.

1925. Man's one-piece woollen suit with striped trim.

White rubber bathing cap.

1922. One-piece bathing suit with skirt, navy with white trim on belt and around neck. Stockings rolled to calf.

1935. Dark trunks and lighter top joined by a zipper so that top may be easily removed

1922. One-piece black wool suit buttoned on shoulders.

1936-7. Green and White knitted wool suit; shoulder straps pass through loop at back to form belt tying at front.

1938. Playsuit, white linen with navy trim and belt.

1936. Matching slacks and shirt worn with yachting cap and silk scarf.

1930. Linen trousers with pleated insets. Waist-length 'bloused' jacket over striped vest.

1939. Matching cotton gaberdine jacket and shorts.

Sporting dress, 1920s and 1930s

1932. Woman's golfing outfit: knitted woollen jacket or cardigan, boldly-patterned skirt. Beret, dark stockings, Oxford brogues.

1927. Golfing outfit: Tweed jacket, plus-fours and waistcoat; fancy socks, two-tone shoes

1937. For golf: blue turtle-neck sweater, tan zip-fastened jacket, grey flannel slacks.

1937. Man's riding costume: tweed jacket, jodhpurs and jodhpur boots; check cap.

1925. Girl's riding costume: grey knitted pullover, fawn cotton corduroy breeches, fawn wool socks, brown leather shoes.

1926. Woman's skiing outfit: long knitted pullover and scarf, felt cap, trousers tucked into heavy socks and boots.

1932-3. Short pleated skirt for skating, knitted wool sweater and cap.

1936. Tennis player in white flannel trousers, short-sleeved shirt.

1919. Tennis dress and 'Lenglen' bandeau.

1936. Man's skiing outfit: double-breasted windproof jacket, dark wool breeches, turtle-neck sweater; cable stitch socks, canvas gaiters.

1938. Tennis dress in cream twilled wool; navy blue eyeshade in straw and ribbon.

Changes in the distribution of wealth and fewer servants after World War I meant that more women had to care for their children's clothes, and the consequent demand for more convenient and easily washable styles, coupled with higher standards of hygiene, resulted in children's clothes becoming steadily more sensible and comfortable.

Until about 1910–12 boys were kept in petticoats up to the age of two years or so, but this practice soon died out; by 1914 small boys were dressed in short trousers and smocks or sailor suits, with straight, loose coats and gaiters for out-of-doors in winter. As previously, but now at a younger age, boys wore jackets like their fathers' with short trousers to just above the knee and long woollen socks, graduating to long trousers when about fourteen years of age. Like men, they suffered the discomfort of hard, stiff collars for party wear, and as part of many school uniforms until comparatively recently. Blazers, caps or straw boaters, with school badges on breast pockets, hat bands or caps, and neckties in the school colours or with the school insignia were usual wear for schoolboys of the middle and upper classes in England. Sports outfits followed those for men, hair was cut short and Oxford shoes replaced boots.

The dress reforms of the 19th century seem to have been revived for girls early in the 20th; easy-fitting dresses hung from shoulder to calf in soft fabrics, and what appear to be pinafore or jumper dresses were worn over a blouse or dress, decorated with embroidery reflecting the Arts and Crafts fashion of the day. To protect dresses, true pinafores were worn as they had been in Victorian times; in France boys and girls wore black ones until the late 1930s.

In the 1920s-30s girls' clothes followed women's fashion: straight, simple, low-waisted short dresses often over matching knickers, sweaters and pleated kilts, straight-cut coats perhaps with a fur trim in winter, berets or tam-o'-shanters, plain, deep-crowned and medium-brimmed hats of felt trimmed with grosgrain ribbon in winter, 'chip' or leghorn straw trimmed with flowers or printed silk in summer, short white socks and Oxford or strapped shoes. From the age of about twelve years, they wore long stockings in white, brown or black – but by the mid 1920s these could be flesh-coloured if not part of school uniform. Hair was worn long, loose or tied back in plaits (braids) with bows of taffeta or moiré ribbon until the fashion for bobbed hair for women was also adopted for girls. In the 1920s bows were perched butterfly fashion on bobbed hair, and in the 1930s the hair tended to be unadorned except for slides.

Boarding schools for girls were on the increase in Europe and most of them demanded a school uniform. This naturally varied from school to school, but the sleeveless gym-slip with box pleats from a narrow, square-necked yoke in navy, dark green or brown was the most usual in British schools and at select girls' schools in Europe, many of whom bought their uniforms in Britain. The gym-slip was worn over a cream or white blouse or shirt, often with a necktie in school colours. Plain, tailored coats or blazers like the boys' were worn out-of-doors with felt or panama hats, round-crowned, medium brimmed and encircled with a striped ribbon in the school colours or with a school badge at the front.

Girls' party dresses with frills and flounces in silk, net, taffeta or muslin were ankle-length at first, then to the calf or knee by the 1920s, and velvet capes lined with silk were usually worn over them.

Look-alike dresses for mother and daughter had a considerable vogue, particularly in the United States during the 1920s.

Children's Wear 1900 - 1940.

1900-10
Girl's pinafore
dresses;
(left) soft silk
with quilted
sections on
sleeves and
front.

1910. Boy's suit
in linen with
tucks on
jacket.

1918. Small
boy's coat in
fine wool,
felt hat.

1914-16. Boy's sailor suit
navy and white.

1905. Laced
Oxford shoe

1920-22.
White
knitted
jumper,
navy wool
skirt'n
mounted
on
cotton
bodice;
navy
tam-o'-
shanter.

1935-40
Boy's party suit:
cream silk shirt,
black velvet
shorts.

1900-20.
Button boots,
patent
leather
and white
kid, silk
tassel.

1905-15
Button
shoes in
black calf.

1926-27.
School uniform:
low-waisted
dress in navy
wool, pleated
skirt; white collar,
navy silk bow;
navy blazer;
panama hat;
black stockings
and shoes.

1922-3. Boy's
grey flannel suit,
school cap and
necktie, 'Eton'
collar.

1915-30
Sandal in
tan leather.

1939. Small boy's
coat in red wool; white
knitted hood and mitts

Gloves throughout the period continued to be essential for ladies. They were short for day, fastened with two to four buttons, sometimes by the mid 1920s replaced by an elastic inset at the wrist. Gauntlets were worn between 1900 and 1910 and again in the 1930s. Evening gloves in black or white kid or silk were very long, with up to twenty buttons, and were worn very wrinkled during the war years. For men gloves became less fashionable after the war, but were worn for warmth or for driving and rarely in summer except on very formal occasions. Both sexes wore knitted and lined gloves in winter. Leather, suede, kid or doeskin gloves were in neutral colours – white, beige, fawn, etc. – or black.

Umbrellas with long handles were carried by men and women; the men's, in black silk or cotton tightly furled when not in use, usually had a crooked handle and took the place of a walking stick in town. Around 1923–5 umbrellas with straight wooden handles about 2 foot long overall called 'cubbies' or 'dumpies', were introduced for women, and by the 1930s women's umbrellas might be made in bright colours, often matching a raincoat.

Early in the 20th century, parasols of lace lined with chiffon or silk, or in chiffon and moiré silk often matching the dress, with exquisite handles of gold, silver, carved ivory or wood with jewelled knobs, were carried by women. They gradually became plainer and lost favour completely in the 1920s when only an occasional paper sunshade might be carried. There was, however, a brief revival in the late 1930s when long-handled lace or organdie parasols matched the long-skirted garden party dresses.

Walking sticks or canes of rattan and malacca with silver handles and tips for town, gold- or silver-mounted ebony for evening, and ash, oak or hazel for the country, some containing pencils or flasks, were carried by all fashionable men until World War I when they began to decline in favour. They continued in fashion longer in Europe than in the United States, but by the end of the 1930s were generally only used at race meetings, for walking in the country, or by the elderly or infirm.

The use of fans gradually declined during this period. Small gauze, lace or hand-painted folding silk fans were used until around 1910, as were large ostrich feather fans which continued to be popular and fashionable, apart from the war years, until about 1923; but fans were rare by the end of the 1920s and throughout the 1930s. Feather boas, often finished with tassels, were extremely fashionable for day and evening wear between 1900 and 1910. In the early 1900s they might reach the ground for evening, but by 1905 they were rarely longer than knee-length for day wear. Gauze and chiffon scarves replaced the boa for evening in the next decade, joined by embroidered Spanish shawls in the 1920s.

The large flat muffs in fur or velvet carried by women in 1900 were replaced by smaller round ones about 1904 but returned to favour, alongside the barrel shape, in 1910, frequently worn with a long matching stole in sable, fox or ermine, a feature being made of the tails, paws, or head of the animal. The fashion for muffs died out during the 1920s and returned only spasmodically during the 1930s, and the stole was replaced in the 1920s by the extremely popular fox fur, usually silver fox, mounted with head, paws and tail, worn slung around the shoulders; more extravagantly, two or three might be worn together.

Handbags were to become an essential as well as fashionable accessory during the 20th century. Between 1900 and 1910 they were fairly large, in suede or leather on a metal frame for day, and brocade, beaded, or chain mesh in gold, silver or gunmetal colour (a fashion lasting until the 1920s) or 'Dorothy' style, gathered at the top, in fabric to match the dress, for evening. Between 1910 and 1920 they hung on long cord handles almost to the ground. The typical 1920s envelope-shaped handbag (pochette), fairly small in leather for day, brocade or bead-embroidered for evening, was clutched in the hand or under the arm. Shoes and handbag often matched by 1929, and during the later 1930s the bag grew in size and became more boxy in shape.

Men's jewelry was so discreet as to be almost non-existent. Finely designed watches tucked into waistcoat pockets were generally replaced after the war by a wrist-watch; after 1925 tie-pins with a simple decorative head were infrequently worn, and cufflinks, although often favoured by the sartorially elegant, were largely replaced by buttoned cuffs. Simple signet rings were worn habitually by most men and the increase in cigarette smoking gave rise to some smart silver or gold cigarette cases.

Women's jewelry, although lavish by comparison, became increasingly modest during the first half of the 20th century, apart from that worn by royalty and for state occasions. Only a few articles of jewelry would be worn at one time, but a choice could be made between clasps, brooches, pendants, necklaces, chains, bracelets, rings and drop or stud earrings (the latter more usual after about 1910). Pearls or precious stones mounted in gold or silver were popular, combined with enamel in Art Nouveau designs around 1900–10. Tiffany in New York was a great interpreter of this style. The influence of Poiret and the Russian Ballet brought an oriental look to jewelry between 1910 and 1914, and by the 1920s artificial pearls, diamanté beads and costume jewelry became acceptable. Long strings of pearls, real or false, hanging to waist level and beyond in the 1920s were followed by the very popular double row worn close to the neck in the 1930s. The nostalgic mood of the late 1930s gave rise to a liking for Victorian jewelry.

Remarkable during the 1920s–30s was the development and gradual acceptance of make-up for women. Apart from a little powder and perhaps the secret use of rouge, make-up since the 18th century had been firmly associated with women of doubtful reputation. The change of attitude must have been influenced by the cinema, and also by a more honest view of make-up as an accessory rather than as an attempted deception. With a growing interest in health, hygiene, and the general care of the body, it was realized that a slim figure and clean skin required careful diet, exercise, cleanliness, fresh air and sun. The sun-bathing cult grew steadily from the 1920s, prompted to some extent by the snobbish idea that a tan suggested a holiday at a smart resort. Fake tans were not unknown for both men and women. 'Handsome men are slightly sunburnt' was a dictum of the time.

The two great ladies of the make-up industry, Elizabeth Arden and Helena Rubenstein, were to become household names during this period; both offered not only attractive colours in rouge and lipstick but creams and lotions to care for and improve the skin. Lipstick was the most obvious aspect of make-up during the early and mid-1920s, with a fashion for a Cupid's bow mouth, but it was soon joined by nail varnish, and artificial eyelashes were available by the mid-1930s. Since the late 1920s the majority of western women have put on their make-up as automatically as they put on their clothes.

FABRICS AND COLOUR

Wool continued to be the material used for men's coats, suits and jackets: vicunas and worsteds for frock coats, melton and serge for morning coats, tweeds, worsteds and striped flannel for lounge suits or jackets, barathea for evening suits; the general tendency was for a lighter weight of cloth for day and evening wear. Colours were dark or neutral with a little brighter colour appearing in blazers, fair-isle sweaters and the checked wool used for country or racing outfits.

On the whole, sheer or thin fabrics – chiffon, lace, muslin, net, mousselaine-de-soie, tulle and taffeta – were favoured for women's evening dress, but moiré, panne-velvet and satin were also used, particularly satin in the 1930s. Silk jersey was introduced by the couturier Alix (Grès) for her beautiful draped dresses in 1937. During the economic depression of the 1930s, some designers introduced wool and cotton evening dresses.

For day wear in summer and for jumpers or blouses there was crêpe-de-chine, foulard, linen, ninon, piqué, poplin and voile, joined in the second decade by cotton drill, georgette and shantung; winter coats, suits and dresses were in alpaca, bouclé wool, cashmere, serge, tweed, velour and velveteen and, by 1910, gaberdine and the increasingly popular wool jersey. Fur fabric, real fur and leather were used from the 1920s, combined with wool or alone for winter or sporting outfits. The manufacture of artificial silk or rayon already envisaged in the 19th century made considerable strides in the 1920s with an improved finish and the quality continued to improve throughout the 1930s; it was marketed under a variety of brand names and extensively advertised, but could never really be compared with real silk and was somewhat snobbishly despised by many women.

It is only possible to generalize about fashionable colours. The choice was very wide, and, as always, individuals followed their own tastes; but black, white and navy were consistently popular and rarely, if ever, out of fashion. At the start of the century there was a great liking for gentle colours, pinks and blues, soft browns and greens, and after the Boer War khaki was popular in England. The pastel shades were overtaken after 1910 by strong, brilliant colours such as emerald, cerise and sulphur yellow, but the colour most associated with the 1920s was beige, which has rarely been considered unfashionable since. The mid to late 1930s brought back vivid colours and strong contrasts – emerald and navy, purple and brown – and Schiaparelli's 'shocking pink', a bright cyclamen, was particularly favoured.

Mention should be made here of a designer eight years younger then Poiret and much admired by him, whose work was rarely illustrated in the influential fashion magazines of his day. Mariano Fortuny, working in Venice, produced dresses and wraps which are as beautiful today as they were when he made them (and possibly easier to wear). He dressed such women as Sarah Bernhardt, Eleonora Duse and Isadora Duncan and more recently Martha Grahame, Greta Garbo, Peggy Guggenheim and Irene Worth, and his clothes have become collectors' items. His most famous dress was the 'Delphos', of finely pleated silk in superb colours, suspended from the shoulders and hanging to the ground, the undulating pleats following the shape of the body; but his coats and jackets, made from fabrics which he designed and printed himself in the style of Renaissance silks and velvets using his own unique methods, are equally beautiful. Artists and the literary set seem to have appreciated Fortuny's work most; but although he had a shop on Madison Avenue and continued making clothes through the 1930s–40s (he died in 1949), he had less impact on fashion than Poiret and others. Nevertheless, he deserves a place in the history of costume as an artist who used dress as his medium, more than for his contribution to fashion.

1940–1980

The first five years of this period, when Europe and the USA were involved in total war, was not, perhaps, a time to think of fashion; but fashion is a resistant force and also an important source of trade, so that even during the war years, in areas away from the worst of the struggle, it continued to have a following. After the fall of France, the Germans wanted to move the Haute Couture to Berlin or Vienna, but Lelong represented the couturiers in negotiating a long, hard bargain to keep it in Paris. He also obtained exemption from restrictions for twelve fashion houses, but in fact ninety-two managed to continue trading and, by supporting each other, saved some 100,000 skilled workers from forced labour in German war industries and ensured the survival of Paris as the centre for women's fashion. After the liberation, the Chambre Syndicale de la Couture Parisienne organized the Théâtre de la Mode, an exhibition of dolls or miniature figures dressed by leading couturiers in settings by artists such as Cocteau, which toured the major cities of Europe and North America, stunning the public with its brilliant design and craftsmanship.

In Britain, clothes rationing was introduced in June 1941 to control not only the number of garments that might be purchased, but also the type and amount of material used in their manufacture, and restrictions were not lifted until 1949. However, the British Board of Trade in 1942–3 sought the co-operation of the newly formed Incorporated Society of London Fashion Designers, consisting of designers such as Norman Hartnell, Molyneux (who had brought his Paris house to London), Victor Stiebel, Creed (also from Paris) and Bianca Mosca, in producing sample models conforming with the regulations. The models, well-designed and easy to manufacture, were then produced in large numbers carrying the 'Utility' label. This link between distinguished designers and the ready-to-wear trade, coupled with an influx of refugee workers from central Europe, many of whom had been trained in dressmaking workrooms in Berlin and Vienna, was to raise the standard of the British wholesale trade and boost the export value of women's clothes to around £3 million by 1958.

In America, where for so long Paris had been considered the main source of fashionable dress for women, the fashion trade was thrown back on its own resources, and a distinctive American look emerged, based on folk fashion: print cotton dresses, such as the early settlers wore, frilled cotton skirts and blouses from Mexico, fringed leather from the American Indian, Stetson hats and boots, and above all T-shirts and the stitched and riveted functionalism of working-men's overalls which, as denim jeans, have become possibly the most universally popular garment ever worn by rich and poor alike throughout the world.

The period since 1940 has been one of great progress in many fields, accompanied by much insecurity and uncertainty. As before, economic pressures and changing social ideals, attitudes and manners have been mirrored in the swiftly changing fashions over the past forty years or so, with fashion journalists and advertisers urging more people than ever before to follow the latest trend.

During the war years, uniforms were seen everywhere and on all occasions. Civilian clothes, in sympathy with the military image, were practical and restrained. Britain's acute shortage of materials gave rise to 'make-do-and-mend': a pair of men's flannel trousers could be turned into a tailored skirt, a knitted jumper unravelled and reknitted to make a child's garment, the best fabric from two old garments would make one new one, a blanket could be dyed and made into a winter coat; ingenuity and inventiveness were never more highly valued, and when stockings became scarce English women painted their legs and drew a seam line down the back. The height of luxury was a pair of 'chiffon lisle' stockings, until the American GIs arrived with gifts of nylon stockings.

Fashion-conscious British women gazed with wistful envy at clothes shown in the American editions of *Harper's* and *Vogue*, not only those manufactured in the USA and designed by such outstanding talents as Claire McCardle, Charles James, Norman Norell and Mainbocher (who had returned from Paris, and designed uniforms for the Women's Forces in America), but also those designed by the Incorporated Society of London Fashion Designers and exported to America. But manufacturers in America also were restricted by rules enforced by the War Production Board, and extravagant styles were certainly not encouraged; the trend was for simplicity, but the shortage of material was less acute than in Britain, as demonstrated by full gathered ballerina-length skirts and a more generous cut.

In both the USA and Britain, Hollywood movies continued to have a strong influence on popular fashion and the elaborately curled and 'piled-up' hairstyles they inspired was one way of achieving glamour in a sad world. From Hollywood also, publicity photographs of pin-up girls such as Jane Russell and Lana Turner emphasized the 'busty' look with high pointed breasts which was to become a feature of the American feminine ideal during the 1950s and cause a boom in the manufacture of the brassière or 'bra'.

Informality in civilian dress increased, of necessity in Britain and by choice in America, for women and whenever possible for men, but it was in America that the first concentrated attempt was made by the less affluent young to create a fashion of their own. When the 'zoot' suit worn by male teenagers in the early to mid 1940s was banned by the War Production Board as an example of wasteful manufacture, teenagers throughout the country registered their outrage – the first sign of the youthful rebellion which has become such a feature of recent years.

In France, with the couture industry virtually in the hands of the Germans after the fall of Paris in 1940, couturiers saw little point in saving cloth or labour to put money into the hands of the occupying power, so their designs featured voluminous skirts and sleeves, elaborate drapery and a general feeling of extravagance. Shortage of material was overcome with inventiveness and a certain bravado, even among those unable to afford Haute Couture. Hats in particular were made from anything women could lay their hands on – old curtains, plaited straw and coloured paper or wood shavings; shoes were soled with wood or mounted on cork. After the liberation in 1944, the press and representatives of the glossy magazines greeted these fashions, so strange and fascinating after years of austerity, with considerable excitement, some enthusiastic and some critical; but the governments of Britain and America were far from enthusiastic and tried to enforce press censorship. The contrast in styling was particularly irritating for the Americans at a time when the French government was keen to import clothes manufactured in the USA for its mass market, for whom there was a severe shortage of garments; the extreme fashions which had greeted the liberators were

1943. Black and white striped wool suit. Green felt hat with matching scarf and gloves. Plaited straw shoulder bag, black shoes.

1940 British WRNS uniform.

1940. British air force and army uniforms

1942. Man's suit conforming to regulations as to use of cloth in the U.S.A.

American army uniform.

American battle-dress

1940-45. Woman's slacks, loose-pleated at waist and with creases down the front, following masculine style.

1942 Dress from 'Utility' range.

R.A.F. pilot's exhaust-heated boot: A rubber tube fed hot air from the engine to keep the feet warm

Boot made in Belsen concentration camp from scraps of cloth and leather, wooden clog sole, string laces.

1940-43. Tailored suit in broadly striped wool with square shoulders, tight skirt and tip-tilted hat typical of war years.

CC41

British Utility symbol.

1941. Woman's laced shoe with thick crêpe rubber wedged sole.

British, 1942-44.
Woollen top coat,
small felt
beret-type hat.

French, 1944.
Tailored coat, hat
trimmed with
ostrich feather.
Huge ermine
muff.

French, 1943.
Draped dress
trimmed with
beads.

French,
Autumn 1943.
Suit with
Persian lamb
collar and muff.

British, 1944-46.
Utility suit.

American, 1947.
Mexican influence.

American, 1946.
Simple styles
suggesting
youthfulness and
independence.

American, 1946.
Little gingham dress
harking back to pioneer days.

Contrast between French couture and British and American styles in the mid-forties.

centered on Paris and restricted to a limited number of people, and in occupied Europe generally clothes were made from recycled waste paper, straw and shoddy and the average citizen was very poorly clad. However, despite the cynics' view that the Paris Couture had done well and saved their own skins and businesses, they had also saved the fashion trade for France, and in the late 1940s, subsidized by an astute government, they produced clothes which fulfilled women's desire for a return to femininity and a development of the trend seen in 1938. The Couture was particularly rich in talent at this time. Most of the great pre-war couturiers were still in business and were joined in 1946 by Pierre Balmain and in 1947 by Christian Dior. They produced clothes of superb craftsmanship and beauty, and in spite of some patriotic resistance from Britain and the USA and a certain resentment from sections of the French working class, those who could afford the prices, together with journalists, buyers and manufacturers, flocked to Paris to buy models or to adapt designs for the ready-to-wear market. By 1948–9 the soft feminine look was firmly established, and for a period of some ten years, against considerable competition from designers in America, Britain and Italy, Paris was once again to direct the female fashion scene with swiftly changing designs of splendour and brilliance.

Men also displayed a yearning for lost elegance, if a little more slowly than women. By around 1949 a style reminiscent of the Edwardian era, originating in England and known as New Edwardian, was favoured by young men about town. Although restricted to the more affluent minority, the movement was to have far-reaching effects.

By the mid to late 1950s a new generation, too young to remember the war, was growing up; rebellious and articulate, scornful of their parents' handling of affairs, they were also more prosperous and independent than young people had ever been and their appetite for innovation was enormous, so manufacturers were quick to exploit the newly named 'teenage' market, especially in the clothing trade. The clothes they chose reflected their attitude to their environment and the establishment and challenged formality, social status and authority.

The increasingly strident voice of youth was to lead to the age of 'op' and 'pop' art, the Beatles, the first discotheques, a new fashion centre in London's Carnaby Street for what *Esquire* called the 'peacock revolution', and the sexual permissiveness which followed the arrival of the contraceptive pill – a period which has become known as the swinging sixties. This emphasis on youth led to a succession of 'pop' trends which undoubtedly influenced the general fashion scene while remaining often a separate and rather idiosyncratic part of it. In their more extreme manifestations, pop fashions from the late 1960s to the 1980s have largely been confined to groups in major cities such as London, New York and Los Angeles, and the rules governing trendy dress among the young are as rigid as any in earlier periods of high fashion.

The styles adopted by young people originated from various sources. In the 1950s from London's East End came the Teddy Boys, dressed in a vulgarized version of the New Edwardian style and encouraged, no doubt, by the success of the zoot suit; in America they were paralleled by Greasers or Rockers who wore similar clothes but favoured leather jackets and, often, trousers. The film *Rock Around the Clock* with Bill Haley and the Comets in 1954 marked the beginning of rock and roll; its popularity spread rapidly throughout America, Britain and France, and its idol, Elvis Presley, like many pop singers a flashy and uninhibited dresser, started a trend for increasing informality with flower-printed shirts, excessively tight jeans, casual sweaters, and garments embroidered or printed with symbols and slogans. The full skirts worn over masses of petticoats by girls in the mid to late 1950s were perhaps a left-over from the New Look, by then discarded by the Couture, but they also owed much to an American/Mexican influence, and the tight bodice outlining high, pointed breasts was pure Hollywood.

Hard on the heels of these rather cheerful fashions came a reaction, originating mainly from the intelligentsia and art colleges and favouring thick, shapeless sweaters, black stockings and tight skirts for girls, corduroy trousers, sandals and beards for boys, duffle coats and untidy hair for both – the 'beatnik' style. Other cult or group styles of the late 1960s included 'bovver boys' or 'skinheads' in England with shaven heads, braces (suspenders), skinny jeans and very thick-soled boots; and Hell's Angels in America, in militarized metal-studded leather motor-cycle jackets, long heavy boots and peaked caps, festooned with chains and Nazi-inspired badges. At the same time a growing disillusionment with modernity and materialism gave rise to the hippy or 'flower children' groups, turning to what they considered a more natural way of life and an interest in the culture of India and Afghanistan, and dressing in ponchos, kaftans, Afghan coats and gleanings from second-hand and Indian shops. The Rolling Stones, with their iconoclastic image, surpassed even the Beatles in popularity, and the pop music scene continued to stimulate crazes and fashions for the young throughout the 1970s and into the 1980s. One of the more sensational in Britain has been the punk style, a deliberately anarchic and ill-assorted assemblage of garments worn by both sexes, including bondage trousers (the legs linked by straps across the back), fake leopardskin, T-shirts sporting aggressive slogans, and safety pins used not only for joining parts of a garment but also worn in the ear or nose as a kind of jewelry; the hair, dyed bright green, pink, purple or orange or sometimes a combination of colours, was stiffened to stand out from the head in uneven lengths or cut to a wide fan shape from forehead to nape with the sides extremely short. The interest in African and Indian cultures gave rise to 'Afro' hairstyles and Indian headbands, and the assertive sexuality of the clothes worn by many pop groups has been adopted by their ardent followers.

Sensitive to the youthful revolt against established values, two designers in particular produced clothes which epitomized the 1960s look for women: Courrèges in France and Mary Quant in Britain. Both expressed the spirit of the age and its desire for physical and social freedom in deceptively simple, pared-down garments with abbreviated skirts (christened by the British press 'the mini') and, in Courrèges' case, pants suits. Both created a complete look, with tights (essential with the mini), shoes, boots, hairstyles and even sunglasses and make-up. Quant appealed directly to the very young; Courrèges, possibly because he was in essence a couture designer (having worked with Balenciaga for eleven years before opening his own house in 1961), to a slightly more mature woman.

The voracious fashion trade demanded new designs with increasing frequency, and some startling 'op' art and see-through styles were produced. The cinema inspired some short-lived crazes such as Tom Jones ruffles and the Bonnie-and-Clyde 1930s look. But as the affluent and optimistic climate of the sixties began to fade the clean-cut mini-skirt image weakened, and skirt lengths ranged from ankle-length to mid-calf where they remained, in general, for day wear during the 1970s. Two strongly contrasted styles in London during the 1960s indicated the desire for change – the Biba revival of a slinky 1930s sexiness, challenged by Laura Ashley's neo-romantic sprigged calico dresses at the end of the decade, which have continued successfully with little variation into the 1980s.

military style helmet

Young Cult Styles
1950 – 1970s

1964. 'Beatle' suit in shiny light-weight fabric, worn on stage, influenced general fashion

Late 1950's 'Hell's Angels': Black leather decorated with badges, metal studs and chains.

Heavy boots.

British, late 1950s, revived in late '70s. 'Bovver boys' or 'skinheads': shaven or close-cropped heads, braces (suspenders) and heavy boots.

Mid-late 1970s. Male and female 'punk rockers': hair dyed in bright colours, arranged to stand out stiffly from the head or partly shaved in 'Mohican' style; patched jeans, or trousers in camouflage fabric; T-shirts printed with symbols; tattoos and earrings.

Late 1960s – 70s. The pop group image: long hair, loose shirts, sleeveless coats, boots and beads, influenced by current interest in India.

Fashion designers seem to have searched rather desperately for new ideas; following the hippy movement of the sixties, the 1970s saw an outbreak of ethnic styles inspired by Persia, Russia, Morocco, India and Japan and echoes from the twenties, thirties and forties. The dominant influence of Paris has now declined and although beautiful clothes are still being made in the couture workrooms it is the prêt-à-porter collections which are more likely to spearhead a new fashion. Highly talented designers are working in France, America, Italy and England, but none appears to be significantly changing the course of fashion. It is interesting to observe, however, that two of the most successful designers in recent years have been from Japan – the highly inventive Kenzo Takada of Jap, and Yuki whose brilliant cut and draped silk jersey dresses have a timeless quality; so perhaps a new influence in Western fashion will come from the East. The young devise their own fashions and obviously feel happier and safer with a group identity, but apart from these groups, any form of dictatorship, whether by a designer or a wealthy elite, is perhaps not acceptable in our present society and people will 'do their own thing' as recommended by Caterine Milinaire and Carol Troy in *Cheap Chic*. But since the urge to copy is strong, fashion will continue to exist whatever its source, and a clear image of the 1980s may yet emerge.

MEN

Changes in men's clothing have been slight in comparison with women's during the last forty years, but both have shown a general trend towards less formality, with men leading the way.

During the 1920s and 1930s manufacturers had endeavoured to improve the fit and general appearance of men's underwear, and from the 1940s a real change was apparent, with Y-front shorts introduced during the late 1930s competing with the 'boxer' style, and neatly fitting sleeveless or short-sleeved vests (undershirts). By the 1950s the short-sleeved T-shirt was doubling as sportswear, in imitation of film idols such as James Dean or Marlon Brando who wore them with blue jeans, and it has remained popular ever since. Earlier, Clark Gable had adversely affected the sale of undershirts or vests for some years by removing his shirt to reveal a bare torso in the film *It Happened One Night*.

Men's underwear was mostly of knitted fabric. Nylon, and later polyester and cotton blends, became commonplace during the 1950s, and some colour appeared, but it was in the 1960s that colour really caught on with co-ordinated shorts and undershirts in bright colours and/or patterns and that bikini briefs and mini-bikini briefs were introduced, creating a trend for underwear that resembled sportswear; even cover-up underwear for winter sports was coloured and featured crew or boat necklines, rib-knitted cuffs and a casual sporty look. Many older men clung to shapeless underpants or shorts and vests in plain white, but the young appreciated the feeling of being well-dressed from the skin out and the sexier appearance of the new styles.

A greater sense of fashion found its way also into the styling of sleepwear and dressing-gowns or robes. Pyjamas held their own against a revival in the 1960s of nightshirts made in brightly coloured patterns or stripes, but were styled to look like a sports shirt and slacks in the late 1940s or might have a collarless top and short trousers in the 1950s–60s or a kimono-style top in the late 1960s–70s. Buttoned elasticated waistbands replaced cord ties. Colours and patterns varied; contrasting piping and binding was used and stripes were particularly favoured. Some dressing-gowns or robes might button but the majority were wrap-over; a kimono shape, usually short to the knee, became popular in the late 1960s–70s when an effort was also made to co-ordinate pyjamas and robe. With more central heating, even in Britain from the 1960s, lighter-weight fabrics replaced the warmer, heavier kind; but owing perhaps to higher fuel costs and economic pressures, track-suit-style pyjamas in warm fabric, closely ribbed at wrist and ankle, have been available for men, women and children since the late 1960s.

The coat-style shirt worn more or less universally from about 1945 was accepted earlier in the USA than in Europe. Separate collars were occasionally worn until the late 1960s, after which all shirts had attached collars. Collars permanently stiffened with a fused interlining and the revolution in easy-care synthetic fabrics made the daily clean shirt a general habit by the 1950s. With fashionable jackets becoming more closely fitted in the 1960s, shirts might be shaped to the body, but the classic straight cut remained popular with the majority of men. The shape of the collar varied slightly from year to year: in general, with widespread points in the late 1940s and early 1950s, high, rounded and sharply cut away in the 1950s–60s, high with long narrow points in the 1970s; it might be outlined with stitching or left plain. Shirts were in plain, striped or geometric-patterned fabrics, and during the 1960s–70s there was a vogue for stripes or plain colours with plain white collars. Short-sleeved shirts in bold prints and colours for beach or resort wear were more readily accepted by Americans than by the British; in the late 1950s and the 1960s, African-inspired prints were often worn with matching shorts, and in the 1960s faded denim shirt-jackets over matching shorts were inspired by a kind of Western cowboy image. The short-sleeved jacket-type or bush shirt with two or four flapped pockets became firmly established for holiday wear in hot climates.

The evening shirt with a wing collar continued to be worn fairly frequently on very formal occasions in the 1950s but has since become increasingly rare. A shirt with a low turn-down collar and narrowly pleated soft front was worn with a dinner jacket (tuxedo) in the 1950s: then, in the late 1950s and 1960s, a combination of ruffles and pleating appeared on evening shirts and even 18th-century style ruffles at the wrist. Lord Snowdon had a turtle-necked evening shirt made for him in woven silk in the late 1960s, and the idea was quickly copied; white knitted lightweight turtle-necked sweaters were worn with dinner jackets for several seasons. Colour has been tried for men's evening shirts, but on the whole white has prevailed.

Wide neckties, sometimes up to 5 inches at the blade end, with bold motifs and colouring were an American innovation at the end of the war and found a certain following in Britain, but a conservative style both in pattern and width became more acceptable during the 1950s and the broadly tied Windsor knot was replaced by the old-style four-in-hand. A narrow knitted necktie with square ends also became fashion-able during the 1950s, and the Teddy-boy 'slim Jim' ties were almost like bootlaces. In the late 1960s, neckties with blades $3\frac{1}{2}$ inches or wider, known in Britain as 'bloater' or 'kipper' ties, returned to fashion and the bow tie, which had begun to be fashionable again in the 1950s, increased in width. Matching bow ties and cummerbunds were worn with evening dress during the mid to late 1950s, and in the 1970s evening bow ties were frequently made of velvet, usually black and 3–5 inches wide.

Although the main construction of men's garments has not varied, and many conservative dressers have changed their style very little, the fit, amount of padding, length of jacket and width of lapel and trouser leg, and the general look, have varied in a number of ways, from the 'bold look' in America during the late 1940s to neo-Edwardian styling and the 'Teds' in Britain in the 1950s, the Italian 'continental' style

1966. Boxer undershorts and T shirt in combed cotton.

1968. Nightshirt in multicoloured striped Orlon.

1948. Collar with widely spread points outlined with stitching.

1953. Button-down collar.

1950-60. Rounded cut-away collar.

1946. 'Y-front' underpants and sleeveless vest or undershirt in knitted fabric.

1971. Pyjama suit with kimono-style jacket.

1964. Shirt-jacket striped seersucker.

1959. Beach shirt printed with travellers cheques in tan, yellow and white on dark grey ground.

1970's Long pointed collar; tie with large Windsor knot.

1957. Silk bow tie with irregular stripes.

1955. Tie with small knot square ends

1969 Large bow ties

Hound's tooth check silk

1956. Australian bush-boot with elastic inset.

1969 Moccasin slip-on shoe and boot with squared toe.

Method of tying a Windsor knot.

Blue silk with beige polka dots.

1940-44. 'Zoot-suit' in broadly-striped cloth; wide necktie, long key chain, two-tone pointed shoes

1955-7. 'Drape-shaped' suit, snap-brimmed hat.

1954. Teddy-boy outfit: long checked wool jacket with velvet collar and cuffs, narrow bow necktie.

1954. Outfit for Ascot in neo-Edwardian style: wing collar, cravat with pearl pin, grey top hat, silk facing on coat lapels.

Early-mid 1950s. Duffle coat popular with students, worn with jeans and slip-on shoes.

Mid 1950s. Sweater and jeans

1950s. Teddy-boy outfit: velvet collar and deep cuffs

Mid 1950s. Teenage style worn for 'rock' sessions: full skirt over frilled petticoats.

1958. Sling-back sandal with grosgrain ribbon front in mauve, pale green, yellow and orange, white leather-covered heel.

1956. Shoe with stiletto heel in pale green leather.

Late 1950s. Straight, striped pinafore dress over black sweater and stockings; typical student style.

1955. Balmain: summer suit in pink silk, wool and Acrilan fabric; hat in fine straw.

of the mid to late 1950s, and the 1960s' peacock revolution associated with Carnaby Street. Most apparent has been the increasingly general acceptance of casual dress for town wear and even for moderately formal occasions. The morning coat is now worn only for such occasions as Royal Ascot and grand weddings in England, and the evening tail coat only for very formal functions; both garments are now often hired for such occasions, and it has been remarked that if a man's morning coat or suit fits well he has hired it, if it fits badly he has inherited it.

In 1941–2 British Utility suits for men were made of cloth with a low wool content in plain weaves restricted to brown, grey or navy, with narrow-cut single-breasted jackets, no buttons on the sleeves, no waistcoats (vests), and trousers without pleats or turn-ups. (Some men bought or had their trousers made too long and then created their own turn-ups.) In America, too, the War Production Board laid down specifications for the use of cloth for men's suits, eliminating such items as patch pockets, trouser pleats, a waistcoat or vest with a double-breasted suit, and restricting trouser lengths and widths. The orders came into effect from 1942, but custom tailors were given longer to conform than those in the ready-to-wear trade. The 'zoot' suit favoured by certain groups of American teenagers in the early to mid 1940s, with its heavily padded jacket and boxy shoulders, tapering to the waist and reaching almost to the knee, and trousers braced high and cut approximately 32 inches at the knee and 12–15 inches at the ankle, was worn with a wide-brimmed hat, pointed shoes, large cufflinks, and in particular a long key chain hanging in a loop to below the knee; often made in boldly striped cloth, it was classified as a glaring example of wasteful manufacture by the War Production Board, and traditionalists referred to it as 'the badge of hoodlums'. The style found its way to Britain in the late 1940s and 1950s; slightly adapted and described as the 'drape shape', it met a demand for sharp dressing, mainly among such groups as the London market traders or barrow boys who often added a wide, flashy necktie, and who became known as 'spivs' or 'wide boys'.

In America during 1948, *Esquire* introduced the 'bold look' for men; like the zoot suit, jackets had wide shoulders and broad lapels, but it was more a move to co-ordinate and draw attention to boldly patterned or shaped accessories, widely spread collars, wide neckties in a Windsor knot, larger buttons, 'snap' brimmed hats with broad binding, wide-ribbed socks, thick-soled shoes and heavy cufflinks and key chains. The New Edwardian style, devised in Britain a little later to capture an air of past elegance, showed a more fundamental change in cut, with slightly flared jacket, natural shoulders, slim waist, tighter sleeves and narrow, straight trousers, usually of dark cloth and worn with a white shirt. With this went a longer hair style, longer, slimmer, single-breasted overcoats with velvet collars and cuffs, and curly-brimmed bowlers.

In the early 1950s a distinctive style, at first favoured by the teenage Teddy Boys of London's East End but spreading both socially and geographically, appears to have had the curious parentage of the drape shape and New Edwardian styles. It consisted of a loosely-cut, broad-shouldered, single-breasted jacket, very long (sometimes almost to the knee), often with a velvet collar, worn with 'drain pipe' trousers or jeans; a fancy waistcoat, fluorescent pink, green or yellow socks, thick crêpe-soled shoes known as brothel-creepers, and a 'slim Jim' or 'bootlace' necktie were often added. The style was à curious mixture of American gangster and Edwardian dandy or 'masher'.

The more extreme fashions were rarely worn by conservative men on either side of the Atlantic. Britons favoured a modified version of the neo-Edwardian style and

Americans the Ivy League look, with natural shoulders and a slim line, the trousers now cut higher in the crotch and much closer fitting, revealing the line of the leg.

Around 1956 a challenge to Britain's domination of male fashion came from Italy, inspired by the designer Gaetano Savini Brioni (whose work as early as 1950 had launched Italy's post-war reputation for men's tailoring). Known as the 'continental' look, the style had broad shoulders, a short three-buttoned single-breasted jacket with a fitted waist, curved fronts, semi-peaked lapels, slanting pockets and short side vents, worn with tapered trousers without turn-ups. Its generally youthful appearance had a strong influence on men's wear during the latter half of the decade, and paved the way for lightweight and brighter suits for men; but its somewhat 'squat' line was not particularly suited to the average British and American physique, and the USA responded gratefully to the 'London line' inspired by Savile Row in 1961 – a longer jacket with wide lapels, fronts moderately cut away and flared skirt with pronounced side vents or centre vent. However, the lead in fashion was to move away from Savile Row as the influence of the dance halls, pop concerts and other activities frequented by the young took over. Zoot suits and Teddy Boys had prepared the way for uninhibited dressing and the beatniks and hippies continued this trend in the late 1950s and early 1960s in a classless style of dress consisting mainly of blue jeans and workmen's shirts combined with Indian and Afghan garments. At the same time, designers such as Hardy Amies, Pierre Balmain, Bill Blass, Pierre Cardin, Oleg Cassini and Emilio Pucci, who had gained prestige in the field of women's fashion, turned to designing for men. The Beatles, in the early 1960s (unlike their earlier beat image or later ethnic fantasies), wore Cardin-inspired short collarless jackets and slim trousers in lightweight fabric, following the 'continental' trend and in line with 'mod' fashion, which may be said to have begun in 1957 when John Stephen opened a tiny boutique in London's Carnaby Street and started what he described as 'a crusade to brighten men's clothes'. Carnaby Street became a tourist attraction, although many of the clothes sold there could be classified as merely fancy dress and were often badly made. Stephen, struggling against the basic inhibitions of many men, retained the traditional scheme of shirt, tie, jacket and trousers but introduced colour and a certain flamboyance: pink and red slacks, frilly shirts, boldly striped and patterned jackets and hipster pants. American visitors to Carnaby Street took home mod clothes which influenced their own manufacturers; and although the mod craze or 'peacock revolution' had faded by the 1970s, it left an indelible impression on men's clothes in the use of pattern and colour, particularly for informal and resort wear, and also in the cut of trousers and jeans. Hipsters, cut with a low rise, were tight fitting and sat low on the upper hip; bell bottoms, introduced around 1966, were reminiscent of Oxford bags but fitted closely over the hips and upper legs; and during the late 1960s and early 1970s the choice included such shapes as baggies, straight-legs, elephant bells and flares.

The hippy interest in Indian culture and religion was reflected in the popularity in western countries of the Nehru jacket, worn for years by Indians, including Prime Minister Nehru after whom it was named. It appeared on the international scene in 1966 in an exact copy of the original made by Pierre Cardin after a visit to India. The jacket was single-breasted with four to five buttons, cut square at the front, slightly fitted, with a $1\frac{1}{2}$-inch stand collar and skirts flared a little over the hips, and was worn with slim tapered trousers. The style spread quickly to Britain (Lord Snowdon wore a black Nehru jacket with his silk turtle-necked shirt) and to America, in a variety of fabrics and colours from flannel and twill worsted in navy, green and shades of brown to linen and cotton in white or tan and, for evening, in velvet or colourful brocaded silk, usually worn with dark trousers. Young men would sometimes wear it with bead necklaces or linked chains with large pendants, another fashion acquired from the hippies. Although the Nehru jacket was immensely popular among the fashion-conscious, its popularity faded quickly and it was rarely seen after the early 1970s.

In 1962 George Frazier wrote in *Esquire* magazine, 'What is nice about men's fashions is that their obsolescence is never obligatory. That is the reassuring thing, that they do not go out of style very swiftly. It is not that they never change but rather that they change so gradually, so almost imperceptibly, that only in retrospect does one realize that there has been a change.' For many men this has undoubtedly been true, and is likely to continue, for the present at least: in spite of fluctuations in youthful trends, young men when they want to dress up a little still put on a suit, even maybe with a waistcoat, that is basically the same as their grandfathers'.

Throughout the war years, men's hair was cut short. This continued into the 1950s when the American crew-cut, very short at the sides and back with a bushy top, found a following in Britain. From it developed the full pompadour and longish sideburns associated with Elvis Presley, while at the same time the Teddy Boys flaunted not only long sideburns but also well-greased quiffs at the front with the sides swept back into a 'D.A.' (duck's arse). Both fashions indicated a trend towards longer hair; but an even shorter version of the crew-cut known as the 'butch' cut was occasionally worn in America.

The fashion for longer hair in the 1960s, whether established by the hippies' long, untidy hair or the Beatles' deep fringes and neat 'pudding basin' style, was accepted in Britain more quickly than in America, although it caused considerable comment – as if men had never worn their hair long before! Apart from the undisciplined manes of the rather scruffy 'drop-outs' or arty groups, the longer styles required more skill in layering and shaping the hair, and men's 'hair stylists' took the place of hairdressers or barbers. Permanent waving for men ceased to be considered effeminate and hairpieces or even wigs became acceptable, particularly for men working in the theatre or films. Apart from the shaven heads of the 'bovver boys' or skinheads first seen in Britain during the late 1960s and the frizzed 'Afro' cut copied by some young white men in the early 1970s, hair has gradually returned to a fairly short cut but usually just covers the tops of the ears and a good part of the forehead.

Moustaches, apart from the full, wide type affected by some British RAF and army officers during the war, went out of fashion until the mid to late 1960s when a drooping moustache like that of the Mexican leader Zapata began to be seen, giving men a slightly sinister appearance. At about the same time long sideburns also had a brief vogue. Beards (except for those worn by the British navy) were on the whole associated during the 1940s–50s with slightly undesirable members of society; but a well-groomed beard became acceptable during the 1970s, although the average fashionable young man of the late 1970s and early 1980s has remained clean shaven.

The hat as an essential accessory for fashionable gentlemen has gradually become obsolete over the last forty years, and during the past decade distinguished statesmen, politicians and leaders of society, if not in uniform, have increasingly appeared bare-headed. The top hat has survived in Britain for Ascot, Royal garden parties and formal weddings, and the bowler (Derby) is still worn by a few men working in the City but has become increasingly rare since the late 1950s. Homburg, trilby or pork pie hats (the latter with the crown tucked in to form a flat top resembling a pork pie), varying in the width of the brim and slope of the crown, have continued mainly for the older generation, in felt, leghorn and baku straw and panama and also, since the 1960s, in fabric such as tweed or corduroy or in suede. A blocked felt cap was fairly popular in the 1950s and caps generally have been worn in the country and for sporting activities, especially with deep peaks or visors for skiing, golf, etc. The boater was revived briefly in America during the late 1950s, and fur hats appeared in America and Britain around that time; but almost unique to America is the cowboy hat known also as a 'ten-gallon', Western or Stetson (the name of its creator), with its wide curling brim and dented crown, worn by ranchers, wealthy Texans and others and symbolic of the classic American 'western' look.

Plain or brogued Oxford and monk-fronted shoes have been worn consistently since World War II, with broad fronts in the 1940s, narrowing in the 1950s to complement the narrower trouser leg and with pointed 'winkle-picker' toes on the more extreme styles. During the late 1960s and the 1970s the toe might have a rather square tip under the flared pants which also encouraged higher heels of up to $2\frac{1}{2}-3$ inches. Marketed first in Britain in the 1940s and quickly spreading to America was the 'Norwegian peasant' shoe (originally hand-made by Norwegian fishermen), a moccasin-fronted slip-on shoe which started a continuing fashion for slip-on shoes. Those of the 1960s were more elegant, often elastic-sided, and elastic insets also appeared on boots, now coming back into fashion. The Australian bush boot appeared in 1956, and the high-heeled pointed-toed Beatle or Chelsea boot in the mid 1960s. Chukka or desert boots extending to the ankle and fastening with a lace through two eyelets, worn as early as the 1940s, became very popular in the 1960s, and the liking for boots increased through the 1970s, the more extreme styles reaching calf level. Sandals for holiday wear had covered fronts and were rather heavy-looking until the mid 1950s; by the 1960s they grew lighter, but a heavier look returned in the 1970s with metallic ornamentation. Specialized footwear has developed for various sports, and the phenomenally successful training shoe, with two-colour finish, low heel and ribbed sole, has become universally accepted for everyday wear among pop stars, television personalities and the young; although much cheaper than regular footwear, its popularity was also part of the fashion revolution which demanded brighter clothes for men and an acceptance of a casual style for almost any occasion.

Apart from some belted coats in the 1950s and the classic trenchcoat, overcoats and raincoats were usually unbelted, double- or single-breasted or with a fly-front fastening, with set-in or raglan sleeves, and grew steadily shorter to reach almost jacket brevity in the mid to late 1960s, casual styles being as a rule shorter than formal. By contrast, some very dashing maxi greatcoats reaching the calf appeared around 1968–9. *Esquire* photographed one made in dark navy wool melton with black military buttons, lined with red wool. Men sufficiently wealthy and audacious might wear a complete fur coat to maxi-length, complemented by a fur hat. By the 1970s, however, top coats had reverted to a conservative length between knee and calf.

As vehicles became better heated, the need for a heavy top coat lessened; long coats could be inconvenient when driving, so many men used short car-coats or garments such as a zip-fronted windcheater (originally intended as a golfing jacket) for additional warmth. The 'British warm', of military origin, a double-breasted coat traditionally made of melton cloth with shaped body lines and a slight flare toward the hem at or above knee level, occasionally with epaulettes, was fashionable in the 1940s and influenced the short coats of the 1960s. The duffle coat, originally worn by British sailors in World War II and also favoured by Field Marshal Montgomery, was a thick wool three-quarter-length hooded coat fastened with loops and toggles of wood or horn; sold at first as Government surplus, it was commercially marketed in 1951 at a modest price and became immensely popular with students and other young men and women, both in Europe and America, and it has continued in use through the last decades. Sheepskin coats worn with the fleece inside were also popular in the 1950s and, like the duffle coat, are still worn, particularly in the country in Britain. The parka, based on an Eskimo coat, thigh-length, hooded and usually zip- or fly-fastened with vertical pockets, in nylon, polyester and cotton, cotton or wool processed for water repellency and intended for winter sports, became popular for utility outer wear. Quilting, also influenced by winter sports wear, has been increasingly used on casual outer wear for men and women. The waist-length leather jacket with fur collar worn by US Air Force pilots was adapted for civilian use; known as a bomber jacket and alternatively made of corduroy or denim, it became popular in the 1970s among the 'jeans generation' in place of a top coat.

WOMEN

The New Look launched in 1947 required little 'waspie' corsets to pull in the waist, returning to a trend started in 1939 (when a photograph of Mainbocher's little pink satin corset was published in *Vogue*). The strapless evening dresses of the late 1940s and the 1950s, although many had built-in support, brought about the development of a combined brassière and suspender belt, a little like some mid 19th century corsets but reaching from above the breasts to about 4 inches below the waist and constructed of stretch materials and non-stretch fabric such as the new Dacron which, unlike nylon, was more resistant to contour changes caused by body heat; some boning was used but the intention, claimed by the advertisements, was 'to hug, not to squeeze'. Manufacturers have aimed over the past forty years to supply women with a kind of controlled second skin, with pantie-girdles with short or long legs, roll-ons, and two-way-stretch belts. But in sympathy with women's growing dislike of such garments, the name corset is now very rarely used, and even 'girdle' has been superseded by names such as 'belt', 'body-garment', 'control garment' or 'body-shaper'. Since the 1960s, diet and exercise rather than restrictive garments have increasingly been considered a better, healthier and more sensible way of achieving the slim, lithe and supple figure judged necessary for the well-dressed.

The introduction of tights in the 1960s removed the need for stocking suspenders and reduced the sale of suspender belts, but the association of suspenders with sexiness (perhaps encouraged by the trade) gave rise in the late 1970s to a revival of these rather ugly garments which, when combined with bikini briefs or panties, form an unaesthetic pattern of straps around the hips – though they are less unattractive with French knickers, also recently revived.

The brassière, abbreviated to 'bra' in the 1950s, is still worn by most women, and from an increasingly early age, in spite of its rejection by militant feminists and the see-through fashions of the late 1960s. During the 1950s Hollywood influenced the popularity of padded and wired bras which helped women emulate well-endowed stars such as Jane Russell, Diana Dors or Jayne Mansfield, but this was a particularly British and American fashion; the French bra encouraged a high but more rounded and natural bust line and the Paris Couture never stressed the high-pointed, somewhat aggressive breasts favoured by movie stars.

Muslin lining in a taffeta jacket, curved padding over shoulder.

Grosgrain corselet with boning

1947 'New Look' foundations

1950s Black strapless corset with lace front.

1947. 'Waspie' and bra in embroidered grey muslin over pink silk.

1965. Bra, panties and knee-length socks in red and white silk.

1967. Stretch Lycra bra with nylon cups, deep blue and pink, with matching pantie-girdle.

1950s. Bra with lace cups.

1956. Waist petticoat in stiffened nylon; bra with stitched cup.

1968. Bra in white tulle with lace flowers

1963. Bra-slip in broderie anglaise.

1970s. Bra, bikini panties and suspender belt in cream satin trimmed with coffee-coloured lace.

1960. Slip and panties in crocus-yellow-coloured nylon trimmed with matching lace.

1970s. Waist slip in pale cream silk with matching lace

1967. Stretch bri-nylon 'cosi-top' and matching long pants or demi-johns in black and blue pattern.

1970s. Moulded bra and panties in cream see-through fabric.

The emphasis on youth in the 1960s demanded an almost adolescent figure as the ideal fashionable shape (the highly successful model Twiggy was only sixteen when she first hit the headlines), so bras were designed to lift the breasts with as natural a look as possible; the trend has continued, with moulded bras that support yet give the illusion that no bra is being worn, the nipple having become unremarkable in the present age.

The full New Look skirts introduced by Dior in 1947 required support, and couture garments were interlined with stiffened muslin and lined with taffeta, but often an additional full petticoat from the waist was also required, and by the 1950s teenagers wore layers of petticoats, some of stiffened net (often known as Dior net) or stiffened 'paper' nylon; some even had hoops inserted which tilted, like the earlier crinolines but with rather more revealing results since skirts were shorter.

The tight calf-length skirts of the late 1940s and early 1950s required lining to prevent 'seating' or, alternatively, a straight underskirt or waist petticoat of firm fabric such as taffeta. The full-length petticoat from above the bust to the hem-line had in the 1930s become more shapely and now began to be called a slip (a name sometimes used in the 18th century for a corset cover), but both names continued, as also for a waist-slip or waist-petticoat. In the 1960s, brassière and slip might be combined as a 'bra-slip'.

Cami-knickers went out of fashion during the 1940s but were revived during the 1970s, together with French knickers, with the return to lace-trimmed and more glamorous lingerie; but the general trend from the early 1950s, with the new stretch fabrics, was for knickers to become smaller and close-fitting and to be known as panties, pants or briefs; the briefest consisted of two triangles, the back slightly larger than the front, joined by elasticated bands across the lower hip. To prevent the pantie-line showing through clinging dresses, control tights were produced with the hip section in an opaque knit as firm as a light girdle; and the body stocking, an almost sheer seamless garment like a one-piece bathing costume or a leotard, was made to wear under the see-through dresses of the late 1960s.

Warm vests and panties in wool or a wool and synthetic mix were available throughout the period though not highly favoured by the young except in the form of demi-johns (close-fitting panties to the knee) and cosi-tops (waist-length vests with built-up shoulders) made in bright colours and lively patterns during the late 1960s; and in times of fuel shortage or extremely cold weather, long johns made originally for wearing under ski pants were worn under trousers, and woollen tights under skirts.

All foundation garments and lingerie have benefited from the development of synthetic fibres and threads which, used alone or combined with natural ones, produce easily-washable, quick-drying fabrics requiring little or no ironing, encouraging a greatly increased standard of hygiene. Pink, cream and white have been consistently popular colours for underwear, but black was rather favoured in the late 1950s and bright, strong colours during the 1960s; deep burgundy, light and dark coffee and rich blues appeared during the 1970s but mainly in the more expensive ranges of lingerie. The new man-made fabrics also brought flimsy and glamorous nightwear within the price-range of most women. Although sheer and delicate-looking, they were remarkably strong and easily washed and drip-dried. The variety of styles has been almost as great as that for day wear, but perhaps particularly notable was the 'baby doll' nightdress or pyjama, first popular during the late 1950s and the 1960s, full and very short, just covering the crotch, with matching panties or briefs.

The line for day dresses and suits during the war years was straight and square. The late 1930s width at the shoulder was often obtained by gathered, pleated or darted sleeve-heads, but the early to mid 1940s shoulder line was more masculine, padded to the tip of the shoulder with the sleeve hanging straight from that point; even with magyar sleeves the shoulder was heavily padded. The shirt-waist dress buttoned to the waist was one of the most frequently worn styles, often with a small shoulder yoke, then gathered or 'soft-darted' to the waist, and with plain, straight, long or short cuffed sleeves, a shirt-type collar and a short straight skirt with a kick-pleat at the back and a hemline about 18 inches from the ground. Two colours, textures or fabrics might be used in one dress, often the outcome of 'make-do-and-mend' economies or as a way of varying a simple design.

Throughout the 1940s the practical pinafore dress, which could be worn with a sweater for warmth or varied with different blouses, found favour on both sides of the Atlantic, as did a bolero effect, fake or real. Jacket-and-dress outfits were popular, and jackets, whether worn with a dress or a matching skirt, were usually single-breasted; British Utility models were restricted to three buttons, fastening high with small collar and revers, and often featured raised or stitched seams and slanting or patch pockets. Suit skirts might be cut with panels but most were plain with one or two inverted pleats.

Afternoon dresses were a little softer, with some gauging or drapery on the bodice and maybe a gentle flare to the skirt in Britain or a more generous one in America. Clothes made in Britain for export to the USA were more elaborate than those for the home market, and evening dresses were more frequently worn in America than in Britain where, by 1943, a long-skirted evening dress was rare at public functions, although still worn for some private parties in very modest styles. A blouse worn with a long skirt was one answer to the problem, as the blouse could be worn with a suit during the day. For evening wear at home, long house-coats, introduced in the 1930s, were convenient and easy to change into; usually of warm material, they were zipped or buttoned down the front, cut with a yoke or with panel seams, belted or unbelted, usually with pockets, and had long or short sleeves, sometimes puffed or of a bishop cut. American influences came not only from Hollywood: cut off from Paris, whose lead they had so assiduously followed, Americans discovered they had some excellent native talent. Outstanding was Claire McCardell, a product of what was to become Parson's School of Design in New York; in the 1940s she was ahead of Dior in discarding shoulder padding and lowering the hemline on full circular skirts; in 1943 she also introduced the leotard, a forerunner of the body-stocking, and flat ballet-type slippers which were to become immensely popular with teenagers in the 1950s. Claire McCardell's simple fabrics – calico, cotton voile, seersucker, dotted Swiss muslin and, above all, denim stitched as on jeans – and her clean-cut, casual chic created an essentially American style, easy, comfortable and confident with perhaps a hint of pioneer days, and based on immaculate grooming. Hard upon her heels was Bonnie Cashin who started designing clothes for films and later opened her own design studio; as well as being one of the first, as early as 1944, to promote boots as fashion accessories, she introduced the layered look a good fifteen years ahead of Europe. To her and to America generally must be credited the later popularity of 'separates' and mix-and-match.

For roughly fifteen years from 1947, in spite of good designers working in Britain and America and a growing challenge from Italy (Pucci in Florence, Simonetta, Fabriani and Galitzine in Rome), it was Paris that provided an unquestioned leadership in women's fashion, with a positive cornucopia of ideas. Cutting skills reached an astonishing level; cloth was moulded with sculptural expertise into beautiful or fantastic shapes and the standard of tailoring, dressmaking and embroidery was impeccable.

Christian Dior's name dominated the headlines from 1947 until his early death in 1957, owing partly at least to his gift for publicity; but Paris almost overflowed with brilliant talent – Balenciaga, perhaps the greatest dress-designer of his day, Alix (Grès), notable for the timeless, classic perfection of her superb draped dresses, Jacques Fath, Givenchy, Balmain, Cardin and Nina Ricci, to mention but a few. In 1954 Chanel re-opened her couture house and within a few years versions of her little understated braid-edged suits were being worn throughout the western world. The greatest impact was that of Dior's New Look in 1947: the slightly sloping shoulders, clinched waist, rounded hips and full, calf-length skirt required not only skilled cutting but an interlining of muslin for bodices and jackets to hold the skin-tight fit, discreet padding over the shoulders and hips, and stiffening to hold out the skirts. Some of Dior's dresses and suits almost stood up by themselves, supported by their foundation fabrics which, together with the quality of cloth, tailoring or dressmaking, were never equalled in copies of the originals.

Competing with the full-skirted styles was a slender line. Dior showed skirts with trouser pleats from the waist tapering to a narrow hemline alongside his full skirts in 1947, and extremely tight calf-length skirts fitting closely down the thighs were featured throughout the 1950s and used by Dior for his H-line in 1954. Model girls were photographed standing with one leg behind the other to help achieve this ultra-slim line; a few strategically placed clothes-pegs often held back the skirt. To make walking easier, slits or, more often, pleats were arranged at the centre back.

Suit jackets worn with the slim skirts between 1950 and 1955 were easy-fitting with a somewhat rounded back but fitted closely around the hips; later in the 1950s they were often short, a few inches below the waist but still fairly loose, just skimming the body; the collar or neckline stood away from the neck, and sleeves were three-quarter length. This length of sleeve and a collarless, standing-away neckline were also a notable feature on suits and some coats during the early 1960s.

Dior's A-line in 1957, close and narrow at the rib-cage, then gently spreading to the wide hemline, reintroduced the wide skirt in couture clothes and also marked a final departure from the tight waistline. Yves St Laurent at the house of Dior developed this line in 1958, after the master's death, in his 'trapeze' dress, a little looser over the bust and firmly lined to hold a triangular shape, with the wide hemline slightly shorter than before. An alternative line, narrow around the hem, was featured by Givenchy and Guy Laroche in 1957 and by Jacques Fath in 1958, among others, in the 'sack' dress with natural shoulders, usually three-quarter-length sleeves and a very loose-fitting body section tapering to just below the knee or high on the calf.

During these years the choice for evening wear was immense. Strapless bodices, supported by boning or mounted on a boned under-bodice, were very popular but not universal, although evening dresses at this time rarely had sleeves. The waist was clearly defined and usually close-fitting, and even with the loose trapeze in 1958 the waistline was often marked at the front. Skirts were slim or full (the fullness balanced equally all round or flowing towards the back) and to the ground, even sometimes trailing, and materials such as satin, taffeta, faille patterned or plain, tulle, lace and exquisite embroidery were used to produce dresses of outstanding beauty. Less formal

Spring 1947. Dior: satin afternoon dress

1950. White dinner jacket (tuxedo) for tropical wear.

Spring, 1947. Dior evening dress in black silk and tulle.

Spring 1947. Dior: cream tussore silk jacket, very full pleated skirt in black wool.

1950-55. Man's formal day wear: coat with velvet collar, fly-front fastening; bowler (Derby) hat.

1945-47 Black satin ankle-strap sandal

1947. Black suede peep-toe shoe with platform sole.

1950. Man's shoe in brushed leather.

Spring 1947. Dior: coat in fine wool with small close-fitting waist and pocket flaps emphasising the roundness of the hips.

Autumn 1947. Ready-to-wear copy of Dior's 'NEW LOOK' suit in navy and white printed rayon.

1950. Mass production copy of Dior dress in black and white patterned and plain rayon.

1954. Balmain: dress and stole in fine wool, stole lined with Persian lamb. Small beret.

1958. Yves St. Laurent for the house of Dior: Trapeze-line dress, collar standing away from neck, with long bow in same fabric. Long ruched gloves.

1958. 'Italian style' suit in worsted wool; short-waisted jacket, tapered trousers without turn-ups.

1959. 'British-style' suit, broad shoulders, peaked lapels, deep side vents on jacket.

1954. Dior: H-line suit; collar slopes to gentle natural shoulder, sleeves cut just above wrist are level with edge of jacket. Hat brim in the popular long-haired felt.

1955. Dior A-line suit; spacing between buttons increases to follow line of three-quarter-length jacket.

1954. Man's felt hat with wide grosgrain ribbon.

1956. Man's pork pie hat with matching felt band.

1950s. Tweed cap with concealed peak.

1957. Balenciaga: Suit with collarless, semi-fitted jacket and narrow skirt.

1958. Griffe: Sack-line dress, cloche felt hat with broad ribbon.

Evening Wear 1950s.

1955. Pale pink silk organza appliqued with satin and embroidered with sparkling beads. Matching pink tulle stole and long kid gloves.

1958. Balenciaga's evening dress line: short skirt flowing to a train, ruffle-edged; high waist with narrow sash.

1958. Ball gown in pink acetate and lurex brocade; short front panel, sides sweeping down to form train.

1956. Balmain: slim line in satin, worn with full-length fur coat and muff.

The hobbled 'puff ball' or bubble line.

1958. Trapeze-line in navy organza with matching stole. Jewel at centre of high bodice.

1960. Italian-designed mule in coral red fabric.

1959. Evening shoe in white satin embroidered in silver and beads with white lace, by Roger Vivier for the House of Dior.

Yves St. Laurent

Givenchy

or 'cocktail' dresses had calf-length skirts, and full-skirted ballerina-length dresses were convenient for dancing. Around 1958 Balenciaga lifted the front hemline of formal evening dresses, retaining the full length or even a train at the back, thus reversing the late-1920s transition from short to long skirts, and St Laurent's trapeze evening dresses were short-skirted. A short skirt was also necessary for the puff-ball style introduced by Givenchy around 1957 and quickly copied throughout the western world: the skirt, gathered or pleated from a tight waist, was also gathered into a band around the knees and mounted on a shorter underskirt to hold the puffed line.

The younger element in society, moving away from the domination of Paris, was at first happy with wide skirts and frilly petticoats but began to revolt as the 'beat' generation began to assert itself, assuming, as do many revolutionary movements, a uniform – black stockings, short hip-hugging skirts or pinafore dresses and loose sweaters – which became known in Britain as the Chelsea Look. To meet this youthful search for an independent fashion, Mary Quant opened her first Bazaar shop in 1955 and became increasingly successful. Yves St Laurent, also sensitive to the new atmosphere, presented a 'beat' collection in 1960 which brought his career at the House of Dior to an abrupt end at the age of twenty-five; he later opened his own fashion house, showing his first independent collection in 1962 and eventually establishing himself as one of the most successful designers of his day, with over a hundred of his Rive Gauche shops all over the world, but his departure from Dior was another signal that a change of leadership in fashion was about to take place and that the influence of the Paris Couture would gradually fade throughout the 1960s.

The trend towards a more youthful style was apparent in Cardin's collection in 1958, but it was Courrèges and Mary Quant who caught the true feeling of the 1960s. In 1964 Courrèges raised skirts above the knee and in the following year Quant raised them a little higher; but the essence of mid 1960s fashion was not only the short skirt. A complete change in the ideal image, from the elegant sophisticate of apparently impeccable background or the sexy 'sweater girl' to an adrogynous childlike creature from almost anywhere, demonstrated the gap in attitudes between the generations in morals, manners and values. Little dresses, coats or suits in simple shirt shapes had narrow shoulders, slim-fitting long or short sleeves (often cap sleeves at Courrèges) or none, skirts varied in length from just above the knee to the upper thigh, and detail was minimal. The Courrèges shifts often flared slightly and his favourite fabric, gaberdine, enabled him to shape them with architectural precision, outlining the construction with welted or raised seams. White was his favourite colour, with pale pink and ice blue close runners-up, and when he used patterned fabric it tended to be boldly and widely striped or checked. Quant's designs and those of her followers were much less sculptured in shape; John Bates in particular showed rather pretty, far less aggressive clothes. Op art patterns were used on the simple shifts, and St Laurent's 1966 collection showed some prints clearly inspired by the paintings of Mondrian.

As an alternative to the leg-revealing mini skirt, trousers became fashionable. They were not new – Chanel had worn them in the 1920s for sailing, there were silk or satin lounging pyjamas in the 1930s, and the Italians made 'palazzo pyjamas' acceptable for evenings at home in the early 1960s, Irene Galitzine lavishly beading and embroidering them and Emilio Pucci using beautiful prints. But in 1964 Courrèges designed trousers to be worn formally or informally for daytime or evening, cutting them pencil-slim, cleverly seamed at the back and front of the leg, the front seam opening at the foot to allow the back to fall over the heel without wrinkling across the ankle and to increase

1964. Plain wool jacket, plaid skirt cut to just above knee, short white boots.

1966. Mini dress with 'op-art' decoration.

1964. Man's elastic-sided 'Beatle' boot.

1966. Mini dress cut with abstract shapes in three colours.

1966. Woman's white plastic boot with black rubber sole.

Mid-1960s. Shoulder bag with Mary Quant daisy motif in black and white PVC

Mid-1960s. Shoulder bags in PVC with chain straps.

1968. White coat and skirt over a knitted cat suit, white boots.

1966. Dress in cream, navy and red bonded jersey.

1966. Nehru jacket with standing collar, worn over polo-neck sweater.

1968. Flared denim slacks, patch pockets with button-down flaps. Broad leather belt.

baggies   straight legs   elephant bells   flares.
Variation in shape of trousers and jeans in mid 1960s

Trousers for Women

1964. Courrèges trouser suit. Trousers cut with seam down front of leg split open over foot.

Mid-1960s. Mary Quant: satin hipster pants and striped shirt.

1967. St. Laurent: three-piece city suit in pin-striped flannel. Platform soled peep-toe shoes

1972. Caped top coat with wide cuffed trousers. Beret pulled down over the ears.

1976-7. silver fox fur coat worn with trousers.

1965. Courrèges trouser suit, forerunner of many tunic and trouser suits. Short white gloves

1976. Shown in 'Vogue': Man's suit, cap, fair-isle sweater and scarf worn by young girl.

1971. Sling-back sandal with peep toe.

1974. shoe in patchwork suede.

1976. Mid-calf-length boot with self stitching.

1982. Shirt with ruffled trim, knickerbockers in indigo blue denim, lace-up boots, red nylon tights.

1964. Courrèges evening outfit: trousers in glittering silver fabric under white satin coat trimmed with silver braid; bonnet to match.

1964. Evening dress and coat in white lace.

Mid 1960s. Mini dress with frills at wrist and hem.

White boots

1967. White turtleneck pullover worn under black striped dinner jacket with satin collar facing and cuffs

Late 1960s – early 1970s. Double-breasted velvet dinner jacket with satin facing on revers. Pleated shirt front, satin butterfly bow tie.

1967. Evening dress in striped glitter fabric and matching tights.

1968. Black culotte evening suit worn with see-through blouse in sheer fabric, satin bow. Sheer black tights.

1967. Paco Rabanne: mini dress made from plastic discs linked by chains.

1969. Men's evening shirts. White batiste with ruffles of eyelet embroidery

Cream coloured sheer cotton with mandarin collar and horizontal narrow pleats

Late 1960s. 'Return-to-the-thirties' look: trousers flared widely from knee in soft printed fabric with very long matching scarf.

1973. Hot pants worn with blouson jacket and knee-high boots.

Late 1960s – early 1970s. Pullover shirt with side vents, broad belt over the hips, boldly checked trousers, white moccasin shoes.

1975. The milkmaid look: pinafore over sprigged cotton blouse and long frilled skirt.

1973. Soft fluid suit in black jersey trimmed black and white feathers. Helmet hat, dark tights, rather heavy shoes

1967. Hippy style: waistcoat in moiré silk with printed silk sleeves and bow fastening, tunic or shirt dress in different printed silk, baggy trousers in semi-sheer striped fabric.

Early 1970s. Shoe with platform sole made of wet-look brown plastic and fake leopard skin.

1971. Dark blue canvas boot laced over metal hooks.

1971. Maxi dress in brown jersey worn over a cream blouse.

the apparent length of the leg. Combined with a flared tunic or tailored jacket, they were an immediate success. Later, Quant's hipster pants and, in 1967, St Laurent's velvet evening trouser suit (*le smoking*) and his rather gangster-like trouser suit in men's striped suiting confirmed the acceptance of trousers or pants as a normal, even essential part of most women's wardrobes.

Short-skirted evening dresses were usual through the 1960s, in fabrics such as lace or satin to give them the required formality; couture models often had matching jackets or coats. They did not completely replace long skirts for very formal or state occasions though these were rare. The mood was set for breaking with convention and for sensationalism. In 1964 Courrèges showed long satin evening coats edged with silver bobble braid, caught by a bow between the breasts, then falling open over nothing but slim, glittering silver hipster pants, with another satin bow poised below the navel; later in the decade he, Feraud, Rudi Gernreich, St Laurent and others showed see-through dresses (some even for day) which veiled the body in sheer or open-work fabric or, in the case of the space-age designs of Paco Rabanne, revealed it through linked plastic discs. These designs were admittedly worn only by the daring: but they defined a trend towards an increasing acceptance of nudity on stage and screen and on some beaches, and eventually even on the street men's bare chests and women with breasts barely covered caused little comment.

By the late 1960s the mood was changing again. Disillusionment among the young with the space-age liveliness of the affluent mid 1960s was creating a need for escape to what seemed a more glamorous or romantic past. A return to what was seen as the sexiness of the 1930s, an odd pastiche of old-style Hollywood vamp with slinky soft fabrics and Art Deco designs, brought a more fluid line, flared skirts, long narrow scarves, drooping brims on hats, dark sludge colours and trousers flared from the knee. Barbara Hulanicki popularized the style, first with a mail order business started in 1964 and then with a boutique called Biba in Kensington, dimly lit with lamps in Tiffany-type shades, which became, like Carnaby Street, a tourist attraction. In 1969 Biba moved to larger premises; but the 1970s brought another change of mood and it was eventually forced to close.

In the late 1960s an idealized dream of country living with home-made bread and pottery, natural wood furniture and the 'simple life' brought success to the Welsh designer Laura Ashley. She insists that her clothes are not fashion but merely an alternative to jeans; but her simple, long-skirted 'milkmaid' dresses in flower-printed calico or with insets of coarse lace, and her pinafores and frilly blouses, have been eagerly bought throughout the last decade and continue to sell in shops throughout the British Isles as well as in Paris, Aix-en-Provence, Washington, Boston and New York. A similar mood was caught by St Laurent in 1964 with provençal cotton print skirts and headscarves, and Oscar de la Renta in the USA presented printed cotton dresses with matching headscarves and frilly petticoats in 1977.

Skirts plummeted almost to the ground in 1967–8. Rather dramatic and exciting maxi coats looked at first a little strange over mini dresses, until skirts also became full-length for a year or so before settling down to a midi-length which remained fairly general throughout the 1970s, apart from the miniscule 'hot pants' of 1971–3. Attempts to revive the mini-skirt had little success until 1982 when the 'ra-ra' skirt, a rather frilly mini, was welcomed by the young for a warm summer. But skirt lengths, and fashion generally, included a fairly wide choice, although the basic garments, as for men, remained much the same with only slight variations. The blazer shown by St Laurent in 1970 and the masculine-styled jacket remained fashionable and popular throughout the decade; the shirt-waist dress or blouse and skirt appear to be perennials, the skirt varying between straight, flared and pleated styles; trousers and jeans were flared widely in the early 1970s, then straight and fairly wide, then narrow; knee-length breeches have proved an attractive style for the very young and skinny since 1979 and the early 1980s brought full baggy trousers gathered to the ankle. Trousers with tunic or waistcoat, high fashion in the 1960s, became almost a uniform for many older women throughout the 1970s, as jeans, T-shirts, men's shirts or skinny sweaters were for the young.

The variety of choice was underlined by the growth of separates and mix-and-match collections, allowing for the layered look advocated by Bonnie Cashin in the 1960s and the fashion for putting different patterned fabrics together which was encouraged by the growth and advances in design of knitwear, the best coming from Italy. Without a clear definition of precise fashion lines or the control afforded by etiquette or social rules, women were left to 'do their own thing', with varying results: some were stunningly successful, others had a piquant, bizarre charm, some were plain dull and many simply a mess. But even in the past, when strong guidelines prevailed, well-dressed women were often rare.

In a period of confusion, disorder, terrorism and violence and some feeling of hopelessness and despair, it is not surprising that since the 1970s fashion has lacked a sense of direction and seemed confused about its function, looking all ways for inspiration and escaping into fantasies which have produced somewhat 'fancy dress' results, often charming or beautiful but divorced from everyday living and therefore at their best for evening wear. Few taboos are left; even the extreme punk style caused only a slightly raised eyebrow, and the cult of the ugly was accepted as part of the violent scene. Baggy running shorts with T-shirts became acceptable wear for girls prancing down Fifth Avenue, crotch-moulding jeans made the bottom the erogenous zone of the 1970s, patches and bleached-out denim became a uniform for the young, and a version of workman's overalls in satin seemed the smart wear for dining out. Practically anything went – and still goes.

Apart from women in the services whose hair had to clear the collar, during the early 1940s the back hair was worn fairly long, rolled smoothly under or in curls, the sides and front swept up to form a waved pompadour or a bunch of curls on the head, occasionally with a fringe. The hair continued to be drawn back from the face through the mid 1940s, with sometimes a bun on top of the head or in the nape of the neck; the hair was drawn through and over false 'doughnut' pads to increase the size of the bun. A short cut was introduced in the late 1940s, sometimes very short with an irregular fringe, known as the gamine or urchin cut.

A neat, fairly small head was a feature of the early to mid 1950s, with mid-length hair drawn into a French pleat, or a bob flicked out or under at the sides, and 'pony-tails' for teenagers, but two innovations towards the end of the 1950s revolutionized hair styling: first, the roller to lift the hair, which was then held out by strenuous back-combing, and second, lacquer spray to hold the hair in place. These led to some towering 'bee-hive' styles between 1959 and the early 1960s. In 1958 Givenchy started a new trend when he gave his models wigs, and Cardin followed suit in 1960; wig departments were to appear in many stores and wigs became fairly common for women during the following two decades.

The crisp, clean lines of the mid-1960s clothes were complemented by the precise

1975-7. Man's waistcoat or vest suit with zipper fastening, worn with patterned shirt.

1977. Blazer in cream shantung, black silk jersey sweater.

Red carnation

Felt Trilby hat

Red pleated skirt, gold kid belt

1980. Woman's zip-fastened dungarees in purple, beige or black fabric with a satin finish. Leather belt and cowboy-style boots.

1976. The layered look: coat in red, navy, beige and green, blouson jacket in beige needlecord, dark kakhi-green trousers, white T-shirt.

Suede hat with cream fur brim

1982. Boots in mixed skins; cuffed boot in purple suede; black and red leather pump.

1982. Pink stretch-cotton top worn with matching mini or 'ra-ra' skirt; pink leather shoes.

1982. Cashmere sweater and leg-warmers in multi-coloured stripes; black culottes and tights; red leather pumps.

1970s. Man's zippered leather jacket with sheepskin lining, collar and cuffs; leather straps to fasten collar.

1976. Ethnic influence: printed wool scarf, fine wool shirt, braided flannel jacket, cream wool skirt, suede boots geometric haircut associated with Vidal Sassoon; brilliant cutting gave body and bounce to a cap-like shape with deep symmetric or asymmetrical fringes. An alternative, much favoured by the 'arty' set, was long straight hair worn hanging down below the shoulders. Italian influence reintroduced more elaborately styled hair at the end of the 1960s, and the 'black is beautiful' movement which brought success to black fashion models also encouraged the frizzy 'Afro' style around 1972 and plaited and beaded hair, worn by black and white girls alike, around 1976. Generally, however, older women throughout the 1970s favoured a shorter cut, often clinging to a rather bouffant look, while most younger women wore their hair fairly long, layered and smooth or very curly; and some fashion models have been photographed looking as if they had just risen from bed after a rough night. However, as with clothes, individualism has allowed a wide choice since the late 1970s.

Hats during the last forty years have gradually ceased to be a vital fashion accessory. Exempt from clothes rationing, they were important during the war to give a lift to old or renovated dresses or suits, perched forward on the head or slightly to one side with tiny crowns and elastic or a band across the back of the head to keep them on. For everyday wear, however, many women wore the more convenient headscarf. In France, women showed their defiance of the occupation with towering turbans, and some rather ugly styles appeared during the mid 1940s. During the late 1940s and early 1950s, millinery complemented dress styles: wide coolie brims reflected the wide skirts, or tiny hats contrasted with them in 1947–8; small neat berets and close helmets set off the huge stoles and wide brims emphasized the narrow H-line in 1954; tiny hats formed the apex of the A-line in 1957; and the sack dress brought with it a return to the cloche hat. Milliners showed themselves as inventive as dress designers but were fighting a losing battle with the increasingly high bee-hive hair styles and the use of wigs. Some extraordinary and rather ugly hats resembling inverted chamber pots or hair dryers enlarged heads still further above the full coats and collarless suits of the late 1950s.

The 1960s look was complete without a hat, but hats if worn were small, youthful and cute – schoolgirl hats, berets and tiny flower-bedecked pill-boxes perched on the back of the head. Wide drooping brims and close-fitting turbans were part of the Biba 1930s revival. Dashing masculine trilbys were worn with trouser suits and the huge fur hats that accompanied long maxi coats were possibly influenced by the film of *Doctor Zhivago*.

Bare heads were very much part of the 1970s image; apart from deep knitted caps or fur hats for warmth, hats were worn only for formal functions. Skilled milliners are still producing some charming hats for such occasions, but with the prevalent lack of formality hats other than the purely practical are superfluous.

The moderately high or low wedge heels on shoes introduced in the late 1930s continued throughout the war years; high platform styles were seen more in France than elsewhere during the mid 1940s. Shoes in Britain were more practical and work-manlike, such as laced Oxfords or the slip-on Norwegian-peasant shoe later adopted by men. Flat-heeled shoes or pumps were popular with the young in the USA. Black, brown and navy were the most usual colours until the late 1950s and the 1960s, when more variety occurred.

The court shoe has been the most consistently fashionable and popular shape throughout the last three decades. The extremely high slender heels in the 1950s required the insertion of a metal spigot through almost the whole length of the heel. Stiletto heels, tapered to as fine a point as possible, did much damage to floors and carpets and many establishments asked women to remove their shoes or wear some protective covering over the heel. Combined in the mid-late 1950s with extremely pointed toes, they were dubbed 'winkle-pickers'. Lower heels and chisel-shaped toes were features of the shoes made by Roger Vivier for Dior in 1957, and he reshaped and lowered the heel further for some beautiful little shoes to be worn with the short evening dresses of 1959. Lower heels found favour in the USA earlier than in Britain, but Courrèges showed low-heeled and blunt-toed shoes with his shortened skirts, and the popularity of mini skirts clinched the change to young-looking shoes with little tapered or broad heels and rounded or blunt toes, in court, bar or T-strap and sling-back styles.

Boots were worn for warmth and protection throughout the 1950s but they became high fashion after Courrèges showed short white boots in his 1964 collection which were copied extensively in waterproof plastic with rubber soles for the less wealthy. Since the mid 1960s boots have remained very much part of the fashion scene, sometimes worn even during hot summer weather. Thigh-length boots worn with mini skirts had a rather buccaneering look, and in the late 1960s high-laced boots were somewhat reminiscent of the Edwardian era, particularly when worn under a long skirt.

High heels and platform soles were reintroduced during the early 1970s for some of the most hideous, clumsy boots and shoes ever produced; difficult to walk on with any ease or grace, they gave girls the appearance of having crippled feet. Fortunately the fashion was short-lived, but it brought high heels back into general wear during the mid 1970s, even with trousers, and they have remained popular ever since, although challenged by lower heels at the end of the decade.

Nylon stockings were available in the USA just before World War II, but wartime restrictions prevented their general use, particularly in Europe, until about 1946–7 when they appeared in a variety of skin tones, although black and white were favoured by 'beat' groups in the late 1950s. They were seamed until 1960 when the seam-free stretch variety took over. Ankle socks were a teenage fancy during the late 1940s and those who wore them were known as 'bobby-soxers'.

In the 1960s, when short skirts centred attention on the legs, tights replaced stockings and new textures and patterns were introduced – stripes, chevrons, lacy patterns, a scattering of applied petals, embroideries, varied colours and heavy ribbed wool or crochet patterns to match sweaters. Knee socks, new in the 1950s, were worn with shorts and with some mini skirts, and proved useful with trousers. Longer skirts and the increasingly popular jeans and trousers phased out the more lively patterned tights, but some colour remained, although skin tones were the most widely worn during the 1970s. Leg warmers – loose footless socks ruched between ankle and knee or thigh as worn by ballet dancers in class – were introduced in 1979–80 and became immensely popular with the young.

Wartime top coats, like the suits, had heavily padded shoulders, often cut with deep armholes and raglan sleeves to allow for the bulky shoulder line of jackets; they were single- or double-breasted, often belted, with a military look. Short, boxy three-quarter or waist-length coats became popular in the mid 1940s, sometimes called jigger coats. These were later known as car coats and were considered the only correct wear with trousers until the 1970s, when it became fashionable to wear a knee- or calf-length coat with pants. Swagger-back loose coats, cut full and flared at the back, appeared at the end of the 1940s, contrasting with those following the New Look line. In the 1950s

Overcoats 1940 - 1970.

1941. 'British warm' top coat in tan fleece has flapped chest pocket

1957. Black and white herringbone tweed coat with collarless neckline.

1957. Top coat in bold check long-haired mohair fabric

1967. Man's felt hat with brim turned up closely at back

1945. Short boxy double-breasted coat with large patch pockets.

1964. White gaberdine coat with belt placed high and sleeves cut short above wrist.

1970s. Man's wide-brimmed hat

1968. Man's maxi coat in wool with a twill weave, large collar and wide lapels, slanted flapped pockets.

Early 1960s. Short top coat in rayon and wool gaberdine, lined with pile fabric sleeves in rayon.

the body and the quilted

Late 1960s Thigh-length boots.

1968. Grey maxi coat worn over mini dress with huge foxfur hat and high black boots.

some sensational coats, often beautifully cut, flowed out to an enormous width from natural shoulders; wide sleeves and high collars standing away from the neck and sloping down to the shoulders emphasized the cape or cloak effect. The late 1950s also produced a number of collarless coats, often with the neckline cut back and raised to frame the neck. Broad stoles matching the fabric of the suit or dress were also fashionable during the mid and late 1950s, particularly effective with evening dresses in satin, faille or sheer fabrics.

The mid-1960s coats were skimpy with small, high-cut armholes, narrow sleeves, small collars and revers, double- or single-breasted and hanging straight or semi-fitted with perhaps a slightly raised waist. In the late 1960s maxi coats were neat shoulded with slim sleeves, the fitted body flaring out to the lowered hemline. As the hemline settled back to a midi length, coats became fairly classic and masculine in style; an endeavour was made to popularize a full wide line again in 1967–7 but no great change occurred. Padded or quilted coats, jackets and raincoats proved popular through the last years of the 1970s and into the 1980s, possibly to combat the mounting cost of woollen cloth; but from the mid 1970s waist-length, three-quarter or calf-length coats in the classic style associated with the names of Burberry and Aquascutum with natural or slightly padded shoulders, rather squared around 1979–80, and moderately wide sleeves, single, double or fly fastened, have been the most generally worn.

Fur coats received a fillip when St Laurent used horizontal bands of fur alternating with stripes of ciré or suede in 1962, and a new attitude to the use of fur, with casual cardigans made of mink and fake 'fun' furs took away some of the 'worn for best' mediocrity into which it had settled in the late 1940s. Long fur scarves were fashionable around 1977–8 and fur was used in a much more imaginative, casual, fashionable and lavish way at the end of the 1970s, but real fur is still restricted to those with ample means, and there is also a growing body of opinion against the use of animal skins for human adornment.

SPORTSWEAR

The development of synthetic fibres has revolutionized the textile industry over the past forty years, resulting in fabrics that will stretch and spring back into shape and can be crease-resistant, drip-dry, non-iron and permanently pleated. These qualities have proved particularly useful in the manufacture of sportswear. Stretch fabric is ideal for ski pants and riding breeches, and practically all tennis clothes are now made of wash-and-wear or drip-dry fabrics. The development of light and non-bulky winter sports wear benefited from experiments made with air-crews' uniforms during the war and more recently an aluminium lining used in astronauts' clothing has provided warmth without bulk in ski jackets.

Unisex design became usual for many sports; riding breeches and the classic jacket, rather long, single-breasted, shaped to the waist, flared over the hips and cut with a deep centre-back vent or side vents are almost identical for men and women, and a reinforced protective riding cap is universally worn by men, women and children. In a craze for Western ranch-style riding outfits during the 1960s–70s in the USA, both sexes wore tight cowboy pants, bold coloured shirts, wide-brimmed hats and rodeo boots, and on both sides of the Atlantic since the late 1950s jeans and a sweater or shirt have become commonplace informal wear for riding, though not yet acceptable on the hunting field or in the show ring. For golf, trousers, zip-front jackets, tailored shirts, plain or patterned sweaters and peaked caps have been worn by men and women since the 1940s, although some women have preferred skirts or culottes, and attempts were made in the 1970s to revive the fashion for knickerbockers or plus-fours (out of favour since the 1950s) in an updated version for men. Bright colours for ski and golf outfits have increased; the Italians first showed brightly coloured ski wear in the 1950s and others were quick to follow. With the popularity of golfing events on television, well-known players have become fashion catalysts and their colourful styles have been taken up by the general public.

Tennis costume has changed little for either sex over the past forty years, though men's shorts have become shorter and crew-necked T-shirts, usually of knitted fabric, often replace the button-through short-sleeved shirt. Pleated shorts and tailored shirts worn by some women in the 1940s were quickly replaced almost universally by thigh-length sleeveless dresses, flared or permanently pleated; the 'A' line of 1957 was particularly appropriate. In 1949 Gussie Moran caused a mild sensation at Wimbledon by wearing lace-edged panties under her short skirt, and in 1972 Chris Evert wore panties frilled across the back; but apart from these and other flights of fancy such as lace outfits and the use of sequinned dresses for matches under artificial lights, simple white dresses and panties for women and white shorts and shirts for men, with perhaps an edging of colour, has been normal wear.

Swimming costumes have become steadily more minimal. Snug-fitting trunks with the leg cut high above the thigh were hailed as the male bikini in the 1960s; then the waist was lowered and the leg openings raised until by the 1970s it consisted of little more than a pouch at the front and a triangle of cloth at the back. Alternatives consisted of boxer-type shorts, worn from the 1950s, easy-fitting shorts to just above the knee in boldly patterned fabric with a concealed cord at the waist in 1966, and an updated one-piece version of the 1930s two-piece, known as a tank suit, in the 1970s. The woman's bikini was launched in Paris as early as 1946 but was not generally worn until the late 1950s, after some costumes with heavy, rigid built-in bras following the fashion for high pointed breasts had been discarded for a more natural style. Rudi Gernreich produced a one-piece suit cut away at the front between the waist and breasts in 1960, and a topless suit in 1964 consisting of a close-fitting lower half and two narrow straps running from the centre front, just above the waist, over the shoulders and down the back: but for topless sunbathing and swimming in the 1970s the lower half of the bikini seemed simpler. Considering the small area to be covered, a great variety of designs has been devised for swimming costumes, but for serious swimming and for the older or more reticent a neat one-piece costume serves a perennial need.

For beach or resort wear in the 1950s brightly-coloured and lively-patterned shirts were worn loose over plain coloured shorts or trousers by both men and women; women's trousers were tight-fitting and short to the calf, and jeans were frequently rolled up to this level. Unisex wraps, long or short and in brightly coloured plain or patterned terry towelling, and a wide choice of strapless or low-cut sun dresses and tops for women, have been popular since the 1940s.

CHILDREN

Easy-care fabrics have proved a boon for children's clothes, which, like adult wear, have become increasingly casual. Children dressed like their elders no longer suffer as earlier generations did; the long-skirted dresses that followed the Laura Ashley trend, though charming, were not entirely practical, but most adult wear such as jeans, bib-and-brace overalls, shorts (the French favour them long to the knee), shirts, sweaters,

Sportswear 1950s – 1980s

Men's golfing outfits: proofed poplin jackets in strong colours; plaid trousers or shorts with high socks; two-tone shoes.

1972. Man's skiing outfit in russet-coloured nylon with double zippered fastening; matching trousers worn over boots.

1954. Man's all-white tennis outfit: shorts have pleat at waist.

Woman's tennis dress in white Terylene with permanently pleated skirt.

Ski goggles

1982. Woman's skiing outfit: cream and blue heavy cotton jacket with detachable down-filled lining; cream cotton dungarees with tartan lining; navy blue knitted sweater and hat; blue and white printed scarf.

1949. Beachwear: multi-coloured plaid shirt worn loose over white shorts; large straw hat, heavy sandals.

1964. Beachwear: Orange and white halter top and knee-length frilled trousers. Button-through dress in black, red and white stripes worn over matching bikini.

1945. A 'make-do-and-mend' suggestion – child's pinafore dress made from adult cotton dress.

1959. Girl's party dress in ruby red or slate blue embroidered in white; lace frill and ribbon bow at neck.

1965. Classic top coat for boys or girls with alternative fastening.

1969. Pink cotton shirt, denim jeans turned up at ankles, navy sneakers.

1945. Striped 'make-do-and-mend' sweater from odd lengths of wool.

1959. Woven black and white striped Everglaze easy-care cotton, trimmed black velvet ribbon and embroidery. Stiff petticoat attached.

1982. Pinafore dress in printed machine-washable cotton baby cord in peach, pale blue, green or clover, worn with co-ordinated sweater and socks.

1945. Grey flannel shorts, knitted pullover, fine wool shirt, Wellington boots over long woollen socks.

1981. Boys or girls dungarees in machine-washable cotton needle-cord in tan, red, beige or green with co-ordinated sweater and socks.

1981 Baby's hooded jacket in striped acrylic fabric with patterned borders, worn with teamed dress and matching tights.

1982. Boys or girl's wool duffle coat lined with acrylic pile fabric, corduroy trousers, striped knitted cap and co-ordinating gloves.

Children's Clothes 1945 – 1980s.

zippered jackets, or blazers are practical and attractive for boys and girls. Boys were for so long dressed like girls, and now girls are often dressed like boys; but a wide variety of dresses, or skirts and sweaters, or practical but attractive pinafore dresses over matching tights and sweaters, is still available for young girls.

Shoes for children have not suffered the distortions devised for women's footwear, and the importance of low-heeled, well-fitted shoes for growing feet is now realized.

ACCESSORIES AND JEWELRY

Handbags have been essential for women, since clothes rarely allowed for sufficient pockets. During the war years, large, practical bags, some box-shaped, were carried or slung from the shoulder, to be replaced during the late 1940s and the 1950s by more elegant designs of medium size, frequently with rigid double handles. In the 1960s a smaller shoulder bag, often slung by a chain, returned in keeping with the youthful image and the shoulder bag has remained a firm favourite, varying slightly in design, throughout the 1970s, particularly suitable with trouser suits. Tiny bags matching the dress, barely large enough for a handkerchief, were popular with teenagers in the 1970s, hung around the neck on a cord. The very close fit of men's Italian-inspired suits allowed little room in the pockets and men in Italy, Germany and France carried masculine-looking handbags, but these never became generally accepted in England or America.

Women crocheted or knitted their own serviceable gloves during the war. As restrictions were lifted, rather long gloves, rucked at the wrist, complemented the outfits of the late 1940s and the 1950s. Short, crisp white gloves were part of the late 1950s–60s youthful look, particularly favoured by Jacqueline Kennedy; as a leader of fashion, her pin-neat appearance was widely copied. With the decline in formality in the 1970s, gloves, like hats, were worn less, mainly for warmth or, especially by men, for driving.

Long-handled elegant umbrellas were carried by men and women during the 1950s but thereafter ceased to be a fashion accessory and were used mainly for protection; a collapsible type fitted into handbags or brief-cases. Wide, bold belts were worn by men and women with hipster pants or jeans, or over long jerseys. Long mufflers have often been part of the student image, but a narrow, limp style popular in the 'thirties revival' of the 1960s, and long fur scarves matched the large fur hats in the 1970s. During the winter of 1981–2 very large square scarves were a feature of most of the dress collections and proved very popular, however inconvenient to wear.

The conservative man's jewelry has been restricted to cufflinks, watches and modest rings, but hippies, pop stars and their followers have sported earrings, large finger rings and bead or chain necklaces, and many young men in the 1970s wore a single gold earring, perhaps harking back to the tough gentleman of the Elizabethan age. Women wore stud earrings for day and a more elaborate chandelier type for evening in the late 1940s and the 1950s, and high dog-collar necklaces were featured with the short evening dresses of the late 1950s. Very little jewelry was worn in the 1960s, but 'body jewelry' was devised to decorate the nipples under the see-through fashions. Brooches have rarely been fashionable since the 1950s, but multiple strings of beads became popular in the 1970s, followed by fine gold chains and several rings worn on one finger.

The cosmetic industry has grown enormously, and fashion in make-up has changed as frequently as in clothes. Great attention has been paid to make-up for the eyes: shadow, eye-liners and artificial lashes produced the worldly-wise self-assured look

Evening Wear 1975 – 82

1976. Black wool crêpe with sequin trimming on sleeves.

1976-7. High-waisted dress in a mixture of textured and patterned fabric with hanging strings of beads.

1971. Mohair and wool suit with faille lapel facings and satin binding

1979. Navy rayon matte jersey with white nylon lace puffed sleeves.

1982. Olive green velvet and taffeta top over matching taffeta skirt.

1979. Dress in either red or white ostrich feathers.

1976-7. Black jersey dress with skirt split to thigh level; khaki-coloured taffeta jacket.

1979. Ruffled strapless dress in red polyester chiffon.

1982. Black velvet jacket and bloomers, the jacket quilted and frogged in gold; gold turban, black stockings, black and pewter satin shoes.

required by the clothes of the 1950s; later the doe-eyed appearance associated with Audrey Hepburn and Sophia Loren was obtained by lifting the shading and outlining at the outer corner of the eye. The 'Chelsea girls' of the late 1950s went to extremes with heavily darkened eyes and pale lips, but their influence was seen in the 1960s when the two most successful photographic models of the period used make-up to enlarge the eyes while keeping the lips pale. Lashes were often quite obviously pencilled in at this time, but the 1970s saw a return to an apparently natural look, personified by the American model Lauren Hutton.

FABRICS AND COLOUR

Fabrics made purely from natural fibres have become increasingly rare and expensive, but the easy-care qualities and warmth without weight of synthetics and mixtures, although lacking some of the beauty of natural fabrics, are of inestimable value. Fabric colours for dress over the past forty years have been fairly muted, apart from those for certain sports and beach wear – a reflection possibly of a general desire for practical clothing.

Current social attitudes mean that, on the whole, extravagant and obviously expensive dress is not often indulged in; and increased travel together with women's greater involvement in business and industry means that both men and women require clothes that are comfortable and practical and can be cared for without the aid of servants. But although it seems unlikely that people of the western world will ever again adorn themselves in the complex and elaborate manner indulged in by their ancestors during most of the time covered by this book, it is to be hoped that fashion in clothes will retain a little beauty, some frivolity and an element of change to offset the sober aspects of the late 20th century.

Select bibliography

HISTORY OF COSTUME
(titles marked * also contain some social comment)

Ashdown, Mrs Charles H. *British Costume during Nineteen Centuries* Jack, London & Edinburgh, 1910
*Barton, Lucy *Historic Costume for the Stage* revised edn, A. & C. Black, London, 1961 (Egyptian to 1900)
*Bernard, Barbara *Fashion in the 1960s* Academy Edns, London, 1980; St Martin's Press, New York, 1978
*Calthrop, Dion Clayton *English Costume* A. & C. Black, London, 1926 (commentary a little dated but interesting)
*Carter, Ernestine *Twentieth Century Fashion* Methuen, London, 1975
 – *The Changing World of Fashion* Weidenfeld & Nicolson, London and Putnam, New York, 1977
Cunnington, C. W. and Phillis *A Handbook of English Mediaeval Costume* Faber, London, 1972
 – *A Handbook of English Costume in the Sixteenth Century* Faber, London, and Plays Inc., Boston, 1970
 – *A Handbook of English Costume in the Seventeenth Century* as above, 1973
 – *A Handbook of English Costume in the Eighteenth Century* as above, 1972
 – *A Handbook of English Costume in the Nineteenth Century* as above, 1970
Cunnington, Phillis and Mansfield, Ann *A Handbook of English Costume in the Twentieth Century* as above, 1973
Cunnington, Phillis *Costume in Pictures* revised edn Herbert Press, London, 1981 (distrib. Universe, New York)
*Davenport, Millia *The Book of Costume* Crown, New York, 1976 (from Persian and Egyptian through European and American costume until the 1860s)
*Dormer, Jane *Fashion in the Forties and Fifties* Ian Allan, London, 1975
Fairholt, F.W. *Costume in England* (2 vols), London 1885
*Glynn, Prudence and Ginsburg, Madeleine *In Fashion: Dress in the Twentieth Century* Allen & Unwin, London, 1978
*Johansen, R. Broby *Body and Clothes* Faber, London, 1968 (history worldwide with comments on distortion of the body)
Kelly & Schwabe *Historic Costume 1490–1790* Batsford, London, 1929
Köhler, Carl *A History of Costume* Constable, London and Dover, New York, 1963 (Egyptian to 1870)
*Kybalová, L., Herbenová, O. and Lamarová, M. *The Pictorial Encyclopedia of Fashion* Hamlyn, London and Crown, New York, 1968 (Egyptian to twentieth century European)
Laver, James *A Concise History of Costume* Thames & Hudson, London, 1969; Scribners, New York, 1974
Piton, Camille *Le costume civil en France du XIIIe au XIXe siècle* Flammarion, Paris, 1926
*Robinson, Julian *Fashion in the 1940s* Academy Edns, London, 1980; St Martin's Press, New York, 1978

MEN'S WEAR

Byrde, Penelope *The Male Image* Batsford, London, 1979
Schoeffler, O. E. and Gale, William *Esquire's Encyclopedia of Twentieth Century Men's Fashion* McGraw Hill, New York, 1973

CHILDREN

Cunnington, Phillis and Buck, Anne *Children's Costume in England* A. & C. Black, London, 1966
Moore, Doris Langley *The Child in Fashion 1850s–1934* Batsford, London, 1953

CUT AND PATTERN

Arnold, Janet *Patterns of Fashion 1660–1860* Macmillan, London, 1972
 – *Patterns of Fashion 1860–1940* as above
Waugh, Norah *The Cut of Men's Clothes* Faber, London, 1964
 – *The Cut of Women's Clothes* as above, 1968

UNDERWEAR

Caldwell, Doreen *And All Was Revealed* Arthur Barker, London, 1981
Colmer, Michael *Whalebone to See-through: a History of Body Packaging* Johnson & Bacon, London, 1979
Ewing, Elizabeth W. *Fashion in Underwear* Batsford, London, 1971
Waugh, Norah *Corsets and Crinolines* Batsford, London, 1970

SOCIAL COMMENT RELATED TO DRESS

Ballerberry, M. & A. *Fashion, the Mirror of History* Columbus, London, 1982
Beaton, Cecil *The Glass of Fashion* Weidenfeld & Nicolson, London and Doubleday, New York, 1954
Bell, Quentin *On Human Finery* revised edn Hogarth Press, London and Schocken, New York, 1976
Boehn, Max von *Die Mode (Modes and Manners)* Harrup, London, 1935
Does, Eline-Canter Cremers van der *The Agony of Fashion* Blandford, London, 1980
Garland, Madge *The Changing Face of Childhood* Hutchinson, London, 1963 (Toys, education, dress, etc.)
Laver, James *Modesty in Dress* Heinemann, London, 1969
Lurie, Alison *The Language of Clothes* Heinemann, London, 1982
Newton, Stella M. *Health, Art and Reason* Murray, London, 1974
Squire, Geoffrey *Dress, Art and Society 1560–1970* Studio Vista, London, 1974

SPECIALIZED DRESS

Williams-Mitchell, Christobel *Dressed for the Job: the Story of Occupational Costume* Blandford, London, 1982
Cunnington, Phillis and Lucas, Catherine *Occupational Costume in England from the Eleventh Century to 1914* A. & C. Black, London, 1967

COSTUME FROM PAINTINGS AND PHOTOGRAPHS

Birbari, Elizabeth *Dress in Italian Paintings 1460–1500* Murray, London, 1975
Dars, Celestine *A Fashion Parade: the Seeberger Collection* Blond & Briggs, London, 1977 (Photographs by the Seeberger brothers 1900–50 with social comment)
Gernsheim, Alison *Fashion and Reality (1814–1914)* Faber, London, 1963
Herald, Jacqueline *Renaissance Dress in Italy 1400–1500* Bell & Hyman, London and Humanities Press, NJ, 1981

FASHION PLATES

Blum, Stella (ed.) *Victorian Fashions and Costumes from 'Harper's Bazaar' 1867–1898* Dover, New York, 1974
Moore, Doris Langley *Fashion through Fashion Plates 1770–1970* Ward Lock, London 1971; Potter, New York, 1972
Nuzzi, Cristina *Fashion in Paris: from the 'Journal des Dames et des Modes' 1912–13* Thames & Hudson, London, 1980

BIOGRAPHY AND AUTOBIOGRAPHY

Balmain, Pierre *My Years and Seasons* Cassell, London, 1964; Doubleday, New York, 1965
Carter, Ernestine *Magic Names of Fashion* Weidenfeld & Nicolson, London, 1980
Charles-Roux, Edmonde *Chanel* Cape, London, 1976
Deschodt, Anne-Marie *Mariano Fortuny 1871–1947* Editions du Regard, Tours, 1979
Dior by Dior Weidenfeld & Nicolson, London and Ambassador, New York, 1957
Hartnell, Norman *Silver and Gold* Evans, London, 1955
Howe, Bea *Arbiter of Elegance: a biography of Mrs Mary Eliza Haweis* Harvill Press, New York, 1967
Quant, Mary *Quant by Quant* Cassell, London, 1976
Schiaparelli, Elsa *Shocking Life* Dent, London and Dutton, New York, 1954
White, Palmer *Poiret* Studio Vista, London, 1973

Index to text

253